Domestic Abuse and Sexual Assault in Popular Culture

Domestic Abuse and Sexual Assault in Popular Culture

Laura L. Finley

Crime in Popular Culture
Laura L. Finley, Series Editor

 PRAEGER™

An Imprint of ABC-CLIO, LLC
Santa Barbara, California • Denver, Colorado

Library of Congress Cataloging-in-Publication Data

Names: Finley, Laura L., author.
Title: Domestic abuse and sexual assault in popular culture / Laura L. Finley.
Description: Santa Barbara, California : Praeger, 2016. | Series: Crime in popular culture. | Includes bibliographical references and index.
Identifiers: LCCN 2015048443 | ISBN 9781440837944 (hardback) | ISBN 9781440837951 (ebook)
Subjects: LCSH: Violence in mass media. | Violence in popular culture—United States. | Women—Crimes against—United States. | Rape in mass media. | Mass media and culture—United States. | Crime in popular culture—United States. | BISAC: SOCIAL SCIENCE / Violence in Society.
Classification: LCC P96.V52 U65 2016 | DDC 362.82/920973—dc23
LC record available at http://lccn.loc.gov/2015048443

ISBN: 978–1–4408–3794–4
EISBN: 978–1–4408–3795–1

20 19 18 17 16   1 2 3 4 5

This book is also available as an eBook.

Praeger
An Imprint of ABC-CLIO, LLC

ABC-CLIO, LLC
130 Cremona Drive, P.O. Box 1911
Santa Barbara, California 93116-1911
www.abc-clio.com

This book is printed on acid-free paper ∞

Manufactured in the United States of America

I dedicate this book to all those tireless advocates and activists who seek to end domestic abuse and sexual assault. As one small form of help, I dedicate all royalties of this book to No More Tears, a South Florida nonprofit organization that assists victims of domestic abuse, dating abuse, sexual assault, and human trafficking.

Contents

Series Foreword   ix

Preface   xi

Acknowledgments   xvii

Introduction   xix

1. Beyond Stupid Sluts and Innocent Children:
   Describing Victims   1

2. Domestic Terrorists and Strangers in the Bushes:
   Describing Offenders   39

3. Tornados Meeting Volcanos and Asking for It:
   Myths about Domestic Abuse and Sexual Assault   67

4. Evil, Ill, or Controlling: Exploring Depictions
   of Criminological Theory   87

5. Calling the Cops and a Day in Court: Depictions
   of Criminal Justice Responses   105

6. Getting over It or Taking Matters into Your Own Hands:
   Victim and Other Responses   119

Conclusion   143

*Appendix A: Films, Documentaries, Songs, and Popular Books
Featuring Domestic Abuse and Sexual Assault*   155

Appendix B: Recommended Resources on Rape, Domestic Abuse,
and Popular Culture   167

Index   183

Series Foreword

Crime is ubiquitous in the United States. From violent assaults to white-collar offenses, and nonviolent drug offenses to juvenile status offenses, the type, characteristics, and frequency of crime are vast. It is more than just a matter for politicians and the criminal justice system to address, as we are all impacted by crime and by efforts to respond to and prevent it, be it directly or indirectly. As such, crime is necessarily a matter of great public concern.

Unlike some topics like schooling or work, most people have little direct experience with crime. That's good news, as it means most of us are neither perpetrators nor victims. What it does mean, however, is that we are reliant on sources outside of our personal experience to tell us about crime. Since most people never study criminology in school or college, that knowledge is typically acquired from media and popular culture. Many studies have shown that these sources do not always accurately portray the scope and extent of each type of crime, who is most likely to commit offenses and why, the groups most likely to be victimized, the criminal justice and other responses to it, and the short- and long-term effects of crime. The titles in this series seek to provide detailed descriptions of not only what is presented in popular culture, but also how those presentations do and do not reflect reality.

Given the prevalence and ever-growing amount of popular culture, it would be impossible for the books in this series to ever be complete! Readers will be presented with a wide array of examples related to each of the selected crime topics so as to provide a broad but not exhaustive assessment. While the specifics vary per book, films, television, song lyrics, video games, advertisements, and popular fiction appear in all. Historical and current examples are included throughout each book in the series.

Each book also includes both "good" or accurate depictions as well as "bad" ones. Importantly, all the books also include an assessment of the explanations offered for why the crime topic occurs, relating those to criminological theory. Additionally, all books in the series include appendices that provide additional examples as well as recommended resources.

Although there are other books and series that focus on crime and popular culture, it is my belief that this series offers a current, nuanced, and critical assessment that I hope is both interesting and useful to students, professors, service providers, criminal justice practitioners, and general readers.

Laura L. Finley
Series Editor

Preface

I have to admit, I thought this book would be easy to write. I have been studying domestic abuse and sexual assault for 15 years; have written books, journal articles, and other entries about these issues; have spent 10 years as an advocate and activist; and have created and implemented many prevention programs. It was not at all easy, however. For one, the content is always emotionally draining regardless of how long or how often one has been exposed to it. The statistics about abuse and assault are sobering, and even a quick perusal of case studies can be deeply unsettling. Second, because the books in this series are focused on how the specific criminal issues are presented in popular culture, I had to continually engage in reading, viewing, and listening to some of the most disturbing presentations of victims. I thought I kind of knew what was "out there": Boy, was that ever an understatement! Although there are definitely positive, accurate, and helpful depictions of domestic abuse and rape, a lot of what is available is a netherworld of nastiness. That comedians continue to find jokes about raping audience members amusing, that music lyrics talk about "slapping hos" if they speak back, or that story lines in popular television shows make it appear that comatose women are actually enjoying unwanted sexual behavior is absolutely sickening. But, it does indeed highlight the need for this book!

Given that popular culture takes so many forms and is virtually never-ending, I do not purport to include every instance of rape or domestic violence imaginable. I had to make choices of what to review and what to include. I began by outlining what I believe people should know about domestic violence and rape. This includes details about victims and offenders, any warning signs and patterns, risk factors, and the types of efforts victims take to get help, including within the criminal justice system, individually and with family and friends, and through other methods like shelters and therapists. I also wanted to include explanations for why these crimes exist, as well as information about social change and prevention efforts. Further, knowing that there are many myths and misconceptions about these crimes, I wanted to address and correct those. I was interested in seeing not only what was presented but also what was missing, as that also speaks volumes about how we understand rape and domestic violence. There are some very important related topics that I simply ran out of space to include. For instance, this book focuses on rape and domestic violence in the United States and uses examples from American popular culture almost exclusively, despite the fact that the problems are global in nature and that popular culture in other countries also presents depictions ripe for analysis. I included examples of rape and domestic violence in the U.S. military but only a limited amount related to rape as a tool of war. I did not include sexual trafficking here, not because it isn't important but because that would be another entire book. Although I reference a few studies of reality TV, it wasn't a significant focus. Surely there are other important topics or popular culture that I didn't include or didn't cover adequately, and for that I apologize.

Starting from that framework, I then reviewed popular books, movies, television programs, and song lyrics, and to a lesser extent, comedians' jokes, video games, and advertisements. I asked people for recommendations, conducted google searches, perused lists of books on Goodreads, and consulted IMDB for film recommendations. I did not review newspaper and magazine accounts, although I did include a few relevant studies that did so, as my focus was on popular culture, not on news media. I have included as many existing studies on these issues as I could, although surely there are more. Typically, one review led to another, as my online searches would result in lists of films or songs, for instance, which would then lead me to others. Again, I do not pretend that this book provides any type of exhaustive list, but I do hope that it proves useful in educating readers about domestic violence and rape and increases the chances that we will be more critical readers, listeners, and viewers. I did include two appendixes that offer additional information for readers who are interested in diving further into the popular culture abyss! I think all of the above makes this book unique. While there are other texts dedicated to reviewing depictions of rape in film and on TV, there are few that address domestic abuse, and none that covers such a wide array of forms of popular culture. Further, these other texts focus heavily on the popular culture analysis and provide little in the way of teaching readers the reality of domestic abuse and rape, as this book does.

The book begins with an introduction in which I first provide basic definitions of domestic and dating violence and sexual assault, followed by some statistics and data highlighting the scope and extent of these problems. The Introduction then reviews the research on how violent media affects consumers. As is clear from the wealth of studies, violent media indeed results in attitudinal and behavioral changes, albeit with variation based on the demographics of the consumer, the frequency of consumption, and other factors. Finally, the Introduction begins to describe the studies addressing consumption of media specifically focusing on rape and domestic or dating violence. This review of literature is also woven into appropriate topics within subsequent chapters.

First, a note on terminology. I have elected to use the term "domestic abuse" in the title of this book because it connotes to some readers that there are many forms of power and control used by abusers. Given that physical violence is just one of these, I wanted to ensure that the book title reflected reality. In the chapters, though, the terms "domestic abuse" and "domestic violence" are both used where appropriate.

In Chapter 1, I provide an overview of victims of domestic abuse and rape. As the chapter details, while anyone can be a victim, certain groups are more or at least uniquely vulnerable. I discuss female victims; male victims; child victims; immigrants; lesbian, gay, bisexual, and transgender (LGBT) victims; black and Native American victims; elder victims; and poor and/or homeless victims. Again, it is important to note that while some of these groups face increased risk of victimization, they may be underrepresented in popular culture depictions, which can have dangerous implications, as can the overrepresentation of other groups as potential victims.

In Chapter 2, I begin with a description of rape culture and how it contributes to the creation of perpetrators. I then examine the depiction of offenders, again contrasting what is known with what is presented in popular culture. Male and female offenders, black offenders, and military, police, athlete, and fraternity members all receive special attention, given that data show members of these groups or institutions are overrepresented as perpetrators. On the other hand, I also give time to the degree and accuracy of depictions related to false claims of abuse and assault.

In Chapter 3, I examine the most prevalent myths about domestic violence and popular culture. I address the influence of what has been called

"rape myths" as well as misconceptions about the dynamics of abusive relationships and why victims remain in them. These myths are both pervasive
and insidious, as the chapter makes clear.

Chapter 4 focuses on the explanations for abuse and assault that are disseminated through popular culture, matching them up against criminno-
logical theory. The chapter examines and critiques biological,
psychological, choice, strain, learning critical, and feminist theories. Given
that beliefs about offenders also shape police, prosecutors, and corrections
officials as well as service providers, a more nuanced understanding of why
people commit abuse and assault can be very helpful.

Chapter 5 examines responses to rape and abuse by police and the criminal justice system. It addresses issues related to reporting, the arrest process, investigating incidents, and analyzing evidence, including rape kits,
prosecutions, the actual trials, and the correctional systems treatment of
offenders. Many of this remains purposely hidden from public view and
thus assessing how it is depicted in popular culture is essential.

In Chapter 6, I review victim, family, and community responses. The
chapter includes victims who fight back, help-seeking at shelters and
through therapists, the responses of family, friends, co-workers and community members, and the short- and long-term effects of abuse and
assault. As is likely obvious, both of these crimes take a huge toll on not
just victims but also those around them, and as is clear in the chapter, on
society as a whole. Yet often depictions of rape and domestic violence focus
largely or exclusively on individual efforts rather than collective ones,
reinforcing a notion that it is a victim's responsibility to fix the problem.

The Conclusion discusses ways we can improve the depictions, and
decrease the actual incidence of these offenses. It presents information
about prevention programs, efforts to challenge stereotypical gender role
norms, community-based programs to raise awareness and educational initiatives, and media literacy initiatives and alternative media suggestions.

Appendix A offers a compendium of films and television shows that
often depict rape and abuse, song lyrics, and popular books, some of which
are mentioned throughout the book and others that are not. Appendix B
offers a list of recommended readings on domestic violence and sexual
assault in general and related to popular culture, specifically.

In sum, as Heller-Nicholas (2011) notes, "Everyone—including
people who rape—construct their idea of what sexual violence 'is' or 'is
not,' not only via personal experience or that of our peers, but through
the stories and representations that circulate around us more broadly"

(p. 1). The same is surely true of domestic abuse. It is my hope that this book proves to be a thought-provoking tool for readers and that it inspires us all to do better—to demand better movies, books, shows, songs, and other forms of popular culture, and to ourselves take action to support victims and prevent abuse and assault.

REFERENCE

Heller-Nicholas, A. (2011). *Rape-revenge films.* Jefferson, NC: McFarland & Co.

Acknowledgments

Once again, I must thank my husband, Peter, and daughter, Anya, for their support while I eke out writing time among my many other obligations. You two are amazing, and I am so happy and proud of our odd little family!

I also want to thank Matthew Johnson for his assistance with the appendix of resources and for his continued advocacy on behalf of domestic abuse and sexual assault victims.

Further, I want to acknowledge Anthony Chiffolo with ABC-CLIO, who has afforded me the fantastic opportunity not only to write this book but also to edit the Crime in Popular Culture series.

Introduction

The crimes of domestic violence and rape have long been among the most frequently occurring, not just in the United States but across the globe. Yet they remain deeply misunderstood. Despite decades of attention to these issues, there are myriad myths and misconceptions about both victims and offenders. These myths and misconceptions are created, spread, and reified through many channels, but chief among them is popular culture. From books to TV, movies, advertisements and music, popular culture is a sometimes careless and occasionally careful teacher about crime. As a significant source of "teaching" about these issues, it is critical that scholars, advocates, activists, and students consider what messages are disseminated and how they may be received.

This chapter begins with a brief overview of the scope, extent, and characteristics of domestic violence and rape. It then provides a summary of the data on the effects of violent and misogynistic media on consumers. Subsequent chapters provide additional data on studies specific to popular culture, domestic violence, and rape, as well as the author's own analysis of these depictions.

DOMESTIC VIOLENCE

The U.S. Department of Justice's Office on Violence against Women defines "domestic violence" as "a pattern of abusive behavior in any relationship that is used by one partner to gain or maintain power and control over another intimate partner" (What is domestic violence, 2014). Domestic abuse does not involve only physical violence. It can also take many forms, including emotional and verbal abuse, sexual assault, financial control, manipulation of children, isolation, and more. Essentially, whatever tactics the abuser finds help him or her obtain and maintain power and control will likely be utilized, typically in conjunction (What is domestic violence, 2014).

Studies have documented very high rates of domestic violence across the globe. An estimated one-third of the world's women will endure an abusive relationship during their lifetime. In the United States, one in four women and one in seven men will be victims of domestic violence, and every 9 seconds a woman is beaten. Some 1,300 people are killed each year by abusive partners. Women are at greater risk in the home than in any other location (Garcia-Moreno et al., 2005).

Dating violence is even more common. The Centers for Disease Control and Prevention (CDC) defines "dating violence" as "the physical, sexual, psychological, or emotional violence within a dating relationship, including stalking. It can occur in person or electronically and might occur between a current or former dating partner" (Teen dating violence, 2015). An estimated 1.5 million high school students experience physical abuse from a dating partner each year in the United States. One-third of adolescents experience some form of emotional, physical, or sexual abuse from a dating partner, rates that are far higher than for other forms of violence experienced by youth (Davis, 2008). Twenty percent of teens admitted to either being a victim or perpetrator of physical or sexual violence on the National Survey on Teen Relationships and Intimate Violence, with almost 60 percent reporting that they experienced or perpetrated psychological abuse (Crary, 2014). Violent dating behavior generally begins when youth are aged 12–18 and in many cases continues into adulthood (Rosado, 2000). Unlike domestic violence, in which females are disproportionately victimized, boys and girls perpetrate and experience dating violence at similar rates, although the most common forms of abuse vary by gender. Boys tend to use more harmful physical forms of abuse, whereas girls are more likely to use verbal or emotional tactics, such as threatening suicide (National Center for Victims of Crime, n.d.).

Pregnant teens are particularly vulnerable to abuse with rates as high as 70 percent (Dancy, 2003). Many times victims believe that their abuser will cease hurting them, at least physically, if they know that it could harm a baby. That does not seem to be the case, however. One study found that 29 percent of young women pregnant as teens reported having been physically abused in the 12 months before the pregnancy. Another study found that 50–80 percent of teen moms said they were in a violent, abusive, or coercive relationship just before, during, or after the pregnancy. Yet another study found that 75 percent of pregnant teens experienced violence in the two years after giving birth (Silverman, Raj, & Clements, 2004).

Studies have found that females generally experience physical injuries more than do males (Avery-Leaf, Cascardi, & O'Leary, 1997; Foshee, 1996; Halpern et al., 2001; Molidor & Tolman, 1998). That is, the violence inflicted by males on females tends to be more severe (Arriaga & Foshee, 2004; Molidor & Tolman, 1998). One longitudinal study found that even after experiencing physical violence, teens are likely to stay with their abusers (O'Leary & Smith Slep, 2003). Arriaga and Foshee (2004) found that friends' experiences with dating violence were a significant predictor of whether adolescents were involved in dating violence themselves.

College students are also at increased risk for dating violence, with some 30–40 percent of college students experiencing some type of abuse from a dating partner (Leonard, Quigley, & Collins, 2002). The Feminist Majority Foundation reported in 2005 that 32 percent of college students are domestic violence victims. Additionally, 16 percent of college women report being sexually abused by a dating partner (Fifth & Pacific Companies, 2010). Smith et al. (2004) found that college women who were abused by a partner were more likely to endure subsequent physical violence. Stalking, a significant predictor of very serious and potentially lethal dating violence, is also prevalent on college campuses. Mustaine and Tewksbury (1999) found 10 percent of women attending nine colleges had been stalked in the previous six months. Victims suffer long-term impact, including increased substance abuse, lowered self-esteem, and increased risk of posttraumatic stress disorder. Abuse also negatively impacts academic performance.

The threat of physical harm is generally greatest when the victim is ending the relationship or immediately thereafter. This has been called "breakup violence." Twenty percent of teenaged girls reported to Liz Claiborne, Inc. (2005) that their boyfriends threatened violence or self-harm when they tried to break off the relationship. Much of the abuse is witnessed by at least one other person, and 42 percent of boys and 43 percent of girls reported that abuse occurs in school buildings or on school grounds (Lockyer & O'Connell, 2004).

Studies have found that only one-third of youth involved in abusive dating relationships tell anyone (Claiborne, 2005). There are many reasons why youth find it difficult to tell others about abuse, including the fact that dating violence is not specifically prohibited in every state (State laws . . . , 2014). Further, few state laws allow victims of dating violence to receive legal assistance such as restraining orders (State laws . . . , 2014). Victims also fear being judged, worry that they will not be believed, think they may suffer from retaliatory violence, and don't know whom to tell.

Several factors appear to increase the risk that someone will be involved in an abusive relationship, either as an abuser or as a perpetrator. Experiencing abuse as a child increases the risk of later involvement in abusive relationships two to three times. Teen consumption of alcohol and marijuana, as well as early engagement in sexual intercourse, has also been found to increase the risk of abuse (Eaton et al., 2007). Involvement in one abusive dating relationship is predictive of involvement in later dating violence. Additionally, bullying is a predictor of dating violence, in particular for boys. Several studies have found that youth who hold more positive attitudes toward the use of aggression, both in general and in relationships, are more prone to use violence in their dating relationships.

Lavoie, Robitaille, and Hebert (2000) found that teens named many factors that result in dating violence, including both pornography and movies. Conversely, Wood and colleagues (2002) asked teens to rank order a list of ten information sources about dating and television was in the top four, along with dating partners, friends, and parents. Such research supports the compelling need for books like this that can offer a critical examination of what is being taught through popular culture.

Sexual Assault

Rates of sexual assault are high as well. According to the CDC, sexual violence involves "sexual activity when consent is not obtained or freely given" (Sexual violence, 2015, para 1). The U.S. Department of Justice defines "sexual assault" as "any type of sexual contact or behavior that occurs without the explicit consent of the recipient." Sexual activities that fall under this definition include "forced sexual intercourse, forcible sodomy, child molestation, incest, fondling, and attempted rape" (Sexual violence, 2015).

According to the Rape, Abuse and Incest National Network (RAINN), a sexual assault occurs every 107 seconds in the United States. Some 44 percent of victims are under age 18, and 80 percent are under age 30 (Statistics, 2014). Forty-four percent of students in grades 7–12 who have been sexually assaulted were assaulted at school (Young, Grey, & Boyd, 2009). Like dating violence, the risk is particularly acute on college campuses (Statistics, 2014), and freshman and sophomores are at greatest risk (Krebs et al., 2007). An often-cited study from 2000 found that for every 1,000 women attending a college or university, there are 35 incidents of rape each academic year (Fisher, Daigle, & Cullen, 2009). A 2007 study by the U.S. Department of Justice found that 20 percent of female college students have been victims of attempted or actual sexual assaults, while one in sixteen college men report being actual or attempted victims (Krebs et al., 2007). Mohler-Kuo et al. (2004) found that women in sororities were 3 times more likely to be raped as were non-sorority members, and women living in dormitories or residence halls were 1.4 times more likely to be raped than women living off campus. Krebs et al. (2007) reported that 89 percent of campus sexual assaults occur when the victim is to some degree incapacitated by alcohol, and Mohler-Kuo et al. (2004) found that women who attended campuses with medium or high binge-drinking rates were 1.5 times more likely to be raped. Often, victims who have been drinking are reluctant to report sexual assault because they fear they won't be believed, will be judged, or will face trouble for their behavior.

An estimated 80 percent of victims know their assailants, while 47 percent of assailants are actual friends or acquaintances (Statistics, 2014). According to a 2000 report from the National Institute of Justice, 90 percent of campus victims of sexual assault knew their assailant (Fisher, Daigle, & Cullen, 2009). Research suggests that 40–62 percent of domestic violence victims have experienced sexual assault as one form of control exercised by their abusers (Tjaden & Thoennes, 2006).

Research has repeatedly documented that domestic violence, dating violence, and sexual assault are among the most underreported crimes. Criminologists refer to this as the "dark figure of crime"; that is, everyone knows far more incidents occur than are reported to authorities, but it is virtually impossible to assess how much. RAINN maintains that 68 percent of rapes are never reported to authorities (Statistics, 2014). Less than 5 percent of campus sexual assaults are reported to authorities, although two-thirds of victims tell someone (typically a friend) about the abuse (Fisher, Daigle, & Cullen, 2009; Krebs et al., 2007). Some people call crisis help lines, which provide another source of data about the incidence of domestic violence, dating violence, and sexual assault. The National Domestic Violence Hotline and the Love Is Respect hotline received, collectively, 377,968 contacts (calls, e-mails, and text messages) in 2014 (A year in review, 2014).

It is clear from these statistics that domestic violence and sexual assault are significant social and criminal problems. Victims, offenders, and the general public learn about these problems from media and popular culture, among other sources. Such depictions can change attitudes and behavior, whether it be to increase awareness, make us more fearful, increase the likelihood that we will perpetrate an offense, reduce or increase our support for victims, alter our understanding of why people offend, or affect myriad other changes. The following segment of the chapter begins with a brief discussion of the scope of popular culture consumption in the United States. Because popular culture that addresses rape and domestic violence is inevitably violent, the chapter provides an overview of literature relevant to exposure to violent media and popular culture, which frames the presentation of examples specific to rape and domestic violence.

MEDIA CONSUMPTION

In 2013, Americans spent an average of 4 hours and 31 minutes per day watching television, with U.S. adults spending almost 12 hours each day using some form of media (Delo, 2013). Children in the United States between ages 8 and 18 spend, on average, 40 hours behind a screen (Grossman & DeGaetano, 2014). One form of popular culture that is used most frequently by teens is video games, with some 97 percent of 12- to 17-year-olds and 90 percent of kids aged 8 to 16 regularly playing (Grossman & DeGaetano, 2014). While popular culture can certainly provide children and teens with heroes and role models, because violence is ubiquitous and is both reflected in and generated by popular culture, it can also cultivate aggressive and antisocial attitudes, beliefs, and behaviors (Giroux, 2013).

It is clear that popular culture has become more violent over time. The National Television Violence Study (NTVS) examined violent content over a three-year period (1996 to 1998). It found that approximately 60 percent of shows on television contained some type of violence (University of California, Santa Barbara, Center for Communication and Social Policy, 1998). On average, these programs had about six instances of violence per hour (University of California, Santa Barbara, Center for Communication and Social Policy, 1998). Some have proposed that networks and media moguls are competing with each other to deliver more sensational television and film to an ultra-desensitized audience, and, increasingly, a global one (Hiltbrand, 2007). While much of the mediated violence is perpetrated by adult characters, a study that utilized the NTVS and focused on the age of perpetrators found that about 7 percent of perpetrators of violence on television were teens. The majority (81 percent) were male, and 60 percent committed violence against another teen (Wilson, Colvin, & Smith, 2002).

It is not that viewing violent media inevitably results in violent thoughts and behaviors. How the violence is presented matters. The setting, tone, story line, character development, and other factors shape how mediated violence will be received by consumers. For example,

Plays such as *Macbeth* and films such as *Saving Private Ryan* treat violence as what it is—a human behavior that causes suffering, loss, and sadness to victims and perpetrators. In this context, with helpful adult guidance on the real costs and consequences of violence, appropriately mature adolescent viewers can learn the danger and harm of violence by vicariously experiencing its outcomes. Unfortunately, most entertainment violence is used for immediate visceral thrills without portraying any human cost and is consumed by adolescents or children without adult guidance or discussion. (Media violence, 2009)

Even children's programs contain violence; in fact, a study by the Kaiser Foundation found more violence in children's television programs than in any other category (Durham, 2008). In the time that children watch television, they observe at least 40,000 simulated murders and 200,000 acts of violence (Grossman & DeGaetano, 2014). It is clear that this will have some type of impact, although children's understanding of television programs and movies depends on their age. While studies have shown that comprehension of televised narratives occurs around age 10, more complicated films may remain difficult for teens to fully grasp. Even during adolescence, comprehension of extremely abstract moral principles, such as forgiveness over revenge and the nuances of good and evil as relative rather than absolute qualities, may still be difficult for youth to understand (Grossman & DeGaetano, 2014). As Grossman and DeGaetano (2014) explain,

> Because the portrayal of dominator/victim relationships is so pervasive in media violence, and because media play such a massive role in the lives of children and youth, there is an implicit social sanction normalizing the violence of the dominator/victim relationship. As children grow into the dominator role, acting it out in peer groups, practicing it over and over with violent video games, bullying others starts to feel normal. (p. 29)

In sum, "There is a generation out there that has been fed violence from its youngest days, and has been systematically taught to associate pleasure and reward with vivid depictions of inflicting human death and suffering" (Grossman & DeGaetano, 2014, p. 5). Groves (2003) explains that consuming violent media is even worse for children who have been exposed to violence in real life—a growing number of children in the United States. For these kids,

> television violence may represent a terrifying and realistic reenactment of their trauma. For these children, television violence precipitates acute

anxiety and fear. It seems that exposure to real-life violence increases vulnerability to the effects of television violence. Family and community violence and television violence thus may have a synergistic effect on children. (p. 25).

EFFECTS OF VIOLENT MEDIA ON CONSUMERS

While pundits and the general public still debate whether violent media has an effect on viewers, three scientific commissions—the Surgeon General's Commission Report (1972), the National Institute of Mental Health Ten Year Follow-Up (1982), and the American Psychological Association's Commission on Violence and Youth (1994)—have concluded that it is connected with increases in violent behavior. Further, the American Psychological Association's commission noted, and many studies have verified, that viewing violence may not only increase violent behavior but also result in desensitization to violence, as viewers who become accustomed to seeing it depicted in media may hold less empathetic views of victims and be less inclined to provide aid to persons in need. More than 1,000 studies have confirmed that television contributes in various ways to violent behavior (Media violence, 2009).

In 2000, six professional organizations issued a joint statement about media violence. The American Psychological Association, the American Academy of Pediatrics, the American Academy of Family Physicians, the American Psychiatric Association, the American Medical Association, and the American Academy of Child and Adolescent Psychiatry noted the more than 1,000 studies that "point overwhelmingly to a causal connection between media violence and aggressive behavior in some children" (in Grossman & DeGaetano, 2014, pp. 37–38). Testifying at a Senate Commerce Committee hearing in 2003, Dr. Michael Rich, director of the Center on Media and Children's Health at the Children's Hospital of Boston, stated that the link between violent media and aggressive behavior is "stronger than that of calcium intake and bone mass, lead ingestion and lower IQ, condom non-use and sexually acquired HIV, and environmental tobacco smoke and lung cancer, all associations that clinicians accept as fact, and on which preventive medicine is based without question" (in Grossman & DeGaetano, 2014, p. 38).

Grossman and DeGaetano (2014) identify four main effects of media violence, all supported by research. First, media violence increases aggression. For instance, a 2008 meta-analysis of 26 studies involving 13,661 participants found a link between violent media exposure and violent behavior like punching, beating, and choking of others. Another study conducted in 2010 which included 130,295 participants around the world found users of violent video games increased aggressive thoughts, physiological arousal, angry feelings, and aggressive behavior. These and other studies find that the earlier a youth is exposed to violent media and the more frequent involvement increases the effects. Second, violent media increases fear (Glassner, 1999). For example, a 2006 study found that 13- to 17-year-olds who watched more news coverage of the Iraq war expressed greater concern than youth who watched less coverage. Media scholar George Gerbner has studied this for decades and found that both adults and young people who regularly watch violent media rate the world as a more dangerous place, what he calls "the mean world syndrome." Empirical data show crime dramas actually increase fear of crime, especially for men (Psychologists study media violence . . . , 2015).

In their book *The Spiral Notebook* (2015) about James Holmes, the shooter who killed 12 and wounded 70 at a movie theater in Aurora, Colorado, on July 20, 2012, Stephen and Joyce Singular examine the influence of violent popular culture on mass shooters. Holmes was obsessed with the Joker character played by Heath Ledger in *The Dark Knight*, whom he emulated not only in his actions but in his dress as well. They explain,

> The filmgoing generation of teenagers and twentysomethings, including Holmes, had been raised under the near-constant threat of disaster in America and imminent collapse. Countless movies and TV programs aimed at them were dystopian, apocalyptic, or post-apocalyptic, populated by zombies, vampires, and huge mechanical monsters storming through cities and wreaking havoc. (p. 70)

Throughout the book they interview teens and college-age students about growing up in this era. One 25-year-old graduate student commented,

> If you don't have close friends or a good relationship with your parents, what do you have? Action characters in video games and movies. The point of these games is violence. You learn to cope through fantasy games and drugs. Through some form of escape. I see this everywhere in people my age. They feel powerless. They have a lot of intelligence, just like James Holmes, but not a lot of tools for coping. The video games cover all the recent wars: Vietnam, Korea, Afghanistan, and Iraq. It's not hard to figure how someone raised on this stuff could act it out in a real way that causes real violence. Holmes's crime is exactly like something out of a video game. He's basically acting out something he's already seen in a fictional scene. (p. 81)

Third, heavy consumers of violent media often become desensitized to violence in the real world. For example, Krahe et al. (2011) measured skin conductance levels of 303 undergraduate students who either watched a sad film clip or a violent one. They found those who watched the violent clip showed evidence of desensitization. Fourth, users of violent media have an increased appetite for violence. A 2013 study analyzed PG 13 movies and found that they contain more violent scenes than did rated R movies from the 1980s, documenting the increase in violence that viewers enjoy.

Durham (2008) explains that while there may not be a causal relationship between media violence and violent behavior, media

> are culture mythmakers: they supply us, socially, with ideas and scripts into our consciousness over time, especially when the myths are constantly recirculated in various forms. They accentuate certain aspects of social life and underplay others. They are a part of a larger culture in which these myths are already at work, making it possible for the myths to find fertile ground in which to take root and flourish. They can reinforce certain social patterns and trends, and invalidate others. They can gradually and insidiously shape our ways of thinking, our notions of what is normal and what is deviant, and our acceptance of behaviors and ideas that we see normalized on television, in films, and in other forms of popular culture. (pp. 148–149)

Lavoie, Robitaille, and Hebert (2000) found that participants said media had the least influence on them; this is a typical response because of what is known as the "third-person effect," which states that people think the media may influence others but not themselves (Davison, 1983). That is, we are prone to believe that we are wiser or more savvy and thus will not allow popular culture to impact our beliefs or behaviors but other less wise individuals will succumb.

The effects of consuming violent media appear to be both short and long term. Huesmann and colleagues (2003) conducted a longitudinal study that followed up on 557 youth aged 6–9 from a 1977 Chicago study in an attempt to ascertain the long-term effects of exposure to violent media. They re-interviewed 329 of the participants who were then in their mid-twenties. They found a clear connection between childhood viewing of violent media and aggressive adult behavior. Men who were "high TV violence viewers" as children were more likely to have pushed, grabbed, or shoved their spouses; to have responded to an insult with physical aggression; to have had a traffic violation; and to have been arrested. The arrest rate for high TV violence viewing men was three times that of other men. Women who were high TV violence viewers were more likely to have thrown something at their spouse; to have pushed, shoved, beaten, or choked someone in anger; to have a traffic violation; and to have committed a criminal act. The reported rate of punching, choking, or beating another adult was four times higher among high TV violence viewing women than other women. In reviewing more than five decades' worth of research, Potter (1999) extended cultivation theory to determine that (1) exposure to violent portrayals in the media can increase viewer aggression and (2) consumption of violent media increased desensitization, and over time, viewers are more accepting of violence.

Characters in popular culture use violence for a variety of purposes, and consumers are supposed to identify, or have allegiance, with them, in large part due to the reasons for their violence. Thus, again, how violence is depicted and who uses it shape the way it will impact consumers. Neuman and Baron (1998) provide a typology of instrumental and expressive violence as it is depicted in films. Instrumental violence is perpetrated for a particular purpose or goal. Instrumental violence is presented in the following ten ways: (1) rebellion against injustice, (2) vengeance, (3) rebellion against bureaucracy, (4) problem-solving, (5) extracting confessions, (6) demonstrate authority, (7) expose corruption, (8) establish order, (9) a higher morality, and (10) conflict resolution. Expressive violence is presented via: (1) stereotyping of ethnic groups, (2) teenage rebellion, (3) nature, (4) the beast, (5) going it one better, (6) war, (7) fun, (8) mysticism, (9) the madman, (10) vengeance, and (11) sex. Films like *Star Wars* tend to emphasize defeating dark, evil, and violent enemies through violent action. As Neuman and Baron (1998) explained, "Evening up the score is a well-established justification for the use of violence, motivated, some would say, by an expressive or emotional urge to correct a deeply perceived wrong" (p. 45). Citing the *Batman* series, Neuman and Baron (1998) explained, "It seems a contradiction in terms to suggest that violence can be used to establish order because we tend most commonly to think of violence as breaking down order, going against it. But, if chaos reigns (or is perceived to reign), then violence is often used as a ploy to introduce order" (p. 47). Similarly, the Harry Potter series shows protagonist Harry and his supporters using similar forms of violence as those characters presented as "evil" yet it is supposed to be considered justified or acceptable because of its benevolent purpose (Finley & Concannon, 2014). American media tend to portray heroes or protagonists with whom viewers or readers are to identify as using violence to "save the day." Such violence is then perceived as just and necessary and is therefore unlikely to be questioned. The 1999 Brad Pitt and Edward Norton film *Fight Club* has also influenced young men to see themselves as heroes for using violence. Singular and Singular (2015) explain, "Fight Club conveys the message that the way to have a real impact on society is to do something huge and bloody. And in some ways, it's a very difficult message to counter. The movie stars who embody this core message naturally become onscreen heroes and role models" (p. 103). Their son, Eric, who was interviewed for their book, explained,

> The movie is about men feeling emasculated because they don't look like the images in Calvin Klein ads. Believe me, this is a big deal to guys, not just to young women. You have no idea. The mass shooters are not alpha males. Young dudes want to feel empowered and the only way some of them can do it is by joining the military, where they'll man you up. Or you can be in the fake military and play violent video games like Call of Duty, which recreate all of America's recent wars. If you're weak in the real world, in that realm you can kill people much bigger than you and feel good about yourself for a while. (p. 105)

One of the problems with media violence is that it is typically presented as if there are no consequences. As Groves (2003) explains, "It is 'clean.' There is a lack of blood, minimal suffering, and often, in the case of television and video games, the cartoon characters are invincible" (p. 26). Violence is frequently rewarded in popular cultures, and it is usually easy to determine who the "good" and "bad" guys are, which is clearly not the case in reality. Gerbner has referred to this as "happy violence," and notes that it is most common in children's programs. Cartoons often show characters getting beaten, falling off cliffs, blown up by dynamite, or facing other forms of violence and then popping back up, same as always.

Popular culture also fails to tell the reality of crime. Violent crimes like murder are overrepresented in dramatic television programming (Estep & MacDonald, 1983; Shrum, 1996) as well as in reality-based television shows and other forms of popular culture (Cavender & Bond-Maupin, 1993). Consequently, viewers may overestimate how much violent crime occurs and misunderstand the nature of it. Not only does this make people more fearful of what they perceive to be a very dangerous world, but also it changes our daily behaviors. People may avoid certain neighborhoods, purchase weapons or other devices for security, or even stay in more often out of fear that they will be victimized. As Surette (1992, p. 296) contends:

> If most of us get our knowledge of crime and criminal justice from the news media and TV programs, which tend to cover or portray only the most sensational kinds of crime and criminal justice activities, it's no surprise that

many of us develop perceptions that may not reflect what is really happening in the world of crime and in the various stages of the criminal justice system.

Violence is often, although not exclusively, depicted in crime-related shows, which have constituted approximately one-third of all television programs since the 1980s (Rader & Rhineburger-Dunn, 2010). These shows provide important narratives about why crime happens, who is a perpetrator, and who is a victim. Studies have shown that victims are often presented in dramatic ways that result in viewers seeing them as dissimilar to themselves, which may result in increased victim-blaming (Berns & Schweingruber, 2007; Best, 1999). Research suggests that most do not blame victims out of malice but instead out of a desire to believe that the world is just and thus people who are victimized are at fault, at least in part (Best, 1999). Research has shown that crime-related television often emphasizes the victimization of white women by black offenders (Chancer, 1998). In reality, however, most crime is intraracial.

Rafter (2000) and Rafter and Brown (2011) have documented how popular movies reinforce dangerous stereotypes about who commits the crime and responses to it. Films are a significant source of people's ideas "about legality and illegality, the volume of various types of crime, and the motives of lawbreakers" (p. vii). Further, "Due to the globalization of film markets, movies also play a major role internationally in the dispersion of images, myths, and values. For many of us, they are a significant source—perhaps the most significant source—of ideas about crime and criminals" (p. vii). Yet, "although film plays a central role in generating representations and understandings of crime, criminologists have traditionally ignored it, clinging to a narrow social science perspective that pays little attention to the interactions of crime and culture" (Rafter, 2000, p. 4). Additionally, the way police and social service agencies react or provide aid to such victims can certainly be shaped and altered by unfavorable depictions seen in media outlets (Farr, 2005). Britto and colleagues (2007) note that the "prescribed formula taken in prime-time crime dramas, which includes an evil offender, a violent crime, at least one go-getter police officer who is willing to bend the rules to serve justice and a just resolution of the case at the end of the program can create powerful ideological images of crime, the efficiency of the criminal justice system, and characteristics of offenders and victims" (p. 40).

Another form of popular culture, video games, is particularly popular with young boys and men. While some video games feature content that is not problematic, and playing games have been found to have some positive effects on specific kids, many games are hyperviolent and misogynistic. Bushman and Anderson (2009) conducted two studies to test whether playing violent video games or viewing violent movies decreased participants' willingness to help others. In one, participants played either a violent or a nonviolent video game. After playing, they overheard a staged fight that resulted in (fake) injury. While more of the nonviolent players pledged to help the injured person, the result was not statistically significant. The people who had played the violent game who agreed to help took longer to do so and rated the potential for injury as less serious, and they were more likely to report that they had not heard the cry for help than the nonviolent players. In the second experiment, they staged a minor emergency outside of theaters that were showing a violent movie (*The Ruins*, 2008) or a nonviolent one (*Nim's Island*, 2008). Participants who had viewed the violent movie took 26 percent longer to offer aid. Anderson and Bushman (2001) conducted a meta-analytic review of studies of violent video games and violent behavior before 2000. They found a statistically significant relationship between video game violence and violent behavior across 33 studies involving 3,033 participants. Both violent thoughts and violent behavior increased when the violence in the game increased among males, females, children, and adults alike. Further, they found a decrease (at least temporary) in prosocial behavior among those who played violent video games.

As Grossman and DeGaetano (2014) explain, "There is a generation out there that has been fed violence from its youngest days, and has been systematically taught to associate pleasure and reward with vivid depictions of inflicting human death and suffering" (p. 5). The popularity of video games, in particular more graphically violent and real-like options, grew tremendously in the 1990s. Games like *Doom*, introduced in 1992, allowed players to kill simulated people instead of just monsters and demons. The *Duke Nukem* series allowed the shooter, "Duke," who looks like the Terminator, to walk through pornography shops and use posters of scantily clad women as target practice. At more advanced levels, Duke is given bonus points for murdering female prostitutes who are generally naked. Throughout the game Duke encounters naked women who are bound, some of whom even plead "Kill me, kill me." The game awards points for rampage shootings, while the game *Redneck Rampage* features kids perpetrating massacres against farmers and farm animals. *Fallout 3* includes "realistic dismemberment" and "slow motion decapitation" (Grossman & DeGaetano, 2014). Durham (2008) notes that a description of *Grand Theft Auto* states, "You can pick up a hooker, take her out in the woods, have sex with her, pull over, beat her with a bat, then you can get into the car and run her over" (p. 141). *Manhunt 2* features a basement sex club that is a torture chamber (Durham, 2008).

Accompanying these games are action figures which are marketed to kids aged 4 and older. The video game industry is lucrative. In 2013, when *Grand Theft Auto V* was released, consumers spent a billion dollars on the game in just the first three days. That game broke seven records according to the Guinness Book of World Records, including being the best-selling video game in 24 hours and the fastest video game to gross $1 billion. Grossman and DeGaetano (2014) note that if it was a film, it would be the highest grossing of all time. Although video games receive ratings, many do not pay attention to them, according to Durham (2008), who notes that 60 percent of all 13- to 18-year-olds in the United States have played violent video games. Grossman and DeGaetano (2014) note that 89 percent of games are violent, and even 98 percent of those rated appropriate for teens. One-third of all video games feature sexual themes, including sexual violence (Durham, 2008). A 2010 study by Dr. Jordan Grafman with the National Institute of Neurological Disorders found that "continued exposure to violent videos will make an adolescent less sensitive to violence, more accepting of violence, and more likely to commit aggressive acts" (in Grossman & DeGaetano, 2014, p. 88). Video games impact users on the neurological, psychological, and sociological levels. Neurologically, violent video games lead viewers to associate violence with feelings of satisfaction. Psychologically, it creates a sense of self that is comfortable being able to inflict pain on others, while sociologically, it reinforces a society in which inflicting pain on others is normal. Kids often relate easily to video or mediated perpetrators of violence. A study of sixth through eighth grade boys found that playing *Mortal Kombat* resulted in increased aggressive behavior (Durham, 2008). Another study in 2004 found that eighth and ninth grade boys who played violent video games "were more hostile . . . [and] were more likely to be involved in physical fights" (in Durham, 2008, p. 144). Anderson and Bushman (2001) conducted a meta-analysis of studies examining effects of video games. They found that video games in which violent action was the focus increased aggressive behavior. Anderson's (2004) meta-analysis echoed those findings.

For example, Eric Harris and Dylan Klebold, the Columbine killers, as well as Adam Lanza, the man responsible for the Sandy Hook Elementary massacre, were all avid players of violent video games that reward players for increased and more grisly kills (Grossman & DeGaetano, 2014). Just one month after Sandy Hook, 15-year-old Nehemiah Griego shot his mother in her bed, his 9-year-old brother, and his two sisters, 5 and 2, before lying in wait for his father, whom he shot in an ambush. Griego was an admitted "violent video game lover" (Grossman & DeGaetano, 2014, p. 9). Grossman and DeGaetano (2014) explain, "Kids immersed in violent entertainment can blur lines between reality and fantasy. They really don't know why they commit a horrendous crime. On March 24, 2013, 13-year-old Noah Crooks shot his mother twenty times with a .22 caliber rifle and then texted his father, 'Dad this is Noah. I killed mom accidentally. I regret it. Come home now please.' " Crooks shot his mother 20 times, something he had practiced when he played *Grand Theft Auto*. He even told the 911 dispatch that he "felt crazy" and "tried to rape his own mom." It turns out his mother had tried to take away his access to video games in weeks prior due to his bad grades (pp. 10–11).

> Since they practice murder in the virtual world to the point of obsessiveness, youth weaned on violent video games carry out their slaughter in ways that closely resemble the world that preoccupies them. That's what John Zahwari did on June 10, 2013, when he turned the beachfront community of Santa Monica, California, into a battlefield. Zahwari, age twenty-three, who was once a bomb-making teen, shot at cars and at anyone in sight after killing his father and brother and burning down their house. By the time he finished, six innocent people were dead, including a sixty-eight-year-old woman whom he shot in the head at point-blank-range. Eyewitnesses and authorities declared the melee as a "copycat of the video game, *Grand Theft Auto*," complete with house burning and carjacking. (p. 11)

On August 23, 2013, an 8-year-old who had been playing *Grand Theft Auto* got up from the console, found the family gun, and shot his grandmother in the head (Grossman & DeGaetano, 2014, p. 13).

In sum,

> While the media may not cause our behaviors, they are culture mythmakers: they supply us, socially, with ideas and scripts into our consciousness over time, especially when the myths are constantly recirculated in various forms. They accentuate certain aspects of social life and underplay others. They are a part of a larger culture in which these myths are already at work, making it possible for the myths to find fertile ground in which to take root and flourish. They can reinforce certain social patterns and trends, and invalidate others. They can gradually and insidiously shape our ways of thinking, our notions of what is normal and what is deviant, and our acceptance of behaviors and ideas that we see normalized on television, in films, and in other forms of popular culture. (Durham, 2008, pp. 148–149)

Popular Culture and Domestic Violence and Rape

Popular culture also features hypersexualized images and messaging, which, coupled with the violence, send powerful and dangerous messages about gender, rape, and domestic violence. Researchers have observed that exposure to sexually violent films, television, song lyrics, and music videos desensitizes consumers to violent behavior (Linz, Donnerstein, & Adams, 1989; Linz, Donnerstein, & Penrod, 1988), increases aggressive beliefs and thoughts (Barongan & Hall, 1995; Peterson & Pfost, 1989), increases negative views of women, decreases empathy for female victims (Krafka et al., 1997; Linz et al., 1984; Linz et al., 1988; Linz et al., 1989), and increases male's belief in their dominance over females (Golde et al., 2000; Mulac, Jansma, & Linz, 2002).

Females are also more likely to be depicted as sexual beings than males, and are often only portrayed as successful when they are young, thin, attractive, and sexualized (Carpenter & Edison, 2005; Smith, Stern & Mastro, 2004). Jean Kilbourne's work has documented how the typical beauty image is a statuesque, very thin and small hipped, extremely attractive female. This body type is found among approximately 5 percent of the world's women (Kilbourne, 1995). Researchers have attempted to assess the effects of viewing, hearing, and reading these stereotypical images. Behm-Morawitz and Mastro (2008) found that viewing teen films contributes to negative gender-role stereotyping among high school students. Attempts to fulfill this body type have been found to be related to body dissatisfaction (Stice & Shaw, 1994), lower self-esteem (Wilcox & Laird, 2000), greater self-objectification (Harper & Tiggemann, 2008), anger and depression (Pinhas et al., 1999), increased self-consciousness (Kalodner, 1997), and signs of disordered eating (Harrison, 2001; Harrison & Cantor, 1997). Despite several decades of attention to these dangerous mediated body images, several studies have found that female images have gotten even thinner and less realistic (Barriga, Shapiro, & Jhaveri, 2009). The hypersexualization and impossible stereotypes of women and girls set the stage for violence to be normalized. Those images that couple sex with violence are said to have the most detrimental effects. Research has found that persons who consume violent, sexualized media can experience reduced empathy for females who are victimized (Linz et al., 1989).

Sexualized images are everywhere and are frequently marketed to children and teens. Abercrombie & Fitch marketed thong underwear for 10-year-olds featuring slogans like "Wink, Wink" and "Eye Candy" while Wal-Mart at one point sold panties for teen girls that read "Who needs credit cards ...?" (Durham, 2008). "Most media aimed at adolescent and preadolescent girls focus on attracting male desire—'how to get the guy.' And the route to that all-important end involves acquiring a specifically contoured body featuring large breasts, flat abs, and slender thighs; facial features approximating a Caucasian ideal; and a wardrobe and cosmetic stockpile whose elements must shift constantly in order to stay au courant," what Durham (2008) calls the "Lolita effect" (p. 39). Durham (2008) explains that although American culture likes to glorify the "Lolita" stereotype, the book by Vladimir Nabokov makes clear that the 12-year-old Dolores Haze, also known as Lolita, was the powerless victim of her stepfather, Humbert Humbert, a predator (Durham, 2008).

The James Bond films, still popular today, feature prominent female characters "who variously tempt, distract, and assist James in his latest mission. Typically, at least one 'Bond girl' is particularly striking—a woman with an adventurous nature, cunning attributes, strong potential for romantic entanglement with Bond, and a sense of self-assurance whose name (Pussy Galore, Honey Ryder, or Holly Goodhead, for example) is as provocative as the character she portrays" (Neuendorf et al., 2010, p. 747). There has never been a Bond film without a "Bond Girl," and it is the casting of these roles that gets most of the media attention before the films are released (d'Abo & Cork, 2003). In their content analysis of James Bond films, Neuendorf et al. (2010) found that the stereotypes remain true of Bond girls, who are still portrayed as young, attractive, slender, and, importantly, disposable. Nearly 20 percent of the Bond girls were presumed to be dead by the end of the films.

When girls and women are constantly told that in order to "get a man" they must be ultra-sexy, and when boys believe that this is what makes a female attractive, it should be no surprise that the objectification continues in personal and intimate relationships. For instance, studies indicate that exposure to sexual media predicts young adolescents' sexual behavior: "kids who watch highly sexualized media are about twice as likely to have sex early as kids who don't. This finding holds true across class and race" (Durham, 2008, p. 50). In *Pornland: How Pornography Has Hijacked Our Sexuality*, feminist scholar Dines argues that images of violence in Internet-based pornography, which typically included choking, gagging, beating, cutting, and forcing women to consume men's bodily fluids, has created unrealistic expectations around sex. Dines interviewed young men who consumed Internet pornography and found that they expect women to engage in violent sexual acts. Their female partners feel pressured to do so (Bonomi et al., 2014, p. 2). Durham (2008) explains:

Images of violence against women are pervasive: on billboards, in magazines, on television. A magazine ad for the upscale Dolce and Gabbana clothing line features a man having sex with a woman, while other men stand around watching. The scene implies a gang rape. The models in the ad are beautiful, and they look intense and turned on. The woman does not appear to be afraid. The gang rape is implicitly justified. An ad for Cesare Paciotti shoes shows a man stepping on a beautiful, red-lipsticked woman's face. An ad for Radeon gaming software depicts a topless young woman with the product's name branded on her back: the brand is red and raw. (p. 148)

Other forms of popular culture often present violence as sexy. Shooting target producer ZMB Industries introduced a line of targets featuring "zombine ex-girlfriends," clad in bras and bleeding from their mouths. While the company claimed it does not condone violence against women, it used the following description in its marketing:

Be warned, hell hath no fury like a woman scorned but a man scorned is nothing to mess with! A young gent from Louisiana, we'll call him Andre to protect his identity, was deeply committed to his one true love and her to him, or so he thought. While partying with her friends during one particular Mardi Gras, she took several suitors over the course of the festivities. Andre felt something odd indeed, so he paid a visit to his great aunt, Marie, who helped him see the truth. With a few eggs, candles lit and kiss upon his forehead, her voodoo curse was set in motion. Late each night while lying in bed, a smile would appear across his face, for a slight breeze would travel through a cracked window bringing with it, a faint whiff of decay and a unnatural cry of regret. (McDonough, 2013)

Movies do the same. Mulvey (1975) argued that, because the United States is an androcentric culture, women in films are always subject to male heterosexual gaze. In *From Reverence to Rape: The Treatment of Women in the Movies*, Molly Haskell (1987) examines the often dichotomous representations of females in films. She notes, "A woman's intelligence was the equivalent of a man's penis: something to be kept out of sight. Ambition in a woman had either to be deflected into the vicarious drives of her loved ones or to be mocked and belittled" (p. 4). Haskell (1987) notes that it is only in the last several decades that males have dominated film. Prior to the 1960s, women were often billed ahead of men, and were, far more than men, "the barometers of changing fashion. Like two-way mirrors linking the immediate past with the immediate future, women in the movies reflected, perpetuated, and in some respects offered innovations on the roles of women in society" (p. 12).

It wasn't always the case that women's sexuality was vilified in popular culture.

Until the Production Code went into full force, between 1933 and 1934, women were conceived of as having sexual desire without being freaks, villains, or even necessarily Europeans—an attitude surprising to those of us nurtured on the movies of another period. Women were entitled to intimate sexual encounters, to pursue men, even to embody certain "male" characteristics without being stigmatized as "unfeminine," or "predatory." Nor was their sexuality thought of as cunning and destructive, in the manner of certain forties' heroines; rather, it was unabashedly front and center, and if a man allowed himself to be victimized by a woman's sex, it was probably through some long-standing misapprehension of his own nature. (Haskell, 1987, p. 91)

Haskell (1987) refers to the thirties and forties as the heyday for the "woman's film." These, she argues, feature four central themes, often found in combination. First, a woman was to sacrifice: herself for her children, her children for their own good, her marriage for her lover, her lover for her marriage or for his own good, her career for love, or her love for her career. Sacrifices tend to end happily, stressing women's so-called joy of suffering. Second, the heroine of women's films is typically struck by some affliction which she typically keeps secret. Third, women in these films typically are pursued by at least two suitors and must choose between them. Finally, the heroine generally meets and competes with the wife or girlfriend of the man she loves. The women often find they like one another better than they do the man (pp. 163–164).

In 1960, the iconic *Psycho* featured nude Janet Leigh being stabbed in the shower, kicking off the popularity of horror/slasher films. While some maintain that these films allow viewers to identify with victims, others note that the girls who are killed are often being "punished" for sexual behavior and/or for other alleged negligence and violations (Durham, 2008). Horror/slasher films equate sex with violence. Most consider John Carpenter's *Halloween* to have paved the way for the slasher film industry. *Halloween*, which was filmed on a mere $325,000 budget, was one of the most financially successful independent films, earning $47 million. The slasher genre was widely popular in the 1980s and waned in the 1990s. It was reinvigorated in the 2000s with the release of *Scream*. Between 2004 and 2006, an average of 20 horror films were released each year (Bowles, 2007). Teens are the biggest consumers of what has been called "torture porn" films like the *Saw* and *Hostel* series. These films are notorious for their depictions of graphic sexual violence (Murray, 2007). Grauerholz and King (1997) found that depictions of the sexual harassment of women "occur with regularity" on prime-time television. Studies also show that adolescents' exposure to violent media content is associated with real-life aggression and violent behavior regardless of the type of media (Potera & Kennedy, 2009; Ybarra et al., 2008).

Welsh (2009) analyzed 50 slasher/horror films from 1960 to 2007. He found a greater number of violent interactions involving female characters, and that they were generally depicted in heightened states of fear or terror and psychological aggression. While the male characters experienced more severe forms of violence, the violence against the female characters took up more screen time. Only female characters were ever shown nude, and they were more likely to be presented in scenes that included both violence and sex. Clover (1992) argued that while male and female characters die at relatively equitable rates in slasher films, the death scenes involving males are almost never set in a sexual context. Heavy consumption of sexual images appears to decrease sensitivity toward sexual aggression victims (MacKay & Covell, 1997), and repeated exposure to filmed violence against women similarly produces desensitization effects (Dexter et al., 1997). Gender role stereotypes portrayed in the media reflect gender stereotypes in society (Signorielli, 1989), as well as stereotypes of crime and victimization. Rape tends to be portrayed as perpetrated by sadistic, psychopathic, or disturbed persons who prey on the relatively helpless (Bufkin & Eschholz, 2000). Numerous studies have reported that sexually oriented violence against female characters in film increases men's negative attitudes toward female victims, distorts their beliefs about women and sexuality, and increases aggressive behavior against women (Barongan & Hall, 1995; Linz et al., 1989).

Linz, Donnerstein, and Penrod (1988) conducted a study with males in which participants were shown five full-length slasher films over the course of one to two weeks. Researchers measured participants' emotional reactions, perceptions of violence, and attitudes toward women after each film. They found that participants perceived less violence in the films and found them to be less degrading to women over time. Further, participants expressed less sympathy toward women who were described as rape victims than did the control group. Linz et al. (1988) explained that, initially, violence against women produces anxiety in viewers but that as they watch more, they become more comfortable with the content and thus it produces less anxiety. Using a similar research design, Mullin and Linz (1995) also found that men exposed to slasher films experienced desensitization.

The desensitization toward victims of domestic violence remained three days after the exposure to the films. Titillating violence in sexual contexts and comic violence are particularly dangerous, because they associate positive feelings with hurting others. One study of nearly 32,000 teenagers in eight different countries, for example, revealed that heavy television-viewing was associated with bullying (Kuntsche et al., 2006).

Weisz and Earls (1995) randomly assigned 193 college students to view one of four films. One (*Deliverance*) featured sexual violence against a male, one (*Straw Dogs*) featuring sexual aggression against a female, another depicting physical aggression (*Die Hard 2*), and the other containing virtually no explicit physical or sexual aggression (*Days of Thunder*). Upon viewing their assigned film, the participants completed a 252-item questionnaire that addressed acceptance of interpersonal violence, rape myth acceptance, attraction to sexual aggression, a hostility inventory, a social desirability scale, and an empathy assessment. Then, participants viewed a reenactment of a rape trial and completed another questionnaire. Males were more accepting of both rape myths and interpersonal violence, were more attracted to sexual aggression, and, after viewing the rape trial reenactment, rated less likely to express sympathy for the victim and to view the defendant as guilty. The effect was the same regardless of whether the film depicted aggression or violence against a male or female. Females were not affected by any of the film types.

Music videos often contain high levels of gender violence. One study found that more than 80 percent of the violence portrayed in contemporary music videos is perpetrated by an attractive male protagonist against women (Rich et al., 1998). Even music videos by female artists may use the same formula. Interestingly, shock rocker Marilyn Manson expressed dismay at Lana Del Rey's video for "Summertime," which features the star being pushed forcibly onto a bed by a man and sexually assaulted. The video ends with her crying while wearing a Texas Chainsaw Massacre T-shirt, bringing together the sex and violence combination. Manson commented, "It wasn't a Marilyn Manson video. This was a grand mistake by the person who put it with my videos but I really had nothing to do with it . . . I'm a person that would beat somebody's ass if they raped somebody I knew" (Denham, 2014).

Music lyrics and videos commonly objectify women, depicting them in hypersexual ways and referring to them as "bitches and hos." One study found that 90 percent of the videos aired on MTV featured sexually explicit content. Plie's "Shawty" discusses raping and beating women who appear to be prostitutes. It's not just rap and hip-hop. Pop star Justin Timberlake's video for "What Goes Around" showed the artist in a violent altercation with a girl who then ends up burning to death. Eminem's video for "Superman" shows him shoving a woman against a wall and ripping off her clothes while rapping "Don't put out? I'll put you out" (Durham, 2008, p. 146). Filmmaker and former professional football player Byron Hurt believes that misogynistic and violent rap music is a factor in the high rates of sexual assault and domestic violence experienced by African American women. He believes that young black men often act out the abusive relationships they see modeled in these videos, and that women may find such behavior more acceptable. Hurt's contentions are supported by a study that found African American girls were more accepting of dating violence after being exposed to rap videos. Other research has found that white, middle-class women who are exposed to these videos are more accepting of real-life interpersonal violence as well (Durham, 2008). Cundiff (2013) analyzed the lyrical content of popular rap and hip-hop songs ($n = 20$) on Billboard's "Hot 100" chart between 2000 and 2010. She found repeated objectification of, power over, and violence toward women. She also conducted surveys with listeners and found a positive correlation between misogynistic thinking and rap/hip-hop consumption.

In a content analysis of six types of media, Pardun, L'Engle, and Brown (2005) found that music contained substantially more sexual content than any other form. Sexually explicit and derogatory lyrics are particularly common in rap music. Young adults between the ages of 16 and 30 are the most likely age group to consume rap/hip-hop music. Because of the volume of this type of music they listen to, they may become desensitized to the derogatory lyrics and to those that condone relationship violence and sexual aggression. Hip-hop culture has been said to "teach men that aggression and violence are closely linked to cultural views of masculinity" (Wood, 2012, p. 105). Rap and hip-hop also celebrate the physical abuse of women, thereby reinforcing models of masculinity that sustain and encourage misogyny. Adams and Fuller (2006) assert that rap music reduces women to objects "that are only good for sex and abuse," which "perpetuate ideas, values, beliefs, and stereotypes that debase women" (p. 940).

Dr. Edgar Tyson (2006) developed a 26-item instrument, the Rap Music Attitude and Perception (RAP) scale, the "only tool available to access an individual's attitude toward and perception of rap music lyrics" (p. 212). The RAP scale contains three constructs: empowerment, artistic aesthetics, and violent misogyny. Gourdine and Lemmons (2011) used the RAP scale to measure "violent, sexist, and misogynistic images conveyed in the lyrics" to examine college students' perceptions of the content through a survey (Gourdine & Lemmons, 2011, p. 65). Using meta-analysis, Timmerman et al. (2008) found that "listening to music generates an effect on listeners consistent with the content of the music," such as when rap/hip-hop artists communicate themes condoning "power over, objectification of and violence against women" (p. 303).

One experimental study examined exposure to the attitude toward dating violence held by teens exposed to rap music videos. Researchers found that females who watched these videos were more likely to consider dating violence as acceptable, and, while that was not the case for males, the researchers noted that men already held much higher levels of acceptance (Johnson et al., 1995).

Armstrong (2001) conducted a content analysis of 490 rap songs from 1987 to 1993, in which 22 percent contained lyrics featuring violence against women including assault, rape, and murder. His study classified rap songs into different categories in which rappers either pride themselves on sex acts appearing to harm women, justify other acts of violence, warn women who challenge male domination that they will be assaulted, and/or seem to invite male violence against women (Armstrong, 2001). Weitzer and Kubrin (2009) conducted a follow-up study analyzing the portrayal of women in 403 rap songs through a content analysis, in which themes of derogatory naming and shaming of women, sexual objectification of women, distrust of women, legitimation of violence against women, and celebration of prostitution and pimping appeared at the greatest frequency. Sexual objectification was found to occur in 67 percent of the misogynistic lyrics in their songs sampled (Weitzer & Kubrin, 2009).

Despite the frequency with which domestic violence occurs in real life, Said (2011) noted that, "Many people first encounter an instance of domestic violence through a mediated source, such as a film, TV show, newspaper, or magazine." While domestic violence once was discussed almost exclusively on women's channels like Lifetime and Oxygen, daytime talk shows, or via soap operas, the topic is now depicted in a variety on a variety of more mainstream television programs. In 2002, Shoos (2003) noted that domestic violence was the topic of popular television dramas like *ER* and *NYPD Blue* as well as the HBO series' *Six Feet Under* and *The Sopranos*. Yet these depictions are not always accurate nor are they helpful in understanding domestic violence. Gender violence is one of the most common themes in popular culture, especially in genres targeted to adolescent audiences. These depictions serve to normalize male violence and therefore "play a critical role in constructing violent male sexuality as a cultural norm" (Katz, 2006, p. 153). According to Berns (2004), the media has a massive influence over perceptions of social problems, including domestic abuse. Berns (2004) argues that women's magazines tell stories about domestic violence that provide an uplifting or hopeful ending. Berns (2004) argues that these are the key ways in which women's magazines frame abusive situations as empowering and "inspirational." With the emphasis in modern media being entertainment, stories about prolonged and ongoing turmoil and abuse are "depressing." Berns argues that the inspirational magazine articles are more attractive and marketable, even if they only report on anecdotal cases that have uplifting and positive endings (Berns, 2004). Women's magazines rarely utilize statistical evidence to show the true scope of the problem. When men's magazines cover these issues, they tend to focus on cases in which males are victims, thereby de-gendering the problem (Berns, 2004). Men's magazines also tend to feature a variety of forms of victim blaming, and to note that society favors women in allegations of abuse, leaving readers with an impression that men are victims of discrimination.

Likewise, as long as rape has been a subject of popular culture, it has also been subject to inappropriate and harmful depictions.

> In short, given the ubiquity of representations of rape, even someone who is a moderate consumer of mass media could have difficulty spending a week (possibly even a day) without coming across the subject. The existence of rape is thus naturalized in U.S. life, perhaps seemingly so natural that many people are unaware of the frequency with which they encounter these representations. (Projansky, 2001, p. 2)

Television situation comedies (sitcoms) often feature jokes about rape. Sexual violence is frequently the focus of shows that are popular with older teens, like *Law & Order: Special Victims Unit* (*SVU*), *Nip/Tuck*, *Gossip Girl*, and *One Tree Hill* (Durham, 2008). Even shows largely devoted to the issue of sexual assault, like *SVU* tend to gloss over the victim's stories in lieu of more titillating approaches. Zimmerman (2015) argues that such an approach fails to explain the complexity of the situation or the psychological challenges of healing and recovery. "In a procedural like *SVU*, rape is so integral to the show that its ubiquity eventually becomes invisibility, and the audience is inured to the violence of the crimes and the real experiences and traumas the actors are reenacting" (Zimmerman, 2015). She argues:

> Whether they're being exploited for the male gaze or for a ratings spike, insensitive and unthorough representations of sexual assault negatively impact both survivors and couch surfers. Using rape as a blasé plotline or for a cheap thrill is an egregious insult to actual survivors. It belittles the

experience of sexual assault, and fails to illustrate the long-lasting effects of trauma. In addition to obliviously bypassing a teaching opportunity, heavy-handed rape plotlines also reinforce a larger rape culture, in which violence is sexy and sex is violent.

Despite the sometimes problematic portrayals of sexual assault and responses to it, the educational nonprofit organization No More has agreed to couple with *SVU* for a "marathon" of episodes about sexual and domestic violence in October 2015.

Another type of popular culture that features excessively violent content and story lines is World Wrestling Entertainment (WWE), which remains popular with teen boys. In their documentary *Wrestling with Manhood*, Sut Jhally and Jackson Katz show that the narratives of the WWE clearly suggest that abuse is normal, that women deserve it, and that violence is sexually gratifying. One study found that high school boys who watched more professional wrestling engaged in more fighting. The authors noted "It should not be a surprise that youth who are exposed more often to TV programs that portray a barrage of severe violence without the expected consequences, the degrading of women, sexuality connected with violence, and extreme verbal intimidation and abuse between wrestlers and their female escorts, are influenced by what they see and hear" (in Durham, 2008, p. 147). DuRant, Champion, and Wolfson (2006) found that high school students who watched professional wrestling were more likely to engage in dating violence, among other forms of violent behavior.

Fiction novels are also important sources that teach people about crime and violence. "Few things reveal social beliefs as effectively as the imaginary realms we choose to escape into en mass. As such, fiction is a rich resource for examining beliefs about partner violence . . . the popularity of some fiction extends its reach considerably farther than that of policy, advocacy or even the law in its likelihood to influence social expectations, norms and values, and beliefs about what is or is not acceptable behavior" (McDaniel, 2013, p. 18). Young adult literature often focuses on social justice issues, which can help young people develop moral and ethical understanding (Sambell, 2003; Wolk, 2009). While fiction novels tend to do a better job of portraying the reality of domestic violence and sexual assault, they also sometimes promote dangerous stereotypes and misconceptions.

This chapter by no means provided an exhaustive review of the scope of the problems of domestic violence and sexual assault nor of the effects of consumption to violent popular culture. It did, hopefully, provide readers with a deeper understanding of these issues that are taken up in far greater detail in subsequent chapters.

REFERENCES

Anderson, C. (2004). An update on the effects of playing violent video games. *Journal of Adolescence, 27*(1), 113–122.

Anderson, C., & Bushman, B. (2001). Effects of violent video games on aggressive behavior, aggressive cognition, aggressive affect, physiological arousal, and prosocial behavior: A meta-analytic review of the scientific literature. *Psychological Science, 12*(5), 353–359.

Armstrong, E. G. (2001). Gansta misogyny: A content analysis of the portrayals of violence against women in rap music, 1987–1993. *Journal of Criminal Justice and Popular Culture, 8*(2), 96–126.

Arriaga, X. B., & Foshee, V. A. (2004). Adolescent dating violence: Do adolescents follow in their friends', or their parents', footsteps? *Journal of Interpersonal Violence, 19*(2), 162–184.

Avery-Leaf, S., Cascardi, M., & O'Leary, K. (1997). Efficacy of a dating violence prevention program on attitudes justifying aggression. *Journal of Adolescent Health, 21*(1), 11–17.

Barongan, C., & Hall, G. (1995). The influence of misogynous rap music on sexual aggression against women. *Psychology of Women Quarterly, 19*(2), 195–207.

Barriga, C. A., Shapiro, M. A., & Jhaveri, R. (2009). Media context, female body size and perceived realism. *Sex Roles, 60*(1), 128–141.

Behm-Morawitz, E., & Mastro, D. E. (2008). Mean girls? The influence of gender portrayals in teen movies on emerging adults' gender-based attitudes and beliefs. *Journalism & Mass Communication Quarterly, 85*(1), 131–146.

Berns, N. (2004). *Framing the victim: Domestic violence, media, and social problems.* New York: Aldine de Gruyter.

Berns, N., & Schweingruber, D. (2007). When you're involved, it's just different. *Violence against Women, 13*(3), 240–261.

Best, J. (1999). *Random violence: How we talk about new crimes and new victims.* Berkeley: University of California Press.

Bonomi, A., Nemeth, J., Altenburger, L., Anderson, M., Snyder, A., & Dotto, I. (2014). Fiction or not? Fifty Shades is associated with health risks in adolescent and young adult females. *Journal of Women's Health, 23*(9), 720–728.

Bowles, S. (2007, May 4). Slasher film corpses pile up at a box office. *Calgary Herald,* C7.

Britto, S., Hughes, T., Saltzman, K., & Stroh, C. (2007). Does "special" mean young, white and female? Deconstructing the meaning of "special" in *Law & Order: Special Victims Unit. Journal of Criminal Justice and Popular Culture, 14*(1), 40–57.

Bufkin, J., & Eschholz, S. (2000). Images of sex and rape: A content analysis of popular film. *Violence against Women, 6*(12), 1317–1344.

Bushman, B., & Anderson, C. (2009). Comfortably numb: Desensitizing effects of violent media on helping others. *Psychological Science, 20*(3), 273–277.

Carpenter, C., & Edison, A. (2005). *Taking it off all over again: The portrayal of women in advertising over the past forty years.* Paper presented at the annual conference of the International Communication Association, New York.

Cavender, G., & Bond-Maupin, L. (1993). Fear and loathing in reality television: An analysis of *America's Most Wanted* and *Unsolved Mysteries. Sociological Inquiry, 63*(3), 305–316.

Chancer, L. (1998). Playing gender against race through high-profile crime cases: The Tyson/Thomas/Simpson pattern of the 1990s. *Violence against Women, 4*(1), 100–113.

Clover, C. (1992). *Men, women and chainsaws: Gender in the modern horror film.* Princeton, NJ: Princeton University Press.

Crary, D. (2014, August 23). New survey details vast scope of teen dating abuse. *Washington Times.* Retrieved September 13, 2015, from http://www.washingtontimes.com/news/2014/oct/23/new-survey-details-vast-scope-of-teen-dating-abuse/?page=all

Cundiff, G. (2013). The influence of rap and hip-hop music: An analysis of audience perceptions of misogynistic lyrics. *Elon Journal of Undergraduate Research in Communications, 4*(1), 4–5.

d'Abo, M., & Cork, J. (2003). *Bond girls are forever: The women of James Bond.* New York: Harry N. Abrams.

Dancy, D. (2003). Dating violence in adolescence. *Family Violence Forum 2.* National Center for State Courts.

Davis, A. (2008). *Interpersonal and physical dating violence among teens.* The National Council on Crime and Delinquency Focus. Retrieved January 7, 2016, from http://www.nccdrc.org/nccd/pubs/Dating%20Violence%20Among%20Teens.pdf

Davison, W. (1983). The third-person effect in communication. *Public Opinion Quarterly, 47*(1), 1–15.

Delo, C. (2013, August 1). U.S. adults now spending more time on digital devices than watching TV. Adage. Retrieved September 13, 2015, from http://adage.com/article/digital/americans-spend-time-digital-devices-tv/243414/

Denham, J. (2014, December 15). Marilyn Manson breaks silence on Lana Del Ray rape clip. *The Independent.* Retrieved September 13, 2015, from http://www.independent.co.uk/arts-entertainment/music/news/marilyn-manson-breaks-silence-on-lana-del-rey-rape-clip-i-wouldnt-make-a-video-of-that-nature-9925891.html

Dexter, H., Penrod, S., Linz, D., & Saunders, D. (1997). Attributing responsibility to female victims after exposure to sexually violent films. *Journal of Applied Social Psychology, 27*(24), 2149.

DuRant, R., Champion, H., & Wolfson, M. (2006). The relationship between watching professional wrestling on television and engaging in date fighting among high school students. *Pediatrics, 118*(2), 265–272.

Durham, M. (2008). *The Lolita effect.* Woodstock, NY: Overlook Press.

Eaton, D., Davis, K., Barrios, L., Brener, N., & Noonan, R. (2007). Associations of dating violence victimization with lifetime participation, co-occurrence, and early initiation of risk behaviors among U.S. high school students. *Journal of Interpersonal Violence, 22*(5), 585–602.

Estep, R., & MacDonald, P. (1983). How prime-time crime evolved on TV, 1976 to 1981. *Journalism Quarterly, 60*(2), 293–330.

Farr, K. (2005). *Sex trafficking: The global market in women and children.* New York: Worth Publishers.

Fifth & Pacific Companies, Inc. (Formerly: Liz Claiborne, Inc.), Conducted by Knowledge Networks. (2010, December). College dating violence and abuse poll. Retrieved January 24, 2016, from https://www.breakthecycle.org/surveys

Finley, L., & Concannon, K. (2014). Potter versus Voldemort: Examining evil, power and affective responses in the *Harry Potter* film series. In S. Packer & J. Pennington (Eds.). *Evil and Popular Culture.* Santa Barbara, CA: ABC-CLIO.

Fisher, B., Daigle, L., & Cullen, F. (2009). *Unsafe in the ivory tower: The sexual victimization of college women.* Thousand Oaks, CA: Sage.

Foshee, V. (1996). Gender differences in adolescent dating abuse prevalence, types, and injuries. *Health Education Research, 11*(3), 275–286.

Garcia-Moreno, C., et al. (2005). *WHO multi-country study on women's health and domestic violence against women.* Geneva: World Health Organization.

Giroux, H. (2013). Violence, USA. Retrieved September 13, 2015, from http://monthlyreview.org/2013/05/01/violence-usa/

Glassner, B. (1999). *The culture of fear: Why Americans are afraid of the wrong things.* New York: Basic Books.

Golde, J., Strassburg, G., Turner, C., & Lowe, K. (2000). Attitudinal effects of degrading themes and sexual explicitness in video materials. *Sexual Abuse, 12*(3), 223–231.

Gourdine, R. M., & Lemmons, B. P. (2011). Perceptions of misogyny in hip hop and rap: What do the youths think? *Journal of Human Behavior in the Social Environment, 21*(1), 57–72.

Grauerholz, E., & King, A. (1997). Prime time sexual harassment. *Violence against Women, 3*(2), 129–148.

Grossman, D., & DeGaetano, G. (2014). *Stop teaching our kids to kill: A call to action against TV, movie, & video game violence.* New York: Harmony.

Groves, B. (2003). *Children who see too much: Lessons from the child witness to violence project.* Boston, MA: Beacon.

Halpern, C. T., Oslak, S. G., Young, M. L., Martin, S. L., & Kupper, L. L. (2001). Partner violence among adolescents in opposite-sex romantic relationships: Findings from the National Longitudinal Study of Adolescent Health. *American Journal of Public Health, 91*(10), 1679–1685.

Harper, B., & Tiggemann, M. (2008). The effect of thin ideal media images on women's self-objectification, mood, and body image. *Sex Roles, 58*(9), 649–657.

Harrison, K. (2001). Ourselves, our bodies: Thin-ideal media, self-discrepancies, and eating disorder symptomatology in adolescents. *Journal of Social and Clinical Psychology, 20*(3), 289–323.

Harrison, K., & Cantor, J. (1997). The relationship between media exposure and eating disorders. *Journal of Communication, 47*(1), 40–67.

Haskell, M. (1987). *From reverence to rape: The treatment of women in the movies.* Chicago: University of Chicago Press.

Hiltbrand, D. (2007). Film and television violence is likely to get more graphic. In S. Des Chenes (Ed.). *Is media violence a problem?* Farmington Hills, MI: Greenhaven.

Huesmann, J., Moise-Titus, J., Podolski, C., & Eron, D. (2003). Longitudinal relations between children's exposure to TV violence and their aggressive and violent behavior in young adulthood, 1977–1992. *Developmental Psychology, 39*(2), 201–221.

Kalodner, C. R. (1997). Media influences on male and female non-eating-disordered college students: A significant issue. *Eating Disorders: The Journal of Treatment and Prevention, 5*(1), 47–57.

Katz, J. (2006). *The macho paradox.* Naperville, IL: Sourcebooks.

Kilbourne, J. (1995). *Slim hopes: Advertising and the obsession with thinness* [Video]. Northampton, MA: Media Education Foundation.

Krafka, C., Linz, D., Donnerstein, E., & Penrod, S. (1997). Women's reactions to sexually aggressive mass media depictions. *Violence against Women, 3*(2), 149–181.

Krahe, B., Moller, I., Kirwil, L., Huesmann, L. R., Felber, J., & Berger, A. (2011). Desensitization to media violence: Links with habitual media violence exposure, aggressive cognitions, and aggressive behavior. *Journal of Personality and Social Psychology, 100*(4).

Krebs, C., Lindquist, C., Warner, T., Fisher, B., & Martin, S. (2007). The campus sexual assault study (CSA). Washington, D.C.: National Institute of Justice. Retrieved January 9, 2016, from https://www.ncjrs.gov/pdffiles1/nij/grants/221153.pdf

Kuntsche, E., Knibbe, R., Gmel, G., & Engels, R. (2006). Who drinks and why? A review of socio-demographic, personality, and contextual issues behind the drinking motives in young people. *Addictive Behaviors, 31*(10), 1844–1857.

Lavoie, F., Robitaille, L., & Hebert, M. (2000). Teen dating relationships and aggression. *Violence against Women, 6*(1), 6–36.

Leonard, K., Quigley, B., & Collins, R. (2002). Physical aggression in the lives of young adults: Prevalence, location, and severity among college and community samples. *Journal of Interpersonal Violence, 17*(5), 533–550.

Linz, D., Donnerstein, E., & Adams, S. M. (1989). Physiological desensitization and judgments about female victims of violence. *Human Communication Research, 15*(4), 509–522.

Linz, D., Donnerstein, E., & Penrod, S. (1988). The effects of long-term exposure to violent and sexually degrading depictions of women. *Journal of Personality and Social Psychology, 55*(5), 758–768.

Liz Claiborne Inc., (2005, February). Teen dating violence survey. Conducted by Teenage Research Unlimited.

Lockyer, B., & O'Connell, J. (2004). *A preventable epidemic: Teen dating violence and its impact on school safety and academic achievement.* California Attorney General's Office and the California Department of Education.

Mackay, N., & Covell, K. (1997). The impact of women in advertisements on attitudes toward women. *Sex Roles, 36*(9/10), 573–583.

McDaniel, D. (2013). Representations of partner violence in young adult literature: Dating violence in Stephenie Meyer's *Twilight* saga. Dissertation submitted to the University of Texas. Retrieved January 7, 2016, from https://repositories.lib.utexas.edu/bitstream/handle/2152/23201/MCDANIEL-DISSERTATION-2013.pdf

McDonough, K. (2013, April 1). Bra-clad "zombie ex-girlfriend" target bleeds when you shoot it. Salon. Retrieved September 2, 2015, from http://www.salon.com/2013/04/01/bra_clad_zombie_ex_girlfriend_target_bleeds_when_ you_shoot_it/

Media violence. (2009). American Academy of Pediatrics. Retrieved July 15, 2015, from http://pediatrics.aappublications.org/content/124/5/1495.full#ref-59

Mohler-Kuo, M., Dowdall, G., Koss, M., & Weschler, H. (2004). Correlates of rape while intoxicated in a national sample of college women. *Journal of Studies on Alcohol, 65*(1), 37–45.

Mulac, A., Jansma, L., & Linz, D. (2002). Men's behavior toward women after viewing sexually explicit films: Degradation makes a difference. *Communication Monographs, 69*(4), 311–328.

Mullin, C. R., & Linz, D. (1995). Desensitization and resensitization to violence against women: Effects of exposure to sexually violent films on judgments of domestic violence films. *Journal of Personality and Social Psychology, 69*(3), 449–459.

Mulvey, L. (1975). Visual pleasure and narrative cinema. *Screen, 16*(3), 6–18.

Murray, A. (2007). *From outrage to courage.* Monroe, ME: Common Courage.

Mustaine, E., & Tewksbury, R. (1999). A routine activity theory explanation for women's stalking victimizations. *Violence against Women, 5*(1), 43–62.

O'Leary, S., & Smith Slep, A. (2003). A dyadic longitudinal model of adolescent dating aggression. *Journal of Clinical Child and Adolescent Psychology, 32*(3), 314–327.

National Center for Victims of Crime. (n.d.) Teen victim project. Retrieved January 9, 2016, from http://www.ncvc.org/tvp

Neuendorf, K., Gore, T., Dalessandro, A., Janstova, P., & Snyder-Suhy, S. (2010). Shaken and stirred: A content analysis of women's portrayals in James Bond films. *Sex Roles, 62*(11), 747–761.

Neuman, J., & Baron, R. (1998). Workplace violence and workplace aggression: Evidence confirming specific forms, potential causes, and preferred targets. *Journal of Management, 24*(3), 391–419.

Pardun C., L'Engle K., & Brown J. (2005). Linking exposures to outcomes: Early adolescents' consumption of sexual content in six media. *Mass Communication & Society, 8*(2), 75–91.

Peterson, D., & Pfost, K. (1989). Influence of rock videos on attitudes of violence against women. *Psychological Reports, 64*(1), 319–322.

Pinhas, L., Toner, B. B., Ali, A., Garfinkel, P. E., & Stuckless, N. (1999). The effects of the ideal female beauty on mood and body satisfaction. *International Journal of Eating Disorders, 25*(2), 223–226.

Potera, C., and Kennedy, M. S. (2009). Sex and violence in the media influence teen behavior. *American Journal of Nursing, 109*(2), 20.

Potter, W. (1999). *On media violence.* Thousand Oaks, CA: Sage.

Projansky, S. (2001). *Watching rape: Film and television in post-feminist culture.* New York: NYU Press.

Psychologists study media violence. (2015). APA. Retrieved January 7, 2016, from http://www.apa.org/action/resources/research-in-action/protect.aspx

Rader, E., & Rhineburger-Dunn, G. (2010). A typology of victim characterization in television crime dramas. *Journal of Criminal Justice and Popular Culture, 17*(1), 231–263.

Rafter (2000). *Shots in the mirror: Crime films and society.* New York: Oxford University Press.

Rafter, N., & Brown, M. (2011). *Criminology goes to the movies: Crime theory and popular culture.* New York: NYU Press.

Rich, M., Woods, E., Goodman, E., Emans, S., & DuRant, R. (1998). Aggressors or victims: Gender and race in music video violence. *Pediatrics, 101*(4), 669–674.

Rosado, L. (2000). *The pathways to youth violence: How child maltreatment and other risk factors lead children to chronically aggressive behavior.* American Bar Association Juvenile Justice Center.

Said, S. (2011). Domestic violence and film. *Academia.* Retrieved January 9, 2016, from http://www.academia.edu/3420656/Domestic_Violence _and_Film_English_

Sambell, K. (2003). Presenting the case for social change: The creative dilemma of dystopian writing for children. In C. Hintz & E. Ostry (Eds.). *Utopian and dystopian literature for children and young adults* (pp. 163–178). New York: Routledge.

Sexual violence. (2015, February 5). Centers for Disease Control and Prevention. Retrieved February 16, 2015, from http://www.cdc.gov/violenceprevention/ sexualviolence/

Shoos, D. (2003). Representing domestic violence: Ambivalence and difference in *What's Love Got to Do with It. NWSA Journal, 15*(2), 57–77.

Shrum, L. (1996). Psychological processes underlying cultivation effects further tests of construct accessibility. *Human Communication Research, 22*(4), 482–509.

Signorielli, N. (1989). Television and conceptions about sex roles: Maintaining conventionality and the status quo. *Sex Roles, 21*(5), 341–360.

Silverman, J., Raj, A., & Clements, K. (2004). Dating violence and associated sexual risk and pregnancy among adolescent girls in the U.S. *Pediatrics, 114*(2), 220–225.

Singular, S., & Singular, J. (2015). *The spiral notebook: The Aurora theater shooter and the epidemic of mass violence committed by American youth.* Berkeley, CA: Counterpoint.

Smith, P., Stern, S. R., & Mastro, D. E. (2004). Gender portrayals across the life span: A content analytic look at broadcast commercials. *Mass Communication & Society, 7*(2), 215–236.

State laws on teen dating violence. (2014). National Council of State Legislatures. Retrieved September 13, 2015, from http://www.ncsl.org/research/health/teen-dating- violence.aspx#State%20Laws

Statistics. (2014). Rape, Abuse and Incest National Network (RAINN). Retrieved February 15, 2015, from https://www.rainn.org/statistics

Stice, E., & Shaw, H. (1994). Adverse effects of the media-portrayed thin-ideal on women and linkages to bulimic symptomatology. *Journal of Social and Clinical Psychology, 13*(3), 288–308.

Surette, R. (1992). *Media, crime, and criminal justice: Images and realities.* Belmont, CA: West/Wadsworth.

Teen dating violence. (2015). Centers for Disease Control and Prevention. Retrieved September 13, 2015, from http://www.cdc.gov/violenceprevention/intimatepartnerviolence/teen_dating_violence.ht ml

Timmerman, L. M., Allen, M., Jorgensen, J., Herrett-Skjellum, J., Kramer, M. R., & Ryan, D. J. (2008). A review and meta-analysis examining the relationship of music content with sex, race, priming, and attitudes. *Communication Quarterly, 56*(3), 303–324.

Tjaden, P., & Thoennes, N. (2006). Extent, nature, and consequences of rape victimization: Findings from the National Violence against Women Survey. Washington, D.C.: U.S. Department of Justice, Office of Justice Programs.

Tyson, E. H. (2006). Rap-music attitude and perception scale: A validation study. *Research on Social Work Practice, 16*(2), 211–223.

University of California, Santa Barbara Center for Communication and Social Policy. (1998). National Television Violence Study. Retrieved January 10, 2016, from https://www.saybrook.edu/sites/default/files/faculty/NTVVSexecsum.pdf

Weisz, M., & Earls, C. (1995). The effects of exposure to filmed sexual violence on attitudes toward rape. *Journal of Interpersonal Violence, 10*(1), 71–84.

Weitzer, R., & Kubrin, C. (2009). Misogyny in rap music: A content analysis of prevalence and meanings. *Men and Masculinities, 12*(1), 3–29.

Welsh, A. (2009). Sex and violence in the slasher horror film: A content analysis of gender difference in the depiction of violence. *Journal of Criminal Justice and Popular Culture, 6*(1), 1–25.

What is domestic violence? (2014). U.S. Department of Justice Office on Violence against Women. Retrieved September 13, 2015, from http://www.justice.gov/ovw/domestic-violence

Wilcox, K., & Laird, J. D. (2000). The impact of media images of super-slender women on women's self-esteem: Identification, social comparison, and self-perception. *Journal of Research in Personality, 34,* 278–286.

Wilson, B., Colvin, C., & Smith, S. (2002). Engaging in violence on American television: A comparison of child, teen, and adult perpetrators. *Journal of Communication, 52*(1), 36–60.

Wolk, S. (2009). Reading for a better world: Teaching for social responsibility with young adult literature. *Journal of Adolescent & Adult Literacy, 52*(8), 664–673.

Wood, E., Senn, C. Y., Desmarais, S., Park, L., & Verberg, N. (2002). Sources of information about dating and their perceived influence on adolescents. *Journal of Adolescent Research, 17*(4), 401–417.

Wood, J. (2012). *Gendered lives,* 10th ed. Independence, KY: Cengage Learning.

Ybarra, M., Diener-West, M., Markow, D., Leaf, P., Hamburger, M., & Boxer, P. (2008). Linkages between internet and other media violence and seriously violent behavior by youth. *Pediatrics, 122*(5), 929–937.

A year in review (2014). National Domestic Violence Hotline. Retrieved September 3, 2015, from http://www.thehotline.org/about-us/year-end-review-2014/#tab-id-3

Young, A. M., Grey, M., & Boyd, C. J. (2009). Adolescents' experiences of sexual assault by peers: Prevalence and nature of victimization occurring within and outside of school. *Journal of Youth and Adolescence, 38*(8), 1072–1083.

Zimmerman, A. (2015, June 2). TV's rape obsession: What "Outlander" got right and what "Game of Thrones" gets very wrong. *The Daily Beast.* Retrieved January 24, 2016, from http://www.thedailybeast.com/articles/2015/06/02/tv-s-rape-obsession-what-outlander-got-right-and-game-of-thrones-gets-very-wrong.html

1

Beyond Stupid Sluts and Innocent Children: Describing Victims

Let me open this chapter with a very important point: Anyone can be a victim of domestic violence or sexual assault. There is no "victim profile," nor would it be helpful to develop such. Data do show, however, that certain groups are more at risk for victimization. Thus I have focused this chapter on describing those groups, and on highlighting the ways that popular culture does and, in some cases, does not present them. Most data clearly show that females are more likely to be victimized than are men; as such, this is the first topic addressed in this chapter. This chapter also addresses the depiction and actuality of poor and/or homeless victims (versus more affluent ones); male victims; child victims; immigrants; lesbian, gay, bisexual, and transgender (LGBT) victims; black and Native American victims; prison rape; and elder victims of abuse and assault. I also include the known risk factors, warning signs, and the most frequently occurring forms of abuse and sexual assault and discuss how accurately popular culture depicts these.

WARNING SIGNS AND RISK FACTORS

Although persons who are immersed in abusive relationships have a hard time seeing the signs, there are a number of red flags that are pretty easily detectable by knowledgeable and observant outsiders.

Although it is impossible to make a complete list of warning signs due to the many forms of control an abuser will use, the following are frequently cited by scholars and advocates: being isolated from family and friends, telling inconsistent lies, making excuses for their partner's bad behavior, having to show your partner your phone or phone records, having the mileage on your car monitored, being humiliated or talked down to in public, constantly being accused of cheating, being allowed to wear only certain clothes and makeup, and the like.

Being female is indeed a risk factor for all forms of gender-based violence across the globe. Additionally, according to the Centers for Disease Control and Prevention (CDC, 2015), the following are risk factors for domestic violence:

- low self-esteem
- low income
- low academic achievement
- young age
- aggressive or delinquent behavior as a youth
- heavy alcohol and drug use
- depression
- anger and hostility
- antisocial personality traits
- borderline personality traits
- prior history of being physically abusive
- having few friends and being isolated from other people
- unemployment
- emotional dependence and insecurity
- belief in strict gender roles (e.g., male dominance and aggression in relationships)
- desire for power and control in relationships
- perpetrating psychological aggression
- being a victim of physical or psychological abuse (consistently one of the strongest predictors of perpetration)
- history of experiencing poor parenting as a child
- history of experiencing physical discipline as a child

Risk factors for experiencing dating violence victimization include lower grades and poor achievement in school (Halpern et al., 2001), lower socio-economic status, eating disorders, religion (Halpern et al., 2001), and associating with peers who drink. Halpern et al. (2001) noted that family composition, race, and ethnicity are associated with increased risk for abuse.

At their root, domestic violence and sexual assault are the result of patriarchal beliefs and ideologies. Like abuse and assault, there are many misconceptions about the term "patriarchy." "Patriarchy" refers to societies that are male-dominated and male-identified (Johnson, 2014). That does not mean that there are numerically more males than females (which is not the case in the United States). It also does not mean that any given man is responsible for gender inequalities and violence. Rather, patriarchy is a structural issue, not one of individual perpetrators. It refers to societies that are set up in ways that what is considered "masculine"—toughness (mental and physical), efficiency, control, practicality, among others—is privileged over what is considered to be "feminine"—emotional, nurturing, cooperative, and idealistic. While these binary notions of gender roles are far from reality, they are indeed pervasive, and many buy into them, at least to some degree.

Patriarchal societies that undervalue women and girls do so in popular culture as well, not surprisingly. In *From Reverence to Rape: The Treatment of Women in the Movies*, Molly Haskell (1987) examines the often dichotomous representations of females in film. She notes, "A woman's intelligence was the equivalent of a man's penis: something to be kept out of sight. Ambition in a woman had to either be deflected into the vicarious drives of her loved ones or to be mocked and belittled" (p. 4). Bleackley (2004) conducted a content analysis of *Pulp Fiction*, *The Accused*, and *Boys Don't Cry*. Although the three featured different types of rapes (*Pulp Fiction* a male–male situation, *The Accused* an account of a real gang rape of a woman, and *Boys Don't Cry* the rape of a transgender woman, also based on a real event), she found that all three promoted binary gender and sex roles.

FORMS OF ABUSE

Domestic violence takes many forms. While it may indeed be physical and include anything from hitting to punching, kicking, biting, scratching, strangling, and more, abuse is also sexual, emotional, verbal, financial, and spiritual. NiCarthy (2004) explains:

> The chronic physical injury from beatings creates an ongoing state of exhaustion. The woman who is subjected to these techniques of brainwashing becomes worn out by her tension, fear, and her continual rushing about in the effort to arrange her partner's world effectively enough to avoid abuse. She must also strain to keep her fear, sorrow, and rage from showing, since any display of emotion is likely to be ridiculed or punished. (p. 260)

Sexual violence might involve anything from completed or attempted forced intercourse to forcing a partner to view pornography (Richards & Restivo, 2015). Stalking is another tactic used by abusers, and one that has repeatedly been identified as a red flag for lethal violence (Tjaden & Thoennes, 2001).

Women who are psychologically abused often feel as though there is something wrong with them, first for choosing the partner who abuses them and also because their abuser typically tells them it is their fault. Similarly, "Crazy-making . . . involves making the victim feel as though she is imagining things. Abusers are often adept at identify particular traits that their victim is pleased with and using those against her" (NiCarthy, 2004, p. 277).

Other forms of abuse include isolating victims from loved ones or supporters, and then manipulating or controlling them through a variety of means. Increasingly, perpetrators use technology to control victims, perhaps purchasing a phone and requiring the victim answer it or give it up for the abuser to assess whom she called or who called her. Social media is used by abusers, both teens and adults, to embarrass, harass, and threaten victims. One of the more common ways that abusers control victims is through use of technologies, including social media. Posting or distributing provocative images that might have been shared with good intent—what is sometimes called revenge porn, cyber harassment, or sexual shaming—is an issue that had gained a lot of attention by 2015. Abusers often share images while also disclosing personal information, like the victim's name, address, phone number, school, or place of employment, thereby jeopardizing his or her economic and social welfare. Although some states now legally prohibit this activity, others still do not have adequate laws to protect victims, in particular for those who are above the age of consent. Importantly, abusers use these methods and more in conjunction with one another to create a pattern of harassment, power, and control.

Power and Control

Power and control are depicted in popular culture, albeit sometimes in far less complex ways than are realistic. One classic film that depicts this exertion of power and control very clearly is *Streetcar Named Desire* (1951). In the film, Blanche goes to stay with her sister Stella and Stella's husband, Stanley Kowalski. Although she is struggling herself, Blanche becomes increasingly concerned about Stanley's outbursts in which he yells at, beats, and intimidates Stella. He even rapes Blanche. Stanley is quick to assert his authority and control, although critics note that the signs of Stella's physical injury are far less than they should be.

Ultimately, power and control are about the dynamics of the abuser–abusee relationship. While I take up the topic of victim-blaming in far greater detail in Chapter 3, it is clear that some forms of popular culture both capture and fail to capture the complex dynamics of abusive relationships. Popular culture usually portrays victims of crime as passive and helpless (Surette, 1998) or, conversely, as crazed people on a mission to seek revenge. What it doesn't do well is capture the daily nuances of abusive relationships that make it hard for victims to get out. From love to fear to financial concerns and more, victims face numerous barriers to leaving abusers, all of which emanate from the fact that the perpetrators are controlling and manipulative individuals.

An example of popular culture that sends mixed messages about power and control is Bessie Smith's jazz song "Outside of That." While it highlights the roller coaster exhibited in such relationships, it seems to suggest that victims are happy to endure the rough times as long as they are occasionally treated decently.

> I've got the meanest man in the land
> But his love is best, thick and grand
> . . .
> People say I'm a fool
> He's heartless and also cruel.
> But outside of that, he's all right with me.
> Outside of that, he's sweet as he can be.

Emotional abuse is frequently depicted as a normal part of relationships. Bonomi et al. (2014) conducted a content analysis of the *50 Shades of Grey* trilogy. They found that emotional abuse dominated the relationship between the main characters Anastasia and Christian, and that it was this form of power and control that set the stage for sexual violence. They concluded that, "Christian controls all aspects of the couple's relationship using the emotional abuse tactics of stalking, isolation, intimidation/ threats, and humiliation" (p. 736). The emotional abuse began immediately after the couple's first meeting, and continues until the end of the book series. Further, they determined that

> Anastasia's reaction to Christian's coercive, manipulative strategies are consistent with those of battered women, including perceived threat (perceptions of impending harm); managing (direct action or inhibition of action to "keep the peace,"); altered identity (changed self-concept/loss of identity from images abusers reflect); yearning (futile attempts to establish intimacy with an abusive partner); entrapment (perceptions of being trapped in the relationship resulting from abuser's control); and disempowerment (loss of power and habitual behavior modification from prolonged exposure to abuse and to fit abuser's desires). (p. 737)

Finally, they found that "Sexual violence is pervasive across the couple's 13 sexual encounters—including Christian's use of alcohol to compromise Anastasia's consent and his use of intimidation (Christian initiates sexual encounters when angry and dismisses Anastasia's boundaries)" (p. 740). Although not officially labeled pornography, the *50 Shades* series surely hovers on the edge. Feminist scholars have argued that the violence that is often depicted in pornographic films has created unrealistic expectations about what an intimate relationship should include, as they emphasize the demeaning of women and degrading, violent sexual acts (DeKeseredy & Olsson, 2011).

PHYSICAL AND SEXUAL VIOLENCE

Although popular culture does address some of the other forms of abuse, it still overwhelmingly focuses on physical and sexual abuse. Songs like Eminem's "The Real Slim Shady" feature lines like "Jaws all on the floor, like Pam, like Tommy just burst in the door and started whoopin her ass worse than before," alluding to the physical abuse that actor Pamela Anderson endured from her former husband Tommy Lee, who was imprisoned for six months for the assault. Ludacris, Mystikal, and I-20's "Move Bitch" says, "I'ma 'bout to punch yo ... lights out." Not only is that line an example of physical abuse but it also shows that abusers intend to inflict harm; they do not simply "lose it."

Young Money's "Every Girl" discusses a perpetrator's sexual intentions: "Open up her legs then filet mignon that pussy, I'm a get in and on that pussy, If she let me in I'm a own that pussy." The song describes in a lewd way women's anatomy aside; it also demonstrates the need abusers have to control, even to "own" women. Trey Songz's "Bottoms Up" talks about tactics for controlling women, "If a bitch try to get cute ima stomp her. Throw alotta money at her then yell fuck Her." Lil Jon, Usher, and Ludacris's "Lovers & Friends" talks about physical abuse as something victims enjoy, a misconception addressed in more detail in Chapter 2. "Be a good girl now, turn around, and get these whippings. You know you like it like that, you don't have to fight back, Here's a pillow—bite ... that."

The Dixie Chicks' (1999) "Goodbye Earl" uses comedy to tell the story of best friends Mary Anne and Wanda as they plot how to kill Wanda's abusive ex-husband Earl, who attacked her, landing Wanda in intensive care. The song shares some of the lengths victims go to in order to cover up the physical signs of abuse, noting that Wanda had only been married two weeks before her husband started hitting her. The lyrics note Wanda's dark glasses, long-sleeved blouse, and makeup that all helped cover her bruises.

Even television shows largely devoted to the issue of sexual assault, like *Law & Order: Special Victims Unit* (*SVU*), tend to gloss over the victim's stories in lieu of more titillating approaches focused on physical violence and extreme or odd cases. Zimmerman (2015) argues that such an approach fails to explain the complexity of the situation or the psychological challenges of healing and recovery—in sum, it does not capture the nuances of power and control. "In a procedural like *SVU*, rape is so integral to the show that its ubiquity eventually becomes invisibility, and the audience is inured to the violence of the crimes and the real experiences and traumas the actors are reenacting." She argues

> Whether they're being exploited for the male gaze or for a ratings spike, insensitive and unthorough representations of sexual assault negatively impact both survivors and couch surfers. Using rape as a blasé plotline or for a cheap thrill is an egregious insult to actual survivors. It belittles the experience of sexual assault, and fails to illustrate the long-lasting effects of trauma. In addition to obliviously bypassing a teaching opportunity, heavy-handed rape plotlines also reinforce a larger rape culture, in which violence is sexy and sex is violent.

STALKING

Stalking can occur in numerous ways, but often happens in or, in particular, at the end of abusive relationships. When it does, it is a huge red flag of a highly dangerous situation, as some 75 percent of domestic violence homicides occur after the abuser has stalked the victim. Popular culture minimizes the dangers of stalking. It often presents images of mentally ill strangers stalking celebrities, rather than the more common stalking that occurs in an unhealthy relationship.

Another way stalking is minimized in popular culture is by depicting it as something that is sexually titillating. Although the data are clear that women are far more likely to be stalked than are men, popular culture depictions suggest the opposite. The image of the female stalker, typically who won't give up on a relationship that her partner wants to end, is a common trope of films like *Fatal Attraction* (1987) and *Basic Instinct* (1992). The song "Every Breath You Take" by the Police was released in 1984 and was on the Billboard Top 100 singles chart for eight weeks. It was written by lead singer Sting just weeks after separating from his first wife, although there is no evidence it was about her. Most listeners loved the song for its melody, but many mistook the message about stalking that smothers someone for a love song. This is the same thing that happens to many stalking victims, especially young people, who mistake the excessive attention by their stalker as a sign of his or her deep love.

Stalking is often portrayed as intimate, romantic, or funny. As described in Chapter 2, the character Edward in the *Twilight* series stalks Bella, using his vampire powers to track where she is at all times. In the film *Legally Blonde*, Elle follows her ex-boyfriend across the country to law school in order to "get him back." In the film, *The Amazing Spiderman*, Peter Parker stalks Gwen Stacy, "putting her picture up as his screen saver, showing up at her work place, and repeatedly using his 'spidey powers' to hang outside her bedroom window without her knowledge or permission" (McDaniel, 2013, p. 47).

WHO TELLS THE STORY

Most forms of popular culture give more time to the voices of perpetrators or respondents, like police or attorneys, than to that of victims. This is often true in real life, where the criminal justice system is the main messenger about abuse and assault, not the survivors themselves. These individuals, in real life and in popular culture, are disproportionately males, and thus it is more often than not a male perspective about abuse and assault that prevails. It is not surprising that popular culture gives more voice to males, as Mulvey (1975) maintained that women in films are always subject to male heterosexual and invasive gaze, as they are created in an androcentric culture. As such, they are the object, not the subject. Although HBO's graphic *Game of Thrones* TV series frequently features brutal violence, including domestic violence and rape, the series actually shows fewer rapes than are in the George R. R. Martin books. In fact, the show contains four times fewer rapes than are depicted in the books, said one analysis. Blogger Takfar, who conducted the analysis, suggested that the findings should make people critical of both the books and the films because of the way that domestic violence and rape are presented. "George R. R. Martin uses nameless women's bodies as character development for male antagonists in A Song of Ice and Fire," she began. "Rape victims serve as props and set decoration to illustrate a man's depravity." In fact, she notes that in only two instances do rape victims tell their stories through narrative, and both are villainous characters. In response to some who argue that Martin is merely trying to depict a particularly brutal time period, Takfar wrote, "Martin is using horrific events from over the course of a thousand years—but squeezing them into a story with about a 2-year span (so far) ... In addition to cherry-picking his horrors, he's also cherry-picking the social elements of society in a way that doesn't stand up to a historical analysis" (Yoder, 2015).

In the Academy Award–nominated *The Accused*, viewers only learn what really happened at Big Dan's the night Sarah was gang-raped through a series of flashbacks, all precipitated when a man named Ken finally agrees to testify. Ken was there and was actually the one who had called 911, but was hesitant to snitch on his friends. By giving Ken's character so much importance, in fact, it is only after he begins that the audience sees a visual depiction of the incident, the film reinforces that Sarah's story could never be credible enough without Ken's confirmation. The emphasis in this visual depiction is on Sarah's behavior—flirting with the men, drinking a lot, her loose tank top falling of her shoulders to reveal no bra. The friend she was there to meet left, and the visual of her is that she is disgusted at Sarah's behavior. Ken's behavior, which was as awful as the other men in that he did nothing to disrupt the rape, appears almost heroic because he gives voice to Sarah and his testimony results in the convictions.

POOR AND HOMELESS VICTIMS

Most studies show that lower socioeconomic status is a risk factor for domestic violence. The American Civil Liberties Union's (ACLU) Women's Rights Project (n.d.) explains that women with household incomes of less than $7,500 are seven times as likely as women with household incomes over $75,000 to experience domestic violence. Women living in financially distressed neighborhoods are twice as likely to be victims of domestic violence as are women living in more affluent neighborhoods. Similarly, victims of domestic violence are overrepresented among the homeless population in the United States. In 2005, half of the U.S. cities surveyed reported that domestic violence was the primary cause of homelessness (ACLU, n.d.). Homeless youth are at greater risk for experiencing dating violence as well. One study found that 70 percent of homeless youth reported physical violence occurring in their relationship(s). By 12 years of age, 83 percent of homeless children have been exposed to at least one serious violent event and nearly 25 percent have witnessed acts of violence within their families.

A lack of affordable housing options and overburdened shelters, coupled with the fact that some landlords can still legally deny housing to victims, are all factors that increase the difficulty for victims trying to escape abuse. In 2005, a federal law prohibited discrimination against victims in Section 8 housing but it does not apply to other types of rentals (ACLU, n.d.).

Popular culture is often silent on the social class of the victims being depicted, although films often imply a poor or disadvantaged victim by showing a setting of disarray, chaos, and even addiction. Books do a better job of discussing the challenges for victims who are poor. In *Bastard out of Carolina*, Anne is a Bastard who is punished by her stepfather for this and for her mother's absence because she is working so much to help pay the bills. Glen molests Anne and constantly tells her how worthless she is. He would tell Anne he loved her, "over and over again, holding my body tight to his, his hands shaking as they moved restlessly, endlessly, over my belly, ass, and thighs" (Allison, 1992, p. 108). As Brownmiller (1975) wrote, rape is often men's way of punishing women for "being uppity, for getting out of line, for failing to recognize one's place, for assuming sexual freedoms, or for behavior no more proactive than walking down the wrong road at night in the wrong part of town and presenting a convenient, isolated target for a group of hatred and rage" (pp. 254–255).

The popular book and film *The Girl with the Dragon Tattoo* shows protagonist Lisbeth Salander as a ward of the state, although her hard work and ingenuity have not necessarily made her poor. *Dragon Tattoo* takes place in Sweden. In 2010, Amnesty International and the European Union produced a report called "Case Closed," which identified the fact that there are twice as many rapes in Sweden than in the United Kingdom, and four times as many as in German and France due to deeply ingrained sexism (Goodfriend, 2011). The Swedish title for the book is actually *Men Who Hate Women*, and the statistics at the beginning of chapters and the footnotes show that while the story is a fiction, it is based on real incidents (Armstrong, 2001). The film *The Color Purple*, released in 1985 as an adaptation of the Alice Walker book of the same name, is set in the early 1900s. It shows widespread abuse in the family, and is clearly set largely among poor, rural people, with a few more affluent characters aside. Academy Award winner *The Accused* tells the true story of a woman who went into Big Dan's bar in New Bedford, Massachusetts, seeking a pack of cigarettes. She was raped by multiple men at the bar amidst a crowd of others who watched and cheered. The media attention to the trial focused on the ethnicity of the assailants and the victim, all of whom were Portuguese, in an attempt to otherize the problem. The film did not include this element, instead having white Jodie Foster portray the victim, Sarah Tobias. Her perpetrators were all white as well. Sarah is clearly poor, and the film makes reference to the fact that she had previously collected welfare. In the actual trial, this and other things about Sarah were used to suggest she was not being truthful. The fact that so many victims are poor and become homeless likely warrants more popular culture coverage than it receives.

MIDDLE- AND UPPER-CLASS VICTIMS

A growing body of literature shows that middle- and upper-class women also experience abuse but may be far less likely to report it to police or seek help through domestic violence hotlines or shelters. As such, their victimization is often not captured in the statistics about domestic violence. In *Not to People Like Us*, therapist Susan Weitzman (2000) discusses what she calls "upscale violence." She elaborates on her website (2013) on the following characteristics: a combined marital income of at least $100,000 per year; marital residence in a neighborhood ranked in the top 25 percent of its statewide area, according to Census data; or in some cases, neighborhoods highly ranked according to commonly held reputation; a self-perception of being upper-middle class or upper class; and a minimum of a bachelor's degree. These women are often used to being successful and thus try to fix things. They may feel trapped by their own privilege and are often disbelieved by others.

Liane Moriarty's (2014) *Big Little Lies* offers a nuanced perspective on domestic violence involving an affluent woman. One of the main characters, Celeste, is known for having it all—she is beautiful and rich, and she and her husband Perry seem to make the perfect pair. Little does anyone know that behind closed doors, Perry has what Celeste at first calls a "temper problem." Each time he slaps her he apologizes, and she, like so many victims, wants desperately to believe him. Perry always buys her expensive gifts afterward, and Celeste has observed that once an "eruption" passes, the power shifts in their relationship. That is, for a short time, Perry will do anything she wants in an effort to smooth things over, albeit until he loses it again. As is the case with many victims, Celeste grapples with what she must be doing wrong to make this "perfect" man act violently toward her, and for the longest time she cannot dream of leaving him because she really doesn't WANT to; she merely wants that portion of their relationship to end. She believes Perry is a good father, and she loves their good times. Perry is careful to ensure that the physical signs of his abuse are minimal and easily hidden or explained, even to Celeste's closest friends. Like this book, studies have shown that coverage of white, upper-class victims is more likely to depict them sympathetically (Ardovini-Brooker & Caringella-MacDonald, 2002).

MALE VICTIMS

Some have argued that most domestic violence is common couple violence, or abuse perpetrated by both male and females in a partnership. This, they maintain, is distinct from intimate terrorism, which is largely perpetrated by men and results in greater physical harm. Others maintain that there is no such thing; that abuse, by definition, cannot be "mutual" (Johnson, 1995), and that abuse disproportionately impacts women.

It is undeniably true, however, that male victims experience unique barriers to reporting and thus the data sets about this issue are far from complete.

According to the CDC (2015), each year approximately 4.8 million women experience intimate partner-related physical assaults and rapes, while men are the victims of about 2.9 million intimate partner-related physical assaults. Although many studies have focused on describing and understanding female victimization, little is known about domestic violence committed by women against men. Some studies have shown that the males most at risk for victimization are young, African American, and unmarried.

Gelles (1974) was one of the first to study male victims. He reported that husbands and wives were abused at approximately equal rates. Using the National Family Violence Survey, Straus and Gelles (1986) found that 12 percent of both husbands and wives were victims of spousal violence in the past year, again indicating equal amounts of victimization. Some believe that when women act violently it is generally in self-defense. Others, like Straus (1993), maintain that females may be the first aggressor, in that 53 percent of women reported hitting their male partner first, compared to 43 percent who reported that their male partner initiated the violence. One of the largest studies conducted on the issue found that women were as likely or even slightly more likely to use physical aggression during conflicts compared to men (Archer, 2000). Douglas and Straus (2003) found that girls were 1.15 times more likely to assault their male partners. Cook (2009) notes that studies show domestic violence is even more underreported for male victims than for female victims, both to police and to crisis lines or domestic violence centers. Cook (2009) explains that many of the same barriers women face in trying to leaving violent male abusers are true for men seeking to leave female abusers as well. Among the top barriers for men are victims' threats to commit suicide, feeling responsible if the victim were to end up on the streets, love for the victim, and concern about the children.

Many victims of male rape experience the same issues as female rape victims, including depression, loss of self-esteem, loss of sexual identity, and posttraumatic stress disorder (PTSD) (Davies, Pollard, & Archer, 2001). The myths surrounding male rape are similar to the myths about female rape that are presented in Chapter 3, although some studies have shown that male rape victims are seen as more to blame than female rape victims when they do not fight back against their attacker (Davies et al., 2001). Men are presumed be more physically able to fend off assaults and are perceived as less masculine when they fail to fight off an attacker (Davies et al., 2001).

Although data are clear that females are at greater risk for experiencing sexual assault, in their analysis of 24 episodes from the 2003–2004 season of *SVU*, Britto et al. (2007) found that the show overrepresented the number of male victims, and the female victims were more likely than the males to be presented as though they contributed to the offense, either by drinking or using drugs, by associating with the wrong crowd, or by talking to strangers. One-third of sexual assault victims in the episodes were male; nearly all victims were white and were victimized by strangers. In contrast, Soulliere (2003) found that the majority of victims were female, white, and under age 25, and knew their offenders, while the majority of offenders were male, white, and young. Additionally, she found that two of the eleven sexual assaults were falsely reported, and that in three of the eleven cases alcohol and/or drugs were present, but in all cases the victims had been drugged by the offenders.

Depictions of males as rape victims are fairly rare. In 2015, the television show *Outlander* featured an episode in which a male character is raped and tortured by another male. While brutal and explicit, some have argued it is serves an important function of showing not only that males can also be raped, but also that rape is about power and control (Zimmerman, 2015). Berns (2001) found that *Playboy* "de-genders" the problems of domestic and sexual violence by overrepresenting the likelihood that males will be victimized.

Pink focused on female perpetrators in "Please Don't Leave Me," which shows the many ways the artist uses violence to stop her partner from leaving. She continually begs her partner to stay with her. Some have maintained that this depiction trivializes the abuse of men, as few even considered it to be domestic violence.

Although women and girls certainly do use physical forms of abuse, most experts say that emotional abuse and verbal abuse are more common among female perpetrators. Green Day sang about physical abuse and the emotional control a female abuser has over her victim in "Pulling Teeth." The song also highlights the complex feelings victims experience, be they male or female. Further, the song addresses the confusion faced by victims trying to understand why the people who are supposed to love them treat them so horribly. It asks whether the perpetrator is just evil, ultraviolent, or mentally disturbed before noting,

> I better tell her that I love her
> Before she does it all over again.

Perhaps the most famous film featuring male rape is *Deliverance*. The film relies on extensive stereotyping: "the inbred-looking Banjo Boy (Billy Redden) who plays 'Dueling Banjos' with Ronny Cox's character, and the mountain men who rape Ned Beatty's character, demanding he 'squeal like a pig.' " University of Tulsa cultural studies professor Robert Jackson explains that *Deliverance* has "had a tenacious hold on people's imaginations, establishing the hillbilly as a kind of menacing, premodern, medieval kind of figure" (Leopold, 2012). "I think John Boorman deserves so much credit," actor Burt Reynolds said in an interview. "I remember that men had not really had a feeling about rape that they got when they saw the film. And it was the only time I saw men, sick, get up and walk out of a theater. I've seen women do that, but to see men do it, I thought maybe this film is more important in a lot of ways than we've given it credit for" (Gilchrist, 2012). *South Park* and other comedies have made male rape jokes about *Deliverance*, while a T-shirt line offers shirts with printed words: "paddle faster, I hear Banjos."

RACE AND VICTIMIZATION

Data are clear that abuse and assault are more common among certain racial and ethnic groups. The Violence Policy Center found that, in 2011, black females were far more likely to be murdered by males than were white females. Black females were murdered by males at a rate of 2.61 per 100,000 in single-victim/single-offender incidents. For white women, the rate was 0.99 per 100,000. In 94 percent of the cases, the murderer was someone known to the victim, with the most frequent perpetrator being a husband, partner, or former husband/partner (Sugarmann, 2013).

Clinton (1994) argued that "slavery systematically fostered patterns of sexual violence" and "slaves saw rape as part of a continuum of humiliation, coercion, and abuse" (pp. 206, 210). Angela Y. Davis (1985) explained that "throughout Afro-American women's economic history in this country . . . sexual abuse has been perceived as an occupational threat" (p. 8). Further, Davis maintains that "the myth of the Black rapist" "makes it difficult for black women to join a 'multiracial antirape movement' that seeks to bring rapists into the justice system, since most men blamed for rape are African American and most rapes discussed are of white women" (p. 7). Black women sometimes find that "the very same white policemen who would supposedly protect them from rape, will sometimes go so far as to rape Black women in their custody" (p. 10).

Adelman (1989) analyzed four films and found that rape victims were typically presented as sexually promiscuous, especially women of color. Meyers (2004) noted that victims of color are even more likely to be presented as though they contributed to the offense. As bell hooks (n.d.) noted in "Selling Hot Pussy," black women face a different challenge dealing with sexuality: "[b]ombarded with images representing the black female body as expendable" and extremely sexual, the public labels black women as transgressive (p. 117). hooks states, "[u]ndesirable in the conventional sense, which defines beauty and sexuality as desirable only to the extent that it is idealized and unattainable, the black female body gains attention only when it is synonymous with accessibility, availability, when it is sexually deviant" (p. 117). Projansky (2001) noted that black women are overrepresented as crime victims but generally lacking voice.

Toni Morrison (2007) addresses victim-blaming of black women in *The Bluest Eye*, which is written through the eyes of a 12-year-old child. After Pecola is raped and impregnated by her father, the neighborhood women blame her by saying "the girl was always foolish" (Projansky, 2001, p. 189). Another questions "How come she didn't fight him?" (p. 189). In *The Street*, set in 1940s' Harlem, Lutie, a single mother, is harassed and sexually assaulted by her superintendent. Yet, she repeatedly wonders "if there was something about her that subtly suggested to the Super that she would welcome his love-making, wondering if the same thing had led Mrs. Hedges to believe that she would leap at the opportunity to make money sleeping with white men" (Petry, 1946, pp. 240–241). At another point two men, Boots and Jones, attempt to rape Lutie. She defends herself and ends up killing the men. As a result of this action, the "only thing she could do was go away and never come back, because the best thing that could happen to Bub would be for him never to know that his mother was a murderer" (p. 433).

Britto et al. (2007) found that close to two-thirds of the victims depicted in the 2003–2004 season of *SVU* were white, despite the fact that in Manhattan (where the show is set) the majority of victims are women of color. Despite the fact that African American women are at greatest risk for sexual assault in Manhattan, they were almost entirely absent from the show. While females perpetrate just 5 percent of the sexual assaults in Manhattan, they were one-third of the offenders. The female offenders were presented as excessively manipulative and cruel. Offenders on *SVU* are almost always apprehended, tried, convicted, and punished. In contrast, in Manhattan less than half of all rape and murder cases are cleared by arrest and only 51 percent of those result in a conviction.

Rader and Rhineberger-Dunn (2010) conducted a content analysis of the depiction of female victims of stalking, rape/sexual assault, and domestic violence during the 2003–2004 seasons of *Crime Scene Investigation*, *SVU*, and *Without a Trace*. Of the victims, 85 percent were white and 48 percent were under 21; 69 percent were single and 67 percent had no children. This depiction does not reflect reality.

When films depict the rape of black women, an overtly evil white man is typically the perpetrated. For instance, in *A Time to Kill* (1996), it was revolting, racist white men who rape an innocent black girl. "The film thus uses and then shifts attention away from African American women, focusing instead on the excessive evilness of (some) white men and on a narrative about deracialized fatherhood and masculinity through which a different white man is redeemed" (Projansky, 2001, p. 164). In his closing argument at the trial of Carl Lee, the girl's father who killed the rapists, attorney Jake (played by Matthew McConaghey) asks the jury to close their eyes and envision that the innocent girl who was raped was actually white, positioning him as the white savior avenger and deracializing the incident. Projansky (2001) notes that rape scenes involving black female victims are often far more explicit than those involving white victims. An exception to this is *The Color Purple*, which tells the story of Celie, who was abused by her black stepfather. He raped her and impregnated her twice, then sent the children to Africa with her sister who was doing missionary work there (Goodman, 2012).

Native American women are far more likely to be victims of rape and domestic violence than any other racial or ethnic group. Studies have found the rates of murder of Native American women to be ten times higher than those involving non-Native women, with the most frequent perpetrators being intimate partners (Bachman et al., 2008). Native women suffer sexual assault at rates two times higher than non-Native women. In South Dakota, Native women are 10 percent of the population but 40 percent of sexual assault victims. Alaskan Natives are 15 percent of that state's population but 61 percent of its sexual assault victims.

Native Women are among the least likely to report abuse or sexual assault to authorities, though they may not trust the police (Thurman et al., 2003; Wakeling et al., 2001) or may believe the response time will be too slow to matter (Wakeling et al., 2001). Further, many Native women who live rurally do not have phones or access to police stations to report abuse (Wakeling et al., 2001). Additionally, few cases are ever cleared with an arrest by police, let alone prosecuted, so victims likely feel there's no point in involving the criminal justice system. Arrests are made in only 13 percent of cases involving Native American women, compared to 35 percent of cases involving black women and 32 percent involving white women. Only 27 of 45 Indian Health Centers conduct rape examinations, resulting in a lack of physical evidence in many cases that dissuades prosecutors from continuing (Williams, 2012).

Similarly, rates of domestic violence are at least 50 percent higher than for non-Native women. A 2009 CDC study found 39 percent of Native women had endured an abusive relationship, which is higher than any other ethnic group. 70 percent of assailants are of a different race, which is not typically true in domestic violence cases. The abuse endured by Native women is more frequently physical and sexual and more injurious than among other racial groups (Williams, 2012).

Despite this overrepresentation in reality, Native women are rarely depicted as victims in popular culture. One recent book, Louise Erdrich's *The Round House*, tells the story of a woman's rape on a reservation. Her husband Bazil, a tribal judge, tries to get his wife, Geraldine, to identify the perpetrator and seeks to work with tribal and other detectives working on the case. Like many victims, Geraldine falls into a deep depression. Her son, 13-year-old Joe who as an adult narrates the story, tries to solve the crime with the help of his friends. The attack occurred near the Round House, a spiritual place. As is true in reality, solving the crime is made more difficult by the complex issues of who has jurisdiction to investigate particular offenses on tribal lands. Another woman, Mayla, contacts Geraldine and they realize it was the same man, Linden Lark, who raped them. He is arrested but not imprisoned for long, and upon his release begins to harass Geraldine. Family members beat him up as a warning to stay away from Geraldine but he is undeterred. When she makes comments suggesting she might have to kill him, Joe decides he should be the one to do it. He and his friend Cappy murder Linden and, while the family and others suspect Joe did it, they try to protect him from the police. The book won several awards.

CHILDREN AS VICTIMS

Estimates vary as to how many children are victimized each year through physical abuse, sexual abuse, domestic violence, and community violence, but the numbers are in the multiple millions (Grossman & DeGaetano, 2014). While children who live in homes where they are exposed to domestic violence may not have actually been abused themselves, they are often negatively affected by witnessing the abuse. They often blame themselves, and suffer from a host of emotional and other challenges. They may be angry at the abuser but also at the victim for staying in the relationship. "Witnessing violence affects a child's developing capacity for reality testing, for understanding what is real and what is fantasy" (p. 47). Children exposed to violence come to believe that adults are not emotionally available to them and cannot afford them protection. "The logical corollary of this theme, of course, is that children come to believe that they must protect themselves and those that they love" (p. 48). In 2009, it was estimated that as many as

14 million children have been exposed to domestic violence in the United States (Groves, 2002). Groves (2002) explains,

> domestic violence ... seems to be the most toxic form of exposure to violence for children. Furthermore, we now believe that young children are far more likely to be exposed to violence in the home than to violence on the street. For many children, the first lessons they learn about violence are not from television or from the streets, but from their parents. These lessons are generally the wrong lessons; that it is acceptable to use threats or force to get one's way, that violence has a place in an intimate relationship, that adults can hurt one another and not apologize or take responsibility for their actions. (p. 50)

Studies of childhood trauma have found that it is very similar to that of adults, and that children too can suffer from PTSD. Many suffer from nightmares, insomnia, and gastrointestinal problems. Children who live with domestic violence usually end up assuming more adult responsibilities (Riger, Raja, & Camacho, 2002). Groves (2002) has found that children who are exposed to various forms of violence feel that their world is unpredictable, dangerous, and hostile. Many take on a constant watchfulness for bad things, a type of hypervigilance that can affect their neurochemical stress responses. "It interferes with their abilities to accomplish learning tasks in school. These children are distractible and unfocused. They do not complete assignments. They may be highly active and restless" (p. 47). Children and adolescents may also become disruptive at school or have other difficulties related to their lack of concentration. They are more likely to be suspended or expelled. Some drop out of school or begin using illicit substances. Girls are more likely to engage in risky behaviors like drinking, drug use, eating disorders, self-mutilation, suicidal ideation, and promiscuous sexual behavior. One of the biggest concerns is that children who are exposed to violence in the home learn and begin to imitate that behavior. Boys who witness their mothers being abused are 700 times more likely to become perpetrators of violence than boys who never observed domestic violence in their homes (Walker, 2009). Further, "Research has found that abused children watch more television than other children do, prefer violent programs, and appear to admire violent heroes. Children who are both abused and watchers of a great deal of television are more likely to commit crimes later in life" (Grossman & DeGaetano, 2014, p. 32).

Witnessing domestic violence also affects a child's interpersonal relationships. Those children are often isolated and may lose trust in others, which may make it difficult for them to interact with others later in life. Frequently the abuse results in disruptions in where children live, and perhaps even in which parent has custody (Riger et al., 2002).

While historically judges have awarded custody to mothers as a way to protect the mother–child bond, in the 1970s, the "best interest of the child" became the standard for awarding custody, and was at least on its face neutral regarding parental rights. Exposure to domestic violence was not originally considered when determining custody, but today it is a significant consideration.

Parents often claim that the children have no idea what is happening, that they saw nothing.

> Mothers say, "We had a huge fight last night, but the kids were asleep and didn't hear it." When we talk to the children separately from their parents, we discover that they were well aware of the fight. However, because none of the adults talked about it the next day, the children believed that this was not a subject they could discuss with their parents. (Groves, 2002, p. 19)

Although it is not always the case, research has shown that 60 percent of perpetrators of domestic violence will also abuse the children in the home. The Attorney General's National Task Force on Children Exposed to Violence (2012) found that of the 76 million children in the United States, 46 million are exposed to abuse, violence, and crime annually. It noted that sexual abuse places children at greater risk for "for serious and chronic health problems, including posttraumatic stress disorder (PTSD), depression, suicidality, eating disorders, sleep disorders, substance abuse, and deviant sexual behavior. Sexually abused children often become hypervigilant about the possibility of future sexual violation, experience feelings of betrayal by the adults who failed to care for and protect them" (p. 3). The Center for Youth Wellness (2014) studied California children's exposure to adverse childhood experiences (ACEs). Often referred to as polyvictimization, these include abuse (physical, emotional, and sexual), neglect (physical and emotional), and household dysfunction (divorce, mental illness, substance abuse, domestic violence, and incarceration). In California, 61.7 percent of adults have experienced one ACE and 16.7 percent have experienced four or more. A person with four or more ACEs is 5.13 times as likely to suffer from depression, 2.42 times as likely to have chronic obstructive pulmonary disease, 2.93 times as likely to smoke, 3.23 times as likely to binge drink, 12.2 times as likely to attempt suicide, 10.3 times as likely to use injection drugs, 7.4 times as likely to be an alcoholic, 2.2 times as likely to have ischemic heart disease, 2.4 times as likely to have a stroke, 1.9 times as likely to have cancer, and 1.6 times as likely to have diabetes (Attorney General, National Taskforce ... , 2012).

Songs often provide more explicit description of abuse about child victims, often from the view of children. In 2012, female rapper Angel Haze, just 21, wrote "Cleaning Out My Closet," in which she detailed childhood sexual abuse: "My heart was pumping it was thumping with like tons of my fear/Imagine being seven and seeing cum in your underwear." She then implores listeners to consider the short- and long-term effects of such abuse.

Busta Rhyme's "Touch It" featured the line, "I'ma hit you and your man and ima hit you where you stand," while Rapper Eminem graphically discussed the effects of witnessing abuse on children in "When I'm Gone," noting the intergenerational cycle of violence, "Daddy it's me, help Mommy, her wrists are bleeding."

Even Broadway show tunes occasionally take up issues like rape and domestic violence. The song "Turn It Off" from the controversial hit "Book of Mormon" features the perspective of a child witness, plus important commentary on how faith can sometimes make matter worse, not better. The child also comments on the array of "triggers" that prompt physical assaults. In this case, dad beats mom every time the Utah Jazz lose.

In 2008, novelist Emma Donoghue heard the story of an Austrian woman, Elisabeth Fritzl, who had finally been freed after being held captive in her father's basement for 24 years, forced to have sex with him and bearing seven children. The man had taken three of the children and raised them, but the other three were with her when she emerged from the dungeon where she had been held. It was the first time those children had ever seen the outside world, and that tragedy served as inspiration for Donoghue's book, *Room*. It is a unique and complex book that is told not from the perspective of a psychopath or as the story of a victim but instead from the point of view of survival. The mother was abducted by her assailant when she was 19, and gave birth in captivity to her son, Jack, who is 5 at the time of the writing. The book literally chronicles what the main character, referred to as Ma, and her son do to make it in their own dungeon, and how they create a rich and vivid life despite the deprivation. But, as Jack gets older things become more confining, and Ma creates a plan for escape. Like many survivors, escape is not perfect, as both have to adjust to the world around them, to the unwanted attention to their plight, and to creating a new world in the real one. *Room* has been made into a feature film that was released in 2015.

Demi Lovato's "For the Love of a Daughter" also presents the child witness perspective.

Four years old with my back to the door
All I could hear was the family war.

The song further addresses the emotional impact of witnessing abuse, as the child inquires as to how someone can physically harm those they profess to love.

Christina Aguilera, herself a sexual assault survivor, penned "I'm OK," which is also from a child's perspective. Aguilera's song also describes the abusive home as a war zone and notes that children feel lost and confused, as they "Never know just where to turn for shelter from the storm."

As noted, although the risk that children who grow up with abuse will become abusers or victims is far greater than for those who come from safe homes, popular culture doesn't spend much time on it. One interesting depiction is in the paranormal film *Sinister 2*, where the main character (Shannyn Sossaman) has fled with her twins from her abusive husband. She is befriended by a former deputy sheriff (James Ransone) who is now a private investigator looking into cases in which a demon is possessing children. Sachs (2015) commented,

> the supernatural horror gains thematic resonance by paralleling a more earthbound horror. One might interpret the demon that Ransone's chasing as a metaphor for domestic violence—it destroys families and haunts whomever survives it. And just as abused children sometimes grow up to be abusers themselves, so too does the demon turn children into monsters.

Christina Aguilera's "Oh Mother" offers the perspective of a child imploring his or her mother to leave an abuser. It discusses how the mother was innocent and thought her future husband was a great guy, until he "took his anger out on her face" for ten years. The child realizes how difficult it was for her mother to survive and to eventually leave, commenting, "Oh mother, don't look back/'Cause he'll never hurt us again."

In the novel *Big Little Lies*, Celeste also naively, but again, like so many victims, believes that her twin boys have no idea about the abuse. As is often the case, Perry's abuse escalates until the injuries are much more pronounced, and Celeste finally starts to accept that she might be a victim of domestic violence. She eventually sees a counselor in a town some distance away, lest anyone see her. It is clear that when she walks in she is grappling with feeling simultaneously superior to the other victims (and even the counselors) while also feeling guilty because she feels that way. This rings true to the literature on upper-class victims, who often take longer or never seek help because they feel that they will be judged extra harshly due to their social status. She makes arrangements to rent a place and plans to leave with the boys, but the plans are thwarted when Perry answers the phone from the property management company. This is a huge error but also one that is quite possible, as unless Celeste told them (which she likely did not) they had no reason to believe it would be dangerous to leave a message with someone else. As is typical, the thought that she plans to leave escalates the abuse, and Perry beats Celeste way worse than he ever had. Even still, Celeste is wracked with guilt, as Perry apologizes and takes care of her. The final straw, however, is when Celeste learns that one of the twins, Max, has been bullying girls at the school. Another boy, the son of newcomer Jane, has been taking the blame for the bullying, and many of the mothers at the school have ostracized Jane and encouraged their kids not to play with her son, Ziggy. Celeste realizes that the boys have indeed seen at least some of the abuse, and Max is replicating what his father does. It all comes to a head at the end, when a scandalous secret about Perry's past is revealed and Celeste publicly outs him as an abuser. Another woman yells at him that the "kids see ... we see everything" before pushing him, which results in his fatal fall off a balcony. The secret was that Perry was the man who had sexually assaulted Jane years prior, resulting in her meek demeanor. Ziggy, it turns out, is Perry's son. Readers learn that Bonnie grew up in a horribly abusive home and suffers from PTSD, which was triggered when she heard Perry justifying his abuse and claiming his behavior had nothing to do with his son's.

Pink's "Family Portrait" documents the fact that children see and hear way more than victims typically estimate. The song also focuses on the confusion children face when they simply want a "normal" and safe home and family. The child hears glass breaking and momma crying and "can't stand the sound." Again, the child compares the home to a war zone, and expresses that she feels great guilt and responsibility for the abuse, saying, "I promise I'll be better, Mommy I'll do anything." At one point the child even runs away. She also notes that the family puts on a happy façade in their "family portrait," and simply wishes that to be her reality.

In *Black and Blue* (1998), Anna Quindlen shares the story of Fran Benedetto's flight from her abusive husband. After years of abuse from police officer Bobby Benedetto, Fran finally contacts a service that offers to relocate women and give them new identities. She and son Robert end up in Florida and begin making a life there. Fran is constantly vigilant, however, as she knows that Bobby will stop at nothing to find them. She hates that she cannot contact her sister or any of her friends, and that Robert, who saw how badly she was hurt the last time, still loves his dad and doesn't really want to be away from him. Fran also replays the emotional abuse she suffered from Bobby, who made it clear it was always "her fault." He taunted her that there was nothing she could ever do, since he was a cop. Just as she predicted, Bobby finds them, as he has both determination and access to people who can help track the phone call Robert made to him one night. He beats Fran badly and by the time she is found by a friend, Bobby has fled with Robert. The book ends with Fran in a new relationship and with a little girl, but still looking for Robert. He called just once and left a message, and she fears he believes her to be dead. In the end, although she is somewhat happy, she cannot truly be because Bobby took so much from her.

Nickelback's (2001) song "Never Again" shares the perspective of a son who hears and sees the abuse committed by his dad against his mom. While the song features some important insights, such as that victims often want to but don't disclose their abuse to medical professionals and that children always know that something is wrong, it also ends with the predictable "fight back" situation in which the mother kills her husband (evidently before the child can). This topic is addressed in detail in Chapter 6.

Other songs show the importance of help from others. The video for country Singer Sam Hunt's "Take Your Time" features a young woman with an infant who's in an abusive relationship. Hunt watches her from afar from different locations, including a bar, Laundromat, and gas station. He witnesses her partner shoving her and yelling at her, until the end, when she tries to get into her car to leave and the man hits her. Hunt intervenes then.

Sexual abuse of children is particularly disturbing. Because it is a largely hidden problem, it is difficult to ascertain how frequently it occurs. Data do show that approximately 70 percent of sexual assaults are of people under the age of 17 (Garland & Policastro, 2015). Although both boys and girls can be victims, data suggest that the victimization of girls is more prevalent (Garland & Policastro, 2015). Many theaters refused to show the 2008 film *Hounddog*, which features Dakota Fanning as a 12-year-old in the Deep South in the 1950s who is raped by a teenage boy. Concerned Women for America (CWA), a Christian group, called for a complete ban of the film. CWA and other conservative groups argued that the film was pornographic and, as such, violated federal antipornography laws. District attorneys in North Carolina, where the film was shot, and Utah, where it was aired at the Sundance Film Festival, declined to pursue these claims. In contrast, the Hollywood chapter of the National Organization for Women applauded filmmaker Deborah Kampmeier for taking on a difficult subject. Chapter president Lyndsey Horvatch argued "We need to be telling stories like this. How Fanning's character transforms from victim to survivor is powerful stuff . . . it's not even close to child porn; that's ludicrous to me. The subject matter was difficult, yes, but it was well told, well done and poignant" (Barbuto, 2008). The film was given an "R" rating by the Motion Picture Association of America due to its sexual content.

Another depiction of very serious sexual abuse is *Precious* (2010), the story of a girl in 1987 Harlem who has two children as a result of rape. She struggles to make it until she is enrolled in an alternate school. It is based on the novel *Push* by Sapphire and won the audience award and the Grand Jury Prize for best drama at the 2009 Sundance Film Festival, as well as a special jury prize for the actor Mo'Nique, who played the mother. Mo'Nique says she took the role, in part, because she was abused by her brother as a child, while director Lee Daniels says he was physically abused by his father. *Precious* received a 15-minute standing ovation at the 2009 Cannes Film Festival (Hirschberg, 2009). Claireece Precious Jones is 16, obese, and illiterate. She lives in Section 8 housing with her abusive and unemployed mother, but flees when her mother attacks her and purposely drops her 3-day-old son. Later, Precious finds out that she, like the father who raped her, is HIV positive. Precious and a social worker confront her mother, Mary, about the years of abuse and neglect, and in the end, Precious announces she is seeking custody of her first son, who is being cared for by her grandmother, is planning to get a GED, and never wants to see her mother again. The film is a tragic but largely accurate depiction of the effects of child sexual abuse. Film critics commented on Gabourey "Gabby" Sidibe's portrayal of Precious as deeply hurt but still with the capacity for tenderness and love (Blankenship, 2011).

Lesbian, Gay, Bisexual, and Transgender Victims

Popular culture almost invariably depicts abuse and sexual assault involving persons of the same sex. In reality, however, domestic violence may be just as common if not more in in LGBT relationships. Likewise, sexual assault rates appear to be similar if not higher for LGBT victims (Guadalupe-Diaz, 2015). Guadalupe-Diaz (2015) notes that

> Several distinct factors place trans populations at higher risk for sexual violence than their cisgender (nontransgender) counterparts. Transphobia, or the feeling of unease or revulsion toward those who express nonnormative expressions of gender identity and expression, may foster intense hatred toward trans individuals and/or foster acceptance of sexual violence as an unavoidable aspect of being transgender. (p. 183)

Studies estimate between 25 percent and 50 percent of gays and lesbians have been victims of domestic violence (Guadalupe-Diaz, 2015).

Many studies have identified that police response to domestic violence or rape involving LGBT persons is deeply problematic. Often, victims are arrested, transported, and housed in the same jail cells as their abusers. In its 2005 report called "Stonewalled: Police abuse and misconduct against lesbian, gay, bisexual and transgender people in the U.S," Amnesty International documented verbal, physical, and sexual abuse by police, in particular of transgender persons. Transgender interviewees told of verbal harassment, demands that they identify as "he" or "she," being arrested for solicitation when they were not, harassed for having identification different than the name they provide, and coerced into having sex with officers to avoid arrest. One interviewee explained, "The police are not here to serve ... they are here to get served. Every night I'm taken into an alley and given the choice between having sex or going to jail" (Amnesty International, 2005, p. 61). Of the 29 police departments included in the study, 72 percent had no policy related with working with transgender victims. Respondents told of police targeting gay bars and establishments as well as widespread use of demeaning slurs, such as "faggot" and "dyke," to refer to LGBT persons.

Another layer of the problem is inadequate response. The Amnesty International report noted that police sometimes fail to respond with due diligence in domestic violence cases involving LGBT persons and conducted cursory investigations (Amnesty International, 2005).

LGBT victims face difficulties outside of criminal justice. There is little shelter space that is welcoming to LGBT victims, and many find it difficult to tell family or friends about the abuse due to societal homophobia.

Boys Don't Cry is one of the few examples in popular culture that address sexual assault and abuse involving an LGBT victim. It tells the true story of Brandon Teena, a transgender teen. Brandon went to stay with a friend, Lisa, who introduced him to others, including ex-convicts Tom Nissen, 22, and John Lotter, 22. Brandon thought of both men as friends. On December 19, 1993, Brandon was arrested for forging checks and sent to the female ward of the Richardson County. The name "Teena Brandon" appeared in the local paper's police blotter, and thus people in the community learned he was transgender. On Christmas Eve, Nissen and Lotter kidnapped and raped Brandon, who managed to escape through a bathroom window to the house of his girlfriend, Lana Tisdel. Her mother then called the police, who asked a variety of offensive, victim-blaming questions. That scene in the film was taken verbatim from the police reports.

Charles Laux: [A]fter he pulled your pants down and seen you was a girl, what did he do? Did he fondle you any?

Brandon Teena: No.

CL: He didn't fondle you any, huh. Didn't that kind of amaze you? Doesn't that kind of, ah, get your attention somehow that he would've put his hands in your pants and play with you a little bit? [...] [Y]ou were all half-ass drunk. I can't believe that if he pulled your pants down and you are a female that he didn't stick his hand in you or his finger in you.

BT: Well, he didn't.

CL: I can't believe he didn't.

Sheriff Laux did not arrest Lotter and Nissen; in fact, he informed them that Brandon had reported the rape. The two shot and killed Brandon on New Year's Eve, 1993, along with two others who were there. A toddler witnessed and survived the incident. Lotter and Nissen were eventually arrested, though, and ended up in prison. Sheriff Laux was later found negligent (Markel, 2014).

IMMIGRANTS

Many studies have affirmed that immigrants are particularly at risk for domestic violence (Erez, 2000). One study of Latina immigrants who in the Washington, D.C., metro area showed that almost 50 percent have been abused physically, 11 percent sexually abused, and 40 percent had been psychologically abused. Yoshihama and Dabby (2009) found that immigrants of Hispanic and Asian/other descent experience a higher risk of homicide in general than persons born in the United States. A study of femicide in New York found immigrants constituted 51 percent of intimate partner homicide victims between 1995 and 2002 (New York City Department of Health and Mental Hygiene, 2008). Immigrant women who have been in the United States for less than three years are less likely to call the police for help because they do not understand U.S. systems, speak limited English, or do not believe police will do anything (Orloff & Garcia, 2013, p. 3).

The following are examples of specific ways in which immigrant women are abused, although the experiences of individual victims will vary from case to case.

- Lying about her immigration status.
- Calling her racist names.

- Telling her that she has abandoned her culture and become "white," or "American."
- Abuser lying about his ability to have the immigration status of his lawful permanent resident abuse victims changed.
- Forcing her to work "illegally" when she does not have a work permit.
- Threatening to report her to immigration authorities if she works "under the table."
- Not letting her get job training or schooling.
- Taking the money that her family back home was depending upon her to send them.
- Forcing her to sign papers in English that she does not understand—court papers, IRS forms, immigration papers.
- Harassing her at the only job she can work at legally in the U.S., so that she loses that job and is forced to work "illegally."
- Threatening to report her to immigration authorities and get her deported.
- Threatening that he will not file immigration papers to legalize her immigration status.
- Threatening to withdraw the petition he filed to legalize her immigration status.
- Threatening to remove her children from the United States.
- Threatening to report her children to the immigration authorities.
- Convincing her that if she seeks help from the courts or the police, the U.S. legal system will give him custody of the children. (In many countries men are given legal control over the children and he convinces her that the same will occur here.)
- Telling her that the police will arrest her for being undocumented if she calls the police for help because of the abuse. (Abuse tactics against immigrant women, 2012, para 1)

Victims who can demonstrate a bona fide marriage and evidence of "extreme cruelty" are eligible, through the Violence against Women Act to self-petition for residency status, which then allows them to obtain a work permit, a driver's license, and other advantageous resources.

Popular culture is largely silent on the issue of immigrant victims. One film that does depict an immigrant's experience is *Not without My Daughter*. It tells the story of Betty Mahmoody, played by actor Sally Field, whose Iranian husband Sayed Bozorg "Moody" Mahmoody, played by Alfred Molina, was always controlling but becomes physically abusive when the couple, with their daughter Mahtob, visit his family in Iran. Moody slaps her and prevents her from leaving the house or using the phone and his family fails to intervene. When she visits an embassy she is told that she is Iranian since she is married to an Iranian citizen and that she cannot leave the country with her daughter unless Moody gives his permission. When Moody learns of her visit to the embassy he threatens to kill her. Betty eventually meets a stranger who helps her and her daughter escape. Although the film does depict some of the essential issues faced by immigrant victims, critics expressed concern that it demonized Iranian culture and Muslims in general.

Since they are not about immigrants but instead set in Afghanistan I will not offer a detailed description or analysis, but Khaled Hosseini's *The Kite Runner*, which was later made into a film, and *A Thousand Splendid Suns* offer interesting and important assessments of rape and abuse. Likewise, the popular and highly acclaimed film *Slumdog Millionaire* shows the reality of sexual abuse of children in the slums of India. These and other films are listed in Appendix A.

PRISON RAPE

The Prison Rape Elimination Act defines "prison rape" as "the rape of an inmate in the actual or constructive control of prison officials" (Worley, Worley, & Mullings, 2010, p. 66). Data from surveys in 2008–2009 show that 4.4 percent of prison inmates and 3.1 percent of jail inmates endured sexual violence, although surely the problem is severely underreported (Garland & Policastro, 2015). In 2011, an estimated 200,000 people were sexually violated in prison. Struckman-Johnson and Struckman-Johnson (2000) studied seven Midwestern prisons and found that 21 percent of respondents had been coerced or sexually victimized at least once. The risk of sexual victimization is greatest in the first five months of incarceration, and while many are victimized by other inmates, some endure sexual abuse by correctional staff members (Garland & Policastro, 2015). The National Crime Victimization Survey identified that a prisoner's likelihood of becoming a victim of sexual assault is roughly 30 times higher than that of a woman on the outside.

There are a number of films that include prison rape as an important component of the story line. Some of these are quite realistic. *Sleepers* (1996) is, according to the author of the book on which the film is based, allegedly a true story that describes the physical and sexual abuse of boys in a juvenile detention center in New York. The Wilkinson Home for Boys is where the four main characters end up after their hotdog stealing prank goes awry in Hell's Kitchen, New York, in the 1960s. They suffer from repeated physical assaults, verbal humiliation, and sexual abuse at the hands of several guards, on whom they seek revenge when they are adults. The film is apt in its recognition that juveniles are even more likely to be sexually victimized in prison than are adults.

The book *Fish* is the memoir of 17-year-old T. J. Parsell, who held up a store with a toy gun and was sentenced to four and a half to fifteen years in prison. On his first night, four older inmates drugged Parsell and took turns raping him, then flipped a coin to decide who would "own" him. Parsell was forced to stay quiet about the abuse, but the release of the book has been credited with prompting much needed conversation about the issue.

Another film that depicts prison rape in a realistic way is Tony Kaye's *American History X*. Edward Norton is Derek Vinyard, a skinhead who learned from his father to hate people of other races and religions. When his firefighter father is killed responding to a situation in a black neighborhood, the distraught but intelligent Derek joins an Aryan group and engages in a variety of crimes, culminating in his murder of a black man who was trying to rob their home. The core drama, however, is Derek's about to face when he ends up in prison. At first he carries on with his racist beliefs, but after befriending a black inmate he begins to soften. The real change, however, occurs when Derek is raped by other skinheads while in the prison shower. The deeply disturbing scene is filmed in slow motion, and ends with a shot of blood rushing down the shower drain. Subsequent conversations reveal that Derek needed stitches to repair the damage.

Sadly, there are even more examples of popular culture that minimize and trivialize prison rape. Prison rape is such a common joke that there is even a board game, created by Kevin Sebelius, the son of Kathleen Sebelius, U.S. Secretary for Health and Human Services, called "Don't Drop the Soap." Likewise, Bruenig (2015) explains that prison rape in television is almost always treated as a joke. Even shows that are supposed to address rape more accurately, like *SVU*, has sometimes includes rape jokes, and in one episode, Christopher Meloni and Ice-T are interrogating a gangster and, while rolling dice, suggest that his cellmates will do the same to determine how he will be raped. So many shows reference cellmates named Bubba and "pretty-boys-like-you." *Horrible Bosses* (2011) has a running joke that the only thing worse than being raped in prison would be if you weren't "cute enough" to be raped (O'Hehir, 2015).

As Bruenig (2015) explains,

> The logic perpetuated by ongoing ease with prison rape is that certain bad people in particular bad settings either deserve sexual assault or do not deserve protection from it. That prison simply *is* a site where rape occurs is given as a deterrent and, in the event that an offender is not deterred, implied to be what they had coming all along. But the notion that prisoners who are raped should have behaved better to be less deserving is the apotheosis of the "asking for it" or "had it coming" arguments so commonly

employed to dismiss victims of rape in the free population. Some crimes are so egregiously heinous that knee-jerk, visceral reactions tend toward the violent, but when we codify primal impulse into popular consensus, we wind up in agreement that rape is sometimes an appropriate punishment. Hatred or indifference to people in prison, therefore, affirms a particularly poisonous view of rape itself: that it has its place in the order of things, especially where badly behaved people are concerned. So long as some 200,000 people are sexually violated in detention centers annually, rape will never really retreat into the realm of the unthinkable, no matter how many perpetrators we turn into victims.

The film *Get Hard*, directed by Etan Cohen and starring Will Ferrell and Kevin Hart, features a variety of rape jokes as Hart, a generally good guy, is employed by the white-collar criminal Ferrell to teach him how to endure his time in prison. Of course Ferrell selected Hart because he is black. In one scene, Ferrell's character is in a gay restaurant and attempts to perform oral sex on a man to "ready himself" for prison rape. When asked about the stereotypes in the film, Cohen commented, "The truth was that this was a really delicate balance. We wanted to think about stereotypes but not go too far." "But at the same time," added Cohen, "prison rape is real. It's still a huge issue. I don't mind having people think about those things as well" (Abramovitch, 2015).

Rape of female inmates is portrayed in less comedic ways, but instead is intended to titillate. Films like *Born Innocent, 99 Women, They Call Her One Eye, Last House on the Left*, and *Chained Heat 2* imply that rape of females in prison is little more than sexual gratification. Clark (2009) explains,

> While sexual abuse and rape have nothing to do with sex, soap-dropping jokes and their ilk permit people to escape their discomfort with male-male sexuality by cloaking it in cheap laughs. In turn, female-female sexual abuse does not register as significant in any way—unless it's sexualized for the enjoyment of voyeurs. It's a self-enforcing cycle—misogyny affirms a narrow view of masculinity as "not womanish" that in turn creates a loathing for the feminization that is presumed to be implicit in male-male sexuality. This idea enforces the notion of femininity as something that is abnormal and lesser, which of course is a misogynistic attitude.

ELDER VICTIMS

Elder abuse was first recognized as a social problem in the late 1970s (Douglass, 1983). According to the Administration on Aging (n.d.), elder abuse or mistreatment refers to intentional actions that cause harm or create a serious risk to a vulnerable elder by a caregiver or other person who is in a trusting relationship with the elder or failure by a caregiver to satisfy the elder's basic needs or to protect the elder from harm. Elder abuse takes different forms and can be physical, psychological, sexual, and financial. Neglect is also a common form of elder abuse.

Elder abuse is one of the most underreported crimes in the United States. Mouton and colleagues (1999) found that 4.3 percent of older women were currently in an abusive relationship. Teaster, Nerenberg, and Stansbury (2003) found that 65.4 percent of abusers were family members or relatives, including adult children (32.6 percent), other family members (21.5 percent), and spouses or partner (11.3 percent). Approximately 14 percent of crimes committed against persons aged 65 or older were considered domestic violence.

Interestingly, while elder abuse is common, it is almost never depicted in popular culture. That likely has to do with the fact that popular culture largely features younger people. The entertainment industry has long been accused of ageism, particularly when it comes to women, so it is not surprisingly that elder victims of rape and abuse are nowhere to be found.

In conclusion, this chapter has focused on the most vulnerable victims, providing basic details on the scope and extent of their victimization and comparing and contrasting that with the depictions in popular culture. As should be clear, some types of victims receive disproportionate attention while others are rarely depicted. Given the overrepresentation of Native American and black women as victims of domestic abuse and sexual assault, it is surprising that so few examples can be found in popular culture. While the depictions of victims are sometimes inaccurate or limited, perhaps the worst is the portrayal of males as victims, which is often the butt of jokes that reinforce the societal trivialization of male victims.

REFERENCES

Abramovitch, S. (2015, March 17). SXSW: If "Get Hard" offends, it's doing it right, says writer-director. *Hollywood Reporter*. Retrieved September 14, 2015, from http://www.hollywoodreporter.com/news/sxsw-get-hard -offends-doing-782553

Abuse tactics against immigrant women. (2012, September 12). Retrieved January 8, 2016, from http://felicityokolo.com/blog/abuse-tactics -against-immigrant-women/

Adelman, S. (1989). Representations of violence against women in mainstream film. *Resources for Feminist Research, 18*(2), 21–26.

Administration on Aging. (n.d.) What is elder abuse? Retrieved January 24, 2016, from http://www.aoa.gov/AoA_programs/elder_rights/EA_prevention/whatisEA.aspx

Allison, D. (1992). *Bastard out of Carolina*. New York: Plume.

American Civil Liberties Union. (n.d.). Domestic violence and homelessness. Retrieved September 5, 2015, from https://www.aclu.org/sites/default/files/pdfs/dvhomelessness032106.pdf

Amnesty International. (2005). *Stonewalled: Police abuse and misconduct against lesbian, gay and bisexuals*. Retrieved January 8, 2016, from https://www.amnesty.org/en/search/?country=38334

Anderson, C. (2004). An update on the effects of playing violent video games. *Journal of Adolescence, 24,* 113–122.

Archer, J. (2000). Sex differences in aggression between heterosexual partners: A meta-analytic review. *Psychological Bulletin, 126*(5), 651–680.

Ardovini-Brooker, J., & Caringella-MacDonald, S. (2002). Media attributions of blame and sympathy in ten rape cases. *The Justice Professional, 15*(1), 3–18.

Armstrong, E. G. (2001). Gangsta misogyny: A content analysis of the portrayals of violence against women in rap music, 1987–1993. *Journal of Criminal Justice and Popular Culture, 8*(2), 96–126.

Attorney General, National Taskforce on Children Exposed to Violence. (2012, December 12). Retrieved January 24 2016, from http://www.justice.gov/defendingchildhood/cev-rpt-full.pdf

Bachman, R., Zaykowski, H., Kallmyer, R., Poteyeva, M., & Lanier. C. (2008, August). *Violence against American Indian and Alaska Native women and the criminal justice response: What is known*. Retrieved February 10, 2011, from http://www.ncjrs.gov/pdffiles1/nij/grants/223691.pdf

Barbuto, D. (2008, September 26). Theaters won't show tough film on child rape. *The State Journal-Register*. Retrieved January 8, 2016, from http://www.sj-r.com/article/20080926/News/309269915

Berns, N. (2001). Degendering the problem and gendering the blame: Political discourse on women and violence. *Gender & Society, 15*(2), 262–281.

Blankenship, J. (2011, May 25). The movie "Precious" tells two stories at once. *Huffington Post*. Retrieved September 6, 2015, from http://www.huffingtonpost.com/mark-blankenship/the-movie-precious-tells_b_350924.html

Bleackley, D. (2004). Representing rape: A semiotic analysis of rape myths in three popular films. Master's thesis, University of British Columbia.

Bonomi, A., Nemeth, J., Altenburger, L., Anderson, M., Snyder, A., & Dotto, I. (2014). Fiction or not? Fifty Shades is associated with health risks in adolescent and young adult females. *Journal of Women's Health, 23*(9), 720–728.

Britto, S., Hughes, T., Saltzman, K., & Stroh, C. (2007). Does "special" mean young, white and female? Deconstructing the meaning of "special" in *Law & Order: Special Victims Unit. Journal of Criminal Justice and Popular Culture, 14*(1), 40–57.

Brownmiller, S. (1975). *Against our will: Men, women and rape.* New York: Ballantine.

Bruenig, E. (2015, March 2). Why Americans don't care about prison rape. *The Nation.* Retrieved September 14, 2015, from http://www.thenation.com/article/why-americans-dont-care-about-prison-rape/

Center for Youth Wellness. (2014). Adverse child experiences study. Retrieved January 8, 2016, from http://www.centerforyouthwellness.org/adverse-childhood-experiences-aces/

Centers for Disease Control and Prevention. (2015). Intimate partner violence: Risk and protective factors. Retrieved September 13, 2015, from http://www.cdc.gov/violenceprevention/intimatepartnerviolence/riskprotectivefactors.html

Clark, A. (2009, August 16). Why does popular culture treat prison rape as a joke? Alternet. Retrieved September 13, 2015, from http://www.alternet.org/story/141594/why_does_popular_culture_treat_prison_rape_as_a_joke

Clinton, C. (1994). "With a whip in his hand": Rape, memory and African-American women. In G. Fabre & R. O'Meally (Eds.). *African American history and memory.* New York: Oxford University Press.

Cook, P. (2009). *Abused men: The hidden side of domestic violence.* Westport, CT: Praeger.

Davies, M., Pollard, P., & Archer, J. (2001). The influence of victim gender and sexual orientation on judgments of the victim in a depicted stranger rape. *Violence and Victims, 16*(6), 607–619.

Davis, A. (1985). Slavery and the roots of sexual harassment. Retrieved January 8, 2016, from https://law.wustl.edu/faculty_profiles/documents/davis/Slavery%20and%20the%20Roots%20of%20Sexual%20Harrassment.pdf

DeKeseredy W., & Olsson, P. (2011) Adult pornography, male peer support, and violence against women: The contribution of the "dark side" of the Internet. In M. Vargas, M. Garcia-Ruiz, & A. Edwards (Eds.). *Technology for facilitating humanity and combating social deviations: Interdisciplinary perspectives* (pp. 34–50). Hershey, PA: IGI Global.

Douglas, E. M., & Straus, M. A. (2003). *Corporal punishment experienced by university students in 17 countries and its relation to assault and injury of dating partners.* University of New Hampshire publications. Retrieved January 24, 2016, from http://pubpages.unh.edu/~mas2/ID13T.pdf

Douglass, R. L. (1983, July). Domestic neglect and abuse of the elderly: Implications for research and service. *Family Relations, 32*(3), 395–402.

Erez, E. (2000). Immigration, culture conflict and domestic violence/woman battering. *Crime Prevention and Community Safety: An International Journal, 2*(1), 27–36.

Garland, T., & Policastro, C. (2015). Victimization of the vulnerable. In T. Richards & C. Marcum (Eds.). *Sexual victimization: Then and now.* Thousand Oaks, CA: Sage.

Gelles, R. J. (1974). *The violent home: A study of physical aggression between husbands and wives.* Beverly Hills, CA: Sage.

Gilchrist, T. (2012, July 3). *Deliverance* stars Jon Voight, Burt Reynolds discuss giving men "A feeling about rape." *Hollywood Reporter.* Retrieved September 13, 2015, from http://www.hollywoodreporter.com/news/deliverance-jon-voight-burt-reynolds-john-boorman-344681

Goodfriend, W. (2011, November 28). Sexism in "The Girl with the Dragon Tattoo." *Psychology Today.* Retrieved January 8, 2016, from https://www.psychologytoday.com/blog/psychologist-the-movies/201111/sexism-in-the-girl-the-dragon-tattoo

Goodman, A. (2012, September 28). Alice Walker on 30th anniversary of The Color Purple: Racism, violence against women are global issues. *Democracy Now!* Retrieved January 8, 2016, from http://www.democracynow.org/2012/9/28/alice_walker_on_30th_anniv_of

Grossman, D., & DeGaetano, G. (2014). *Stop teaching our kids to kill: A call to action against TV, movie, & video game violence.* New York: Harmony.

Groves, B. (2002). *Children who see too much: Lessons from the child witness to violence project.* Boston, MA: Beacon.

Guadalupe-Diaz, X. (2015). Disclosure of same-sex intimate partner violence to police among lesbians, gays and bisexuals. *Social Currents,* 1–12. Retrieved January 6, 2015, from http://www.academia.edu/19566904/Disclosure_of_Same-Sex_Intimate_Partner_Violence_to_Police_among_Lesbians_Gays_and_Bisexuals

Halpern, C. T., Oslak, S. G., Young, M. L., Martin, S. L., & Kupper, L. L. (2001). Partner violence among adolescents in opposite-sex romantic relationships: Findings from the National Longitudinal Study of Adolescent Health. *American Journal of Public Health, 91*(10), 1679–1685.

Haskell, M. (1987). *From reverence to rape: The treatment of women in the movies.* Chicago: University of Chicago Press.

Hirschberg, L. (2009, October 21). The audacity of *Precious. New York Times.* Retrieved September 6, 2015, from http://www.nytimes.com/2009/10/25/magazine/25precious-t.html?_r=0

hooks, b. (n.d.). Selling hot pussy. Retrieved January 8, 2016, from http://www.feministes-radicales.org/wp-content/uploads/2010/11/bell-hooks-Selling-Hot-Pussy-representation-of-black-womens-sexuality.pdf

Johnson, A. (2014). *The gender knot: Unraveling our patriarchal legacy,* 3rd ed. Rutgers, NJ: Temple University Press.

Johnson, M. (1995, May). Patriarchal terrorism and common couple violence: Two forms of violence against women. *Journal of Marriage and Family, 57*(2), 283–294.

Leopold, T. (2012, April 14). The South: Not all bubbas and banjos. CNN. Retrieved January 8, 2016, from http://www.cnn.com/2012/04/14/us/bubba-southern-stereotypes/

Markel, K. (2014, January 9). The legacy of the "Boys don't cry" hate crime 20 years later. BuzzFeed. Retrieved January 8, 2016, from http://www.buzzfeed.com/katrinamarkel/the-legacy-of-the-boys-dont-cry-hate-crime-20-years-later#.nnDJ40OByy

McDaniel. D. (2013). Representations of partner violence in young adult literature: Dating violence in Stephenie Meyer's *Twilight* saga. Dissertation submitted to the University of Texas. Retrieved January 7, 2016, from
https://repositories.lib.utexas.edu/bitstream/handle/2152/23201/
MCDANIEL-DISSERTATION-2013.pdf

Meyers, M. (2004). African-American women and violence: Gender, race and class
in the news. *Critical Studies in Media Communication, 21*(2), 95–118.

Morrison T. (2007). *The bluest eye.* New York: Vintage.

Mouton, C., Rovi, S., Furniss, K., and Lasser, N. (1999). The associations
between health and domestic violence in older women: Results of a
pilot study. *Journal of Women's Health and Gender-Based Medicine, 1*(9),
1173–1179.

Mulvey, L. (1975). Visual pleasure and narrative cinema. *Screen, 16*(3), 6–18.

New York City Department of Health and Mental Hygiene. (2008). Intimate
partner violence against women in New York City. Retrieved January 8,
2016, from http://www.nyc.gov/html/doh/downloads/pdf/public/
ipv-08.pdf

NiCarthy, G. (2004). *Getting free: A handbook for women in abusive relationships.*
Berkeley, CA: Seal Press.

O'Hehir, A. (2015, March 26). *Get Hard* is a bloated, lazy, prison rape-joke train-
wreck. Salon. Retrieved September 13, 2015, from http://www.salon.com
/2015/03/26/get_hard_is_a_bloated_lazy_prison_rape_joke_trainw reck/

Orloff, L., & Garcia, O. (2013). Dynamics of domestic violence experienced by
immigrant victims. Legal Momentum. Retrieved January 8, 2016, from
http://iwp.legalmomentum.org/cultural-competency/dynamics-of-violence
-against-immigrant-women/1.1-Dynamics-of-Domestic-Violence-in-Immigrant
-Families-MANUAL-BB.pdf

Petry, A. (1946). *The street: A novel.* New York: Mariner.

Projansky, S. (2001). *Watching rape: Film and television in post-feminist culture.*
New York: NYU Press.

Rader, N., & Rhineberger-Dunn. (2010). A typology of victim characterization in
television crime dramas. *Journal of Criminal Justice and Popular Culture,
17*(1), 231–263.

Richards, T., & Restivo, L. (2015). Sexual violence among intimates. In
T. Richards & C. Marcum (Eds.). *Sexual violence: Then and now* (pp. 69–81).
Thousand Oaks, CA: Sage.

Riger, S., Raja, S., & Camacho, J. (2002). The radiating impact of intimate partner violence. *Journal of Interpersonal Violence, 17*(2), 184–205.

Sachs, B. (2015, August 25). The horror film *Sinister 2* considers the real-life horror of domestic violence. *Chicago Reader.* Retrieved January 8, 2016, from
http://www.chicagoreader.com/Bleader/archives/2015/08/25/the
-horror-film-sinister-2-considers-the-real-life-horror-of-domestic-violence

Soulliere, D. (2003). Prime-time murder: Presentations of murder on popular
television justice programs. *Journal of Criminal Justice and Popular Culture,
10*(1), 12–38.

Straus, M. (1993). Physical assaults by wives: A major social problem. In R. Gelles & D. Loseky (Eds.). *Current controversies on family violence* (pp. 67–87). Newbury Park, CA: Sage.

Straus, M. A., & Gelles, R. J. (1986). Societal change and change in family violence from 1975 to 1985 as revealed by two national surveys. *Journal of Marriage and the Family, 48*(1), 465–479.

Struckman-Johnson, C., & Struckman-Johnson, D. (2000). Sexual coercion rates in seven Midwestern prison facilities for men. *The Prison Journal, 80*(4), 379–390.

Sugarmann, J. (2013, October 24). Black women face a greater risk of domestic violence. *Huffington Post.* Retrieved September 13, 2015, from http://www.huffingtonpost.com/josh-sugarmann/black-women-face-a-greate_b_4157659.html

Surette, R. (1998). *Media, crime, and criminal justice*, 2nd ed. Belmont, CA: Wadsworth Publishing.

Teaster, P. B., Nerenberg, L., & Stansbury, K. (2003). A national study of multi-disciplinary teams. *Journal of Elder Abuse & Neglect, 15*, 91–108.

Thurman, P. J., Bubar, R., Plested, B., Edwards, R., LeMaster, P., Bystrom, E., Hardy, M., Tahe, D., Burnside, M., & Oetting, E. (2003). *Violence against Indian women, final revised report*. Washington, D.C.: National Institute of Justice.

Tjaden, P., & Thoennes, N. (2001). Stalking: Its role in serious domestic violence cases. National Criminal Justice Reference Service. Retrieved January 8, 2014, from https://www.ncjrs.gov/pdffiles1/nij/grants/187446.pdf

Wakeling, S., Jorgensen, M., Michaelson, S., & Begay, M. (2001). *Policing on American Indian reservations*. Washington, D.C.: National Institute of Justice.

Walker, L. (2009). *The battered woman syndrome*, 3rd ed. New York: Springer Publishing.

Weitzman, S. (2000). *Not to people like us: Hidden abuse in upscale marriages.* New York: Basic.

Weitzman, S. (2013). What is upscale abuse? Retrieved January 7, 2016, from http://drsusanweitzman.com/what-is-upscale-abuse.html

Williams, T. (2012, May 22). For Native American women, scourge of rape, rare justice. *New York Times.* Retrieved September 13, 2015, from http://www.nytimes.com/2012/05/23/us/native-americans-struggle-with-high-rate-of-rape.html?_r=0

Worley, V., Worley, R., Mullings, J. (2010). Rape lore in correctional settings: Assessing inmates' awareness of sexual corrections in prisons. *Southwest Journal of Criminal Justice, 7*(1), 65–86.

Yoder, K. (2015, May 28). "Game of Thrones" books boast 4 times more rape than TV. NewsBusters. Retrieved January 9, 2016, from http://www.newsbusters.org/blogs/katie-yoder/2015/05/28/game-thrones-books-boast-4-times-more-rape-tv-show

Yoshihama, M., & Dabby, F. (2009, September). Facts & stats: Domestic violence in Asian, Native Hawaiian and Pacific Islander homes. San Francisco, CA: The Asian & Pacific Islander Institute on Domestic Violence.

Zimmerman, A. (2015, June 2). TV's rape obsession: What "Outlander" got right and what "Game of Thrones" gets very wrong. *Daily Beast*. Retrieved January 24, 2016, from http://www.thedailybeast.com/articles/2015/06/02/tv-s-rape-obsession-what-outlander-got-right-and-game-of-thrones-gets-very-wrong.html

2

Domestic Terrorists and Strangers in the Bushes: Describing Offenders

Just as anyone can be a victim, anyone can be a perpetrator of sexual assault or domestic violence. That being said, the bulk of media and popular culture coverage, hence public opinion, is focused on male offenders who perpetrate violence and rape against female victims. While statistics generally bear out that this is the most common victim–offender dynamic, it is by no means the only one. This chapter begins by addressing male offenders, focusing first on how these offenses are presented. The chapter then discusses female perpetrators, black male perpetrators, and the issue of false accusations. It also discusses groups that are overrepresented as assailants, including military, athletes, and fraternity members. Additionally, the chapter further includes a segment on sexual abuse in religious institutions.

First, though, I provide a description of the primary warning signs of an abusive relationship and the data on risk factors for perpetration of abuse and assault.

Warning Signs and Risk Factors for Perpetration

Warning signs of an abusive person include but are not limited to the following:

- very clingy
- constantly wanting to call
- excessively questioning one's actions and whereabouts

- randomly showing up at places of work or school
- surprising one in a way that feels like stalking
- insisting that things should be done his way
- unpredictable behavior
- short temper or snaps at the slightest thing
- wanting to have sex for the wrong reasons
- threatens to commit suicide if one leaves
- increased use of drugs and/or alcohol
- teach the other person to respect him
- wants the other person to fear the abuser as a way of showing respect
- blaming the other person for things out of their control (Finley, 2013).

It is clear, as was presented in Chapter 1, that the most common situation is a male perpetrator assaulting or abusing a female victim. Pennington (2014) explains,

> The majority of incidents of sexual violence are perpetrated by men, against women. To take this message further, in order for women to be "truly" safe, they should avoid being around men. How realistic is that? Unfortunately, abusers do not have a special marking that means we can avoid being in their presence. Living an ordinary life means you are going to come into contact with men, even if you do not have relationships with them. These men will be driving your taxi, investigating your symptoms as a medical professional, serving you alcohol in your local pub, being your father, brother, friend, carer, colleague of casual acquaintance. (pp. 46–47)

Like victimization, there are a number of myths about offenders. In his widely used book, *Why Does He Do That? Inside the Minds of Angry and Controlling Men*, Lundy Bancroft (2003) identifies a variety of myths associated with abusers:

1. An abuser holds in his/her feelings.
2. Abusers often have aggressive personalities.
3. Abusers lose control.
4. Abusers suffer from too much anger.
5. The abuser is mentally ill.
6. Male abusers hate women.
7. Abusers are afraid of intimacy and abandonment.
8. Abusers have low self-esteem.
9. Abusers have a stressful work life.
10. Abusers have poor communication skills.

11. There are as many abusive men as there are abusive women.
12. Abuse is just as bad for the perpetrator as it is for the victim.
13. The abuser is a victim of racism or other prejudice.
14. The abuser is dependent on alcohol or drugs.

Bancroft (2003) and others have debunked or unpacked them, but the myths remain common in depictions of domestic violence and sexual assault. Bancroft (2003) explains that many of these myths are used as justifications or excuses as to why the abuser should not be held accountable for his or her actions. Similarly, the popular culture picture of domestic violence is an out-of-control man whose rage prompts his assault. One expert commented about this misconception after the high-profile domestic violence incident perpetrated by NFL star Ray Rice:

> Domestic violence is a pattern of behavior in which one exerts power and control over another individual . . . To use the phrase "He's out of control" isn't accurate. Everything about this person is about control, actually. There are a lot of strategies that an abusive partner uses in order to control their partners aside from physical violence—verbal abuse, isolation, controlling the finances, reproductive coercion, sabotaging birth control so a partner gets pregnant and he's saying she has to stay home with the baby. It's not usually a one-time incident. In the 18 years I've been doing this, I've never worked with a victim who said it was only one time. Maybe there was one physical abuse incident, but she usually speaks to the isolation, the verbal abuse, the fear, the threats. (Filipovic, 2014)

Some of the risk factors for victimization are the same for perpetration and are true of rapists as well. These include depression or suicidal thoughts, academic achievement, sexual behavior, low self-esteem, and substance use (Foshee et al., 2001). According to Perpetrator Risk Factors for Violence against Women (n.d.), approximately one-third of convicted rapists are under the age of 25 and one-fifth of all sexual assault perpetrators are aged 18–21. The typical male stalker is in his thirties.

One of the biggest predictors that someone will be a perpetrator is previous acts of violence against women. Individuals with a history of domestic violence are 13 times more likely to commit future acts of violence against a partner. Men who adhere to rigid notions of masculinity and hold stereotypical gender roles are at greater risk for perpetrating violence against women. Experiencing childhood abuse increases the risk of perpetration as well.

Abusers and rapists almost always claim it is the victim's fault, not theirs. "Abusers may claim to have supernatural powers. Usually they claim to be superior intellectually and to know the ways of the world. Because the abused woman has been brought so low herself, she may come to believe this" (NiCarthy, 2004, p. 259). Because they are manipulative and calculating, abusers seem to be able to sense when a victim might be trying to leave and either come through with some indulgence or, conversely, amp up their techniques such that she is fearful of ending the relationship (NiCarthy, 2004). While physical abuse can be very damaging, "Emotionally abusive people are sometimes remarkably imaginative. They can be just as frightening to their partners as are physically violent partners" (NiCarthy, 2004, p. 260).

RAPE CULTURE

One of the biggest contributors to the prevalence of rape and domestic violence is what has been called "rape cultures." The term was created to

> describe a culture in which sexual violence is normalized phenomenon, in which male-dominant environments (such as sports, war, and the military) encourage and sometimes depend on violence against women, in which the male gaze and women as objects-to-be-looked-at contribute to a culture that accepts rape, and in which rape is one experience along a continuum of sexual violence that women confront on a daily basis. (Projansky, 2001, p. 9)

Rape culture refers to the notion that, while rape can happen anywhere, there are indeed locations and contexts in which it is more common. More broadly, though, it can be argued that the United States itself is a rape culture in that the normalization of abuse and assault is endemic across so many institutions, not least of which is media and popular culture. Harding (2015) noted that while the term has been around since the later 1970s, it did not receive popular attention until more recently. As she observes, "we live in a culture that claims to abhor rape yet adores jokes about the prisoner who 'drops the soap,' the trans woman who discloses to a date that she has a penis and gets punished for it, the altar boy who follows a priest into the back room" (p. 1).

Rape culture is ubiquitous such that it is rarely even recognized, and most don't even question it. It is manifest in many ways, but as Harding (2015) notes, "its most devilish trick is to make the average, non-criminal person identify with the person accused, instead of the person reporting a crime" (p. 4). That is, rape culture creates a situation where the initial response to victims is often disbelief and blame while the first thought is that the poor man must have been wrongly accused.

Because it is so much a part of our lives, Harding (2015) comments, "every boy who doesn't grow up to rape anybody deserves a big gold star" (p. 38). We claim to detest rape but at the same time are titillated by images of sexual violation. Should people not watch, read, or purchase sexually misogynistic materials, profit-motivated industries would produce different content. But, as a whole, we do not. We continue to buy products like Belvedere Vodka, which in 2012 featured a campaign with a tagline that it "goes down smoothly," superimposed on the image of a clearly fearful woman who is try-ing to escape from a man's grasp. T-shirt companies make, retailers sell, and people buy shirts with lines like "No means yes" (Harding, 2015).

In rape cultures, men feel entitled to grope women at bars or women who are wearing revealing clothing. These men believe they can get away with it because such behavior is considered normal for men; it's what they see on all their favorite shows, films, and music videos. That is, when peo-ple refuse to call out others for such men's behavior or attempt to inter-vene, they are complicit with the rape culture.

Rape cultures make sexual assault the topic of jokes, as if being violated is funny. In 2014, Fox aired its long-awaited *Simpsons/Family Guy* cross-over episode. In one scene, Bart Simpson is instructing Stewie Griffin about prank calls. Bart prank calls Moe, the owner of Moe's Tavern, and everyone laughs. Then Stewie tries, prank-calling Moe and announcing that "Your sister's being raped." Supposedly the joke is on Stewie, as he is clearly not good at prank-calling. Some groups, like the Parents Television Council, learned about the joke before the episode aired and attempted to have it removed (Gajewski, 2014). As was noted in Chapter 1, jokes about prison rape are common across many types of popular culture.

South Park, the adult comedy show that is well known for pushing the boundaries in its comedic assaults on both liberals and conservatives, once featured an episode in which Indiana Jones was repeatedly raped by George Lucas and Steven Spielberg. It was intended as a spoof on the rape scenes from *Deliverance* and *The Accused* and was, according to represen-tatives of *South Park*, intended to poke fun at the fourth Indiana Jones film that was released in May 2007. The episode ends with Spielberg and Lucas being arrested after police find them raping a storm trooper (Elsworth, 2008). The show also used the repeated rape accusations against actor and comedian Bill Cosby as fodder in December 2014. The show featured Cosby giving pop music star Taylor Swift a drink and suggesting he was attempting to rape her.

Rape culture is even marketed as wearable. Lhooq (2015) comments on a photograph from the music festival Coachella, on which a man is wearing a shirt reading "Eat Sleep Rape Repeat." She notes, "The dude is grinning widely and throwing deuces, looking thoroughly satisfied with himself. This nauseating celebration of rape culture combined with his unabashed smugness set off a Twitter firestorm, which turned into a viral tornado show once the picture hit Buzzfeed, Jezebel, and beyond." Her colleague who took the picture said the guy who was with a girl at the time seemed "stoked" to be asked about it. Lhooq (2005) explains,

> Here's the thing about rape jokes: most of them aren't funny. Of course, there shouldn't be a unilateral ban on rape jokes ... because one of the essential purposes of comedy is to call out the shittiest parts of life, which includes rape. But there is a time and place for nuance, and a music festival filled with thousands of fucked up people gyrating to throbbing bass is not it.

Further, she explains that women are subject to widespread harassment and assault at music festivals. "But women at festivals are still made to feel uncomfortable and violated all the time—whether it's some guy groping you as he brushes by in a crowd, making unsolicited comments about your body, or taking your enthusiastic dancing as an open invitation to touch you without consent."

Etsy, the online shop in which users can sell and purchase used, vintage, and handmade creations, came under fire when it was revealed that several offensive, prorape shirts were available for sale on the site. One read, "Autumn is perfect for date rape," while another stated "I'm a sensitive guy, I only rape pregnant women." Still one more proclaimed, "Old people are useless. You can't even rape them." Etsy has since removed the shirts, but the question remains as to why anyone would produce them in the first place (Bastenmehr, 2013). Another T-shirt maker has taken the popular phrase "Keep calm and carry on," first produced for a World War II propaganda poster and changed it to read, "Keep calm and hit her." This and "Keep calm and rape a lot" were available for a time on Amazon before outrage prompted their removal. Oddly, the T-shirt maker apologized and argued that the words were computer-generated (Quirk, 2013). SM Department Store was found to be selling a T-shirt reading, "It's not rape it's a snuggle with a struggle," in the boy's section no less. SM pulled the shirt and issued an apology, although the design also appears on foulmouthshirts.com (Astig, 2014).

Although the conversations about rape culture had barely begun, the depictions in 1980s' hit movies surely featured them. For instance, *Sixteen Candles* glamorizes nonconsensual sex between a sober guy and a drunk girl when the uber-popular Jake tells nerdy Ted he could do whatever he wanted with his passed out girlfriend, and then hands the keys over to the freshman and wishes him good luck (Mierlak, 2014). More recently, in *Pitch Perfect 2*, an exchange between "Fat Amy" and her lover "Bumper" suggests that "no" isn't really no if it is said with a wink (Kingkade, 2014).

Rape culture allows people to believe offenders and find justifications for not believing victims. For instance, as of this writing, 45 women have accused comedian and actor Bill Cosby of rape and sexual assault. Yet, despite the volume of accusations and the creepy similarity of their allegations, other celebrities seem determined to defend him. Comedian Damon Wayans said "I just don't believe it. I think it's a money hustle" and "And some of them, really, is unrapeable. I look at them and go, 'No, he don't want that. Get outta here!'" (Edwards, 2015). Although in a less offensive way, comedian and actor Whoopi Goldberg also defended Cosby.

Similarly, when filmmaker Roman Polanski was arrested for statutory rape, celebrities and pundits came out en masse to point out that the victim, who was just 13, looked much older. Many resisted referring to Polanski as a rapist, and some celebrities even started a petition to support the filmmaker. Directors Pedro Almodovar, Martin Scorsese, David Lynch, Jonathan Demme, Wim Wenders, and Woody Allen all signed it, as did more than a hundred celebrities (Harding, 2015).

Harding (2015) shares more examples of how rape culture prevents us from seeing offenders as they are. Further, she notes that the United States is a culture in which people are quick to give rapists like Mike Tyson a second chance. He now has quite an acting career and even ironically played a victim of sexual abuse on an episode of *Law & Order: Special Victims Unit*.

In 2012, Rainn Wilson, an actor on the former hit show *The Office*, tweeted that he'd like to be date-raped to the Led Zeppelin song "Whole Lotta Love." Like so many, he later apologized and then deleted the tweet. But as Romano (2012) noted, Wilson is a repeat offender. She cited these two as examples: "Rape is never funny. Unless it involves IBM's 'Watson'" and "I'm on @ConanOBrien tonight. I'm going to not 'rape' Andy, but consensually 'take' him, you know?" The TV show *2 Broke Girls* is considered to be one of the worst offenders due to the frequency of rape jokes it airs. At one point the main characters state that they wouldn't call it rape if the assailant was "hot," for example. Some female comedians and writers argue that rape jokes can indeed be funny, and that they can serve as a way of take the power out of something that makes women feel powerless (Romano, 2012). Most do not, however, and thereby affirm and contribute to rape culture.

What stories are NOT told are also important. The summer 2015 box office hit *Straight Outta Compton* brought in $56.1 million in its debut weekend. The film, which chronicles the rise and influence of the gansta rap group N.W.A. in the 1980s, met with rave reviews. Yet others have criticized the film for leaving out important parts of the group's history, most notably, the abuse an R&B singer endured during her six-year relationship with one of the group's rappers, Dr. Dre. Michel'le has been vocal about the abuse she endured at the hands of her one-time fiancé, claiming in March 2015 on *The Breakfast Club* that Dre gave her five black eyes and several times broke her ribs. Blay (2015) reports that Michel'le commented, "I was just a quiet girlfriend who got beat on and told to sit down and shut up." The rapper was never charged with domestic violence, although he did have to complete community service and probation for a 1992 assault on a female journalist. Others note that gangsta rappers in general, and N.W.A. specifically, have a long history of misogynistic lyrics that should have been discussed in the film (Blay, 2015).

SICK VERSUS EVIL

While there is often a dichotomy in how victims are portrayed, offenders tend to be portrayed in binary ways as well. They are either understandable because they are addicted or mentally ill, or because their victims precipitated the action, or they are falsely accused, or they are presented as purely evil and not fixable. Patrick Bateman, the protagonist of Brett Easton Ellis's (1991) *American Psycho*, is a wealthy, successful, and handsome serial killer and torturer. While he maintains a facade of political correctness, he, like his colleagues, hates minorities, homosexuals, the homeless, and women. Bateman generally has sex with the female victims before he murders them, and the description of the sexual acts, while often beginning consensually, is essentially pornographic. Bateman brags to his colleagues that he "likes to dissect girls." In the film made a decade later, Bateman (played by Christian Bale) works out at his home while watching videos featuring anal rape (Travers, 2000). Simon & Schuster backed out of the agreement to publish the book and the National Organization for Women called for a boycott of it after it was released by Vintage. In the *Girl with the Dragon Tattoo* series, Lisbeth Salander's legal guardian Nils Bjurman is evil epitomized. He was appointed ostensibly to look after her but instead violently rapes her, gaining sadistic pleasure in violating the girl left in his care (Goodfriend, 2011).

Elizabeth Haynes's *Into the Darkest Corner* depicts a psychotic abuser who will stop at nothing to control his victim. Catherine Bailey is elated to begin dating the handsome and mysterious Lee Brightman, who is so into her. Fairly quickly, however, Catherine realizes that Lee is a sadistic abuser who gets worse whenever she threatens to end the relationship. After she finally escapes and Lee is sent to prison, Catherine finally begins to relax and even think about a new relationship. But Lee tracks her down and she must again fight to stay alive.

Similarly, Martin in *Sleeping with the Enemy* has been described as little more than a psychotic jerk. Gleiberman (1991) comments,

> For the movie to be anything more than a mechanical stalker thriller, we need to experience Martin as a teasingly ambiguous figure—frightening, yes, but attractive as well. We need to see him as a kind of male equivalent of the Glenn Close character in *Fatal Attraction*: a quasi-sympathetic monster whose dementia is really a twisted form of emotional pain. Instead, he's just a repulsive psycho. In an early scene, Martin socks Laura in the head for disobeying him. The movie plays off Roberts' status as America's sweetheart: How can you look at a man who would whack Julia Roberts and feel anything but loathing? (Gleiberman, 1991)

In some cases, offenders are presented as masculine heroes who merely keep women in line. For instance, Eminem, Dr. Dre, and 50 Cent's "Crack a Bottle" describe the offender as almost a hero to be applauded: "The moment you've all been waiting for. In this corner: weighing 175 pounds, with a record of rapes, 400 assaults, and 4 murders, The undisputed, most diabolical villain in the world: Slim Shady." In an episode of CW's *Gossip Girl*, the character Chuck Bass showed his "love" for his former girlfriend Blair Waldorf, played by Leighton Meester, when he attempts to punch her. He misses but shatters a window behind her and a shard of glass cuts her face. Yet he is depicted as a good boyfriend otherwise.

The song "Polly" by Nirvana was written after lead singer Kurt Cobain read a newspaper article about the abduction, torture, and rape of a 14-year-old girl. She eventually escaped from her assailant, who was prosecuted for the crime. The song was one of the few to take the perspective of an offender, with lines like "Polly wants a cracker/Maybe she would like some food/She asks to untie her/A chase would be nice for a few." After the song's release, the band began playing for benefits for rape crisis centers.

Music and music videos often focus on perpetrators. Armstrong (2001) analyzed 490 gangsta rap songs from 13 artists during the years between 1987 and 1993. He found that 22 percent of the songs contained violent and misogynistic lyrics. Half of the songs discussed assaulting women; 31 percent, the murder of women; 11 percent, the rape of women; and 7 percent, rape followed by murder. Many of the songs focus on pimp–prostitute violence, but a good proportion address domestic situations, largely by glorifying the physical and sexual violence as if it is a badge of pride for abusers. In "6 'N the Mornin'," Ice-T beats a woman he doesn't know because she called him a name. "Boyz-N-the-Hood" suggests abuse of women who "talk shit" is justified. Dr. Dre presents the same message in "Nuthin' but a 'G' Thang," the No. 1 rap song of all time (Krohn & Suazo, 1995). In gansta rap, talking and showing disrespect prompt men's violence against women. Women are also not allowed to reject a proposition, as evidenced through these Too $hort lyrics:

> You fuck with us, bitch, something gettin' broken
> Your leg, arm, jaw, nose, pick a part.

Women are portrayed as money-hungry or stuck up, and therefore due whatever the men want to give them. N.W.A.'s "A Bitch Iz a Bitch" recommends "Slam her ass in a ditch." Too $hort slaps women who act "shitty" or are too bold. Physical punishment is the result when one's girlfriend talks to another man, and pregnancy is not a deterrent to abuse, as Ice Cube plans to end a pregnancy by kicking a woman "in the tummy" and by looking in a closet "for the hanger." False accusations are handled with violence as well, as in when the Geto Boys handle a false paternity claim by trying to break the woman's neck. Too $hort deals with a similar situation by surprising the woman "like a mack" and then dropping "her ass off at Kaiser [hospital]." Women are hit, slapped, smacked, tossed, thrown into a trunk, and kicked, typically for no reason other than that they are women. Too Much Trouble notes that "a bitch is just like glass—easy to break." N.W.A. tells of a woman who "got a black eye cause the dope man hit her." Too $hort says he will beat his victim's "ass with a billy-club." In "Ever so Clear," Bushwick Bill arrives at the home of a girlfriend, then he "provoked her, punched her, kicked, and choked her." She shoots him in the eye when he tries to throw her baby out a window.

Marriage is almost always described as including violence. Too $hort "kicks women's' ass like a world champ." In "Bitches 2" Ice-T tells of his friend, who routinely "kicks his wife's ass." Sexual abuse is common as well, as in when Ice Cube nearly breaks "that thing in half" during sex while Scarface brags that "bitches walk out of the crib with a limp." Too Much Trouble says that after oral sex, they "leave some stretch marks" on a woman's jaw. Ice-T describes the dirty work of Evil E, who "fucked the bitch with a flashlight." Because he left the batteries in, "the bitch's titties started blinkin' like tail lights."

Willie D and Too $hort promote raping women who do not submit to their sexual advances. In "She Swallowed It," N.W.A. describes a sexual attack on a 14-year-old in which they punch the girl and then rape her by forcing her to perform oral sex.

These lyrics are all deeply disturbing in their viciousness and in the way that they normalize a description of women as worth nothing more than a vehicle for men's sexual release. It would be difficult for listeners of this type of music not to be affected in some way by these messages.

Young adult literature is sometimes thoughtful and accurate in its discussion of abuse, rape, and offenders in general. Alex Flinn's popular novel *Breathing Underwater* (2001) offers the perspective of a male abuser trying to come to terms with his behavior. It is held up by many domestic violence advocates as an important tool for teaching about dating violence. Nick Andreas, 16, is in court because he hit his girlfriend, Caitlin. The story unfolds through the journal that the judge orders him to keep. Nick is good looking, athletic, and popular, but he is also the recipient of his father's abuse. Nick becomes jealous as Caitlin becomes popular and fears losing her. He insists that Caitlin have no friends and does nothing without him. He criticizes her weight in front of friends and makes her feel bad about her body. When Caitlin goes against Nick's wishes and sings in a school event, Nick beats her brutally.

Yet other popular young adult fiction is rife with problems. Durham (2011) discussed an analysis of the perpetrators and victims in the *Twilight* series. He noted that the violence used by the male protagonists was presented as acceptable, justified, and masculine. The main vampire, Edward, is presented as a "sympathetic vampire," or one who is "persecuted or soulful" (Williamson, 2005), thus he is perhaps more likeable than the weak and boring Bella. In the third novel, *Eclipse*, another main character, the werewolf Jacob, forcibly kisses Bella. She is unable to physically resist due to his strength, but then she ends up kissing him back. Later, after Bella views the postwedding night bruises inflicted by Edward, "like a classic battered wife, Bella figures out ways to hide her bruises and glory in the experience of sex, as physically painful and potentially life-threatening as it is. The bruising is portrayed as an expected and acceptable aspect of heterosexual intercourse" (Durham, 2011, p. 10). Critics have expressed concern that teen readers, many of whom were female, would see the relationship between Edward and Bella as a romance, not as an unhealthy exercise of power and control.

FEMALE OFFENDERS

As was noted in Chapter 1, statistics show that the majority of domestic violence and sexual assault offenders are male. Dating violence, as was noted, is committed at males and females at more equivalent rates. Numerous studies have found that prime dramas do typically focus on male offenders (Bufkin & Eschholz, 2000; Soulliere, 2003) yet also, as was noted in Chapter 1, may overrepresent male victims. In general, female offenders are presented as beautiful, resourceful, and violent, which is influenced by the fact that television mostly depicts young, white, stereotypical females (Cecil, 2007). They are calculating and will stop at nothing. Female offenders are most often presented as murderers who seek revenge on partners who they feel jilted or wronged them, with the most prominent depiction as the femme fatale. Chesney-Lind (1999) commented, "if Hollywood's representation of crime were accurate, unruly women who were not busy trying to kill men would be stalking (*Fatal Attraction*) or sexually harassing them (*Disclosure*)" (p. 120).

Female rapists are more prone to use verbal manipulation, blackmail, and deception than are male rapists. Because of the size and physical strength differential, few female rapists overpower their victims, but many take advantage of intoxicated males. Many have written about the double standard when it comes to depictions of female rapists. Storylines often imply or even state that if a man is raped by an attractive woman he is lucky, and other male characters typically express jealousy. In an episode of *True Blood*, a male character was tied to a bed and gang-raped by a pack of female were-panthers. Clark-Flory (2011) includes the following comment:

> Obviously if you're watching a scene with a woman tied to a bed while a man forces sex on her, the final act of that movie will involve said man getting shot in the face by Bruce Willis. If, on the other hand, it's a *man* being tied down and forced into sex by a pretty lady, well, you're watching a wacky romantic comedy.

Horrible Bosses 2, the sequel to the 2011 hit, uses rape as a punch line for several jokes and gags. In one scene, a person who is in the hospital, unconscious, wakes up to realize she was sexually assaulted. These and other rapes are depicted as nonproblematic because the person who commits the offenses is so attractive all the characters are supposed to "want it." Film critic Mark Hughes (2014) explains,

> To anyone who responds by claiming I need to lighten up, that it's just comedy, or other excuses to defend reliance on rape as a running gag in films, let me make something perfectly clear right off the bat: If someone would laugh at a scene of someone being knocked unconscious and being sexually assaulted; if someone would laugh at people describing the sex organs and

experiences of children in profane graphic sexual detail; if someone would laugh at someone repeatedly attempting to blackmail and otherwise force an unwilling person to have sex against their will; if someone would laugh at racist jokes; and if someone would laugh about women being objects men can just acquire if they are manly enough to be assertive and take what they want, then *I'm* not the one who needs to reconsider my sense of humor *they* are.

Further,

there's a secondary trick going on, because the themes about being "manly" and having "balls" are all tied into the rape humor. Men resisting sexually aggressive, attractive women and who get raped by women are presented as wimpy saps who are the butt of jokes, and then those same men are fearful of rape at the hands of other men as an additional form of "emasculation." Consider that when the man finally becomes sexually aggressive to the woman himself, it's a signal he's taking the initiative and finally being "a man" (even though things don't pan out as it seems).

Clearly popular culture does a very poor job of presenting female offenders, relying instead on silly stereotypes that trivialize the issue. These depictions contribute to the difficulties men have in reporting abuse and assault and in seeking help. Few even want to tell friends, as they fear that they will be laughed at.

NON-WHITE OFFENDERS

The 1915 landmark film *The Birth of a Nation* helped reinforce the white Southern notion that "the idealized white woman under assault by a sexually lusting black man was the biggest threat to the nation" (Haggard, 2014, p. 83). The 1896 Supreme Court decision in *Plessy v. Ferguson* that upheld racial segregation laws furthered the notion that black men were to be kept apart from white women. Popular media continued to conjure up the big black buck as boogie man, and D. W. Griffith's film brought that image to life in *Birth of a Nation*. Although there is no actual sexual assault depicted in the film, viewers are shown Gus's

bulging eyes watching her (Flora Cameron), his erratic movements that focus on his body, his hand on her forearm, his words of marriage, her hand clasping her mouth in shock, her arms flailing, his pursuit, her suicide, his "trial," and his dead body dumped on the steps of Silas Lynch's mansion. *Birth of a Nation*, which bore all the common hallmarks of Southern "folk pornography," transposed its racialized sexual logic throughout the nation: a black buck in the presence of a white woman must be a rapist and therefore justifiably sentenced to death. (Haggard, 2014, p. 88)

Film historian David Bogle (2001) referred to these characters as "brutal black bucks," describing them as "big, baaaaaad niggers, oversexed and savage, violent and frenzied as they lust for white flesh" (p. 14). The film reified the myth of the black rapist, which was often presumed true even if no rape actually happened. According to Haggard (2014), it wasn't until some 250 years after the first African men were captured and forced into slavery in the American colonies that the alignment of black men as hypersexualized emerged. The concern was the miscegenation between black men and white women would create a class of "free Negroes" who would be poised to challenge the social and economic structure. To deter such interactions, white men passed laws prohibiting sex between black men and white women. Following the abolition of slavery in December 1865, the fear of black men amped up and so did the rhetoric. George T. Winston, president of the University of North Carolina, gave a speech utilizing the black buck scare tactic: "The southern woman with her helpless little children in a solitary farm house no longer sleeps secure … The black brute is lurking in the dark, monstrous beast, crazed with lust. His ferocity is almost demonical. A mad bull or a tiger could scarcely be more brutal" (Hall, 1983, p. 14). Haggard (2004) notes that

> Local gossip, public speeches, folklore, and newspaper reports repeatedly told tales of a pure young white girl, the prettiest in town, with a "wreath of golden hair" and "drooping eyelashes," attacked by an "insolent negro!" or a "big burly black brute." Unlike actual instances of rape, the lack of corroboration or proof became a staple in these alleged attacks. The details of the violent sexual act itself are missing and left to the imagination. Instead, descriptions of the stock image of a brutal black buck with the young beautiful blonde girl in hysterics signified a crime and served as a sexual story to justify segregation and legitimate reactionary violence. (p. 86)

In the 30 years before World War I, there was at least one vigilante murder of a black man each week. The Tuskegee Institute counts 3,381 reported lynchings of black men between 1882 and 1935 (Haggard, 2014).

> The vast number of lynchings worked to naturalize the belief that black men were in fact raping white women everywhere and all the time, branding all black men as imminently dangerous threats to white families and society.

The immense fear and anxiety of rape also worked to control white women's behavior, keeping them away from black men and dependent on white men to uphold "the protection of white womanhood." Yet, as Ida B. Wells uncovered in her antilynching campaign of the 1890s, less than one-fourth of lynchings were enacted because of an alleged rape, although the image of the brutal black buck served as the rhetorical justification for almost all lynchings. (Haggard, 2014, p. 87)

Haggard (2014) notes that as lynchings decreased, the death penalty took their place for black men, as 405 of the 455 men who were executed for rape convictions between 1930 and 1967 were black. A 2015 report by Equal Justice Initiative explains the cost of false allegations against black men, noting that almost one-quarter of the lynchings of black men between 1888 and 1950 were the result of sexual assault claims, and that a mere accusation of a white woman against a black man was often enough.

The situation that resulted in a lynching was usually the same:

Typically, a black man was accused of a crime, often of rape—although no actual crime or proof of guilt was requisite; a group of prominent white men went to his house or the jail where he was held, and with the compliance of the sheriff/judge/mayor, the man was taken by force to a central location. Along the way, he was beaten with anything from sticks to crowbars to barbed wire. His clothes were torn from him and he was further savaged with knives, bullets, even the bites and kicks of children. His body was dragged before a crowd of people from as far away as the next state. Lynchings were often announced beforehand in newspapers and radio broadcasts and special excursion trains were made available. He may have been castrated, which was especially likely if there was a sexually-based "crime" involved; a rope or a chain was hung from a tree, his fingers and hair would be cut for souvenirs. The white victim might be there to identify him, and he might be made to confess, feigning elements of the judicial system. Condemned, they would hoist the man up and sometimes a pyre was lit. In the aftermath, he might be re-clothed so as not to often viewers of the photograph that was being taken, which was set up to show the best angle of the carnage with the reaffirmation of the gathered crowd often looking directly into the camera lens. The photographs were reproduced, sometimes mailed as postcards. The bodies were left there as warning and as a trophy. Family members gathered to collect the remains for burial when it was safe to do so. (Turner, 2014, pp. 361–362)

The controversial antilynching song "Strange Fruit" is a powerful examination of the issue, although it didn't specifically address the rape allegation component. The song started as a poem written by Abel Meeropol to raise awareness about the 1930 lynching of two black men who were executed for rape and murder without due process. Meeropol, a Jewish English teacher, is often overlooked as the author of "Strange Fruit" since he asked Harlem jazz singer Billie Holiday to sing it, and she often told people she had written it. Holiday claimed she had been beaten and raped and eventually was sent to a school for "wayward" black girls (Turner, 2014). Turner (2014) noted that, "As in Billie Holiday's time, many contemporary performers are not willing to take on the emotional and political weight of the song, while others are eager to make social commentary or a political point" (p. 367). R&B artist Dwayne Wiggins repurposed part of the song, while rapper Common worked with singer/songwriter/pianist John Legend to feature a reworked version produced by Kanye West.

In *Native Son*, Richard Wright took up the myth of the black rapist. Although there was no sexual contact between Bigger Thomas and the white daughter of his boss, whom he accidentally suffocates, everyone assumes that Thomas raped her, and the imagined rape becomes Bigger's primary offense. Bigger is convicted despite any evidence of rape, and thus he was transformed "from a man who accidentally killed someone into the archetypal buck" and is sentenced to death (Haggard, 2014, p. 89).

The big black buck archetype did not end with the civil rights movement. In 1967, American author William Styron won the Pulitzer Prize for his novel *The Confessions of Nat Turner*, which depicted the antislavery activist as a man who spent his time lusting for white girls. In the 1972 film *Bone* by Larry Cohen, a black character even states "I'm just a big black buck doing what's expected of me," while he pins down a screaming white woman. Haggard (2014) explains "In the face of rising black-white relations, these films revived and popularized the image of the degraded white woman who beds a black man, which had lingered since pre-emancipation" (p. 91).

Similarly, the 1982 film *Death Wish 2* featured a group of black men brutally raping women in a scene reminiscent of *Birth of a Nation*. Andrew Taslitz (1999) explains that the big black buck archetype is frequently invoked by prosecutors, and that in allegations of black on white rape, it is often enough for jurors to convict regardless of physical or other types of evidence. When a white woman, Trisha Meili, was beaten, raped, and abandoned in New York's Central Park in 1989, the arrest of a group of black and Hispanic boys ignited national conversations that invoked rhetoric of "wildings" that was clearly racially coded, while the popular television show *21 Jump Street* aired an episode depicting the incident. The five boys who were originally convicted of the offense were later exonerated. Haggard (2014) explains, "The 'white woman in peril' headlines that once fueled lynch mobs now serve as rallying points for manhunts, courtrooms, and public dramas. Through repeated tropes and themes, the image of the brutal black buck character has promoted the myth of the black rapist for over a century" (p. 92).

Based on an actual incident, *Rosewood* tells the story of Fanny Taylor, a white woman who was beaten by the white man with whom she was having an affair. In order to hide the affair from her husband, she claims the assailant was a black man. Although almost everyone but her husband knows she is lying, the town takes her accusations as an excuse for a massacre of virtually the entire African American population of the town. Although Taylor was not raped and did not claim to be, the sheriff and townspeople presume that she was.

Even thoughtful films or shows can sometimes reinforce the dangerous myths about black males. For instance, although many have praised the film *What's Love Got to Do with It*, Shoos (2003) argues, "while the graphic sounds and images accompanying Ike's rape of Tina in the sound studio convey the inhumanity and degradation of domestic violence, they are also consistent with the racial stereotype of the black man as savage animal. On this level, what the film tells us is what we already assume about the volatility and violence of black heterosexual relationships" (p. 71).

In "Seduced by Violence No More" (1993), black feminist bell hooks explains that even black males reinforce these stereotypical images, often through the music they create (some of which were described earlier). She notes that it should not be surprising that disenfranchised black men find that one of the few areas in which they can assert their patriarchal power is in misogynistic rap.

Popular culture definitely still overrepresents black males as sexual assault perpetrators. Eschholz, Mallard, and Flynn (2004) analyzed 20 one-hour episodes of *NYPD Blue* and 24 one-hour episodes of *Law & Order* during the 2001 season. They found statistically significant disproportionate representation of nonwhites as offenders. Males were far more likely to be shown as offenders than were female, and when females were main or speaking characters, they were more likely to be criminal justice personnel or victims of crime. These crime dramas depict New York City as more violent than it is in actuality, and at the same time they show the criminal justice system as being more effective than in reality. NYPD typically concludes with the arrest of the "bad guy" while the most frequent conclusion to *Law & Order* is a conviction.

Although depictions of black male rapists have received the most attention, other men of color are also likely to be depicted as perpetrators. In the 1910s, films like *Her Debt of Honor* (1916), *The Border Raiders*

(1918), and *Cora* (1915) depicted Native American, Chinese, and Mexican men as perpetrators. Projansky (2001) explains:

> The western, in particular, is a genre in which men of color, usually Native American men, regularly appear as villainous rapists while it is women of color's racial identity that makes them vulnerable to victimization. A few films in the 1930s, 1950s, and 1960s use rape to critique racism, showing unfair lynchings and depicting men of color as falsely accused, such as *Within Our Gates* (1919), *Eskimo* (1934), *The Sun Shines Bright* (1953) and *To Kill a Mockingbird* (1962). The latter three "support antiracism by depicting an African American man falsely accused of rape but defended in court by a liberal white man. While these films confront racism, they also take place in a former era, making the false accusation and racist legal system appear to be a thing of the past. As a result, the films implicitly suggest that the legal system contemporary to the era in which the film is produced need not be similarly examined for racism." (pp. 43–44)

Films in the 1910s often linked rape to immigration, suggesting that reform was needed because rape was rampantly perpetrated by immigrant men. In these plots, white women are attracted to the violent immigrant man. "These films intersect with those that define rape as a danger faced by women who actively express their sexuality in a U.S. context, but here women's sexual desire is particularly dangerous because it is both cross-racial and cross-national, thus threatening the loss of white U.S. (or British) citizenship" (Projansky, 2001, p. 47). Such is the case with *Barbary Sheep* (1917), *The Arab* (1915), and *Flame of the Desert* (1919). The 1920s picked up on the "Arab sheik" theme. Not surprisingly, during wartime, especially World War I and World War II, films tended to depict members of the enemy as rapists, relying heavily on images of German and Japanese perpetrators.

How we discuss rape shapes both public policy and public opinion. Smith (2005) argued that 18th-century colonists told stories about Native American men raping white women so that they could justify violence against Native Americans, while at the same time soldiers and white men actually raped Native women as a tool of control. Parent and Wallace (1993) maintain that rape and the threat of rape by slave owners of black female slaves was a tool of social control yet images of black men as rapists were widely disseminated so as to justify repressive laws and sanctions. Likewise, Davis (1985) notes that the myth of the black male rapist, virginal white woman, white male savior, and oversexed, harlot black woman were used to justify discrimination. Postslavery, narratives about the black male rapists were used to promote a return to slavery, as some asserted that it was only after they obtained freedom that black men began to rape white women (Davis, 1981).

ATHLETES AS OFFENDERS

Studies seem to clearly show that certain types of athletes are overrepresented in allegations about domestic violence and sexual assault. According to the National Coalition against Violent Athletes, which publicizes studies and examples of sexual assault and domestic violence perpetrated by athletes, one-third of college sexual assaults are committed by athletes, and a college athlete will rape at least seven times before he is caught (Statistics, 2012).

Chris Lynch's *Inexcusable* is a young adult novel focusing on date rape involving a high school football player. Protagonist Keir Sarafian is a great high school football player with a college scholarship. His family and the community at large love him, the result of which is that Keir takes no responsibility for his behavior. When he leaves an opposing player horribly injured after a dubious play, he rationalizes that he was only doing what was expected on the field. The one thing Keir wants that he doesn't have is Gigi Boudakian. When he encounters her upset at a party because her boyfriend didn't show up, Keir pins her to the bed and forces himself on her, all the while convincing himself that it is consensual. Keir repeatedly tells himself that he is a good guy who can do no wrong, and therefore did not in this case, either.

Rachele Alpine's *Canary* tells the story of Kate, who after a rough time in her family begins dating a star basketball player at the exclusive Beacon Prep, where players are idolized. Not only do they get away with whatever they want at school, but outside of school they cause all kinds of trouble with no consequence because, as Kate's girlfriend explains, "Those cops aren't stupid enough to screw around with the team during the season" (p. 206). Luke, another player on the team, sexually assaults Kate who feels like no one will believe her amidst the rape culture. Her own father is the coach of the team and fails to hold the players. When Kate finally tells him that she was assaulted, he sides with his player: "Listen. Do you understand what would happen if you told people about this? It would be worse for you than anyone else. You'd have to tell your story to everyone. Do you really want to talk about it again? Especially in front of Luke?" (p. 396).

FRATERNITIES AND SEXUAL ASSAULT

Despite many studies showing that fraternity members are overrepresented as assailants, and that sorority members are at increased risk for being victimized, there are few depictions featuring Greek organizations in popular culture. Valenti (2014) maintains that fraternity guys commit 300 percent more rape than do nonfraternity members. In 2013, three sexual assaults were reported at one Texas fraternity within a single month. At Georgia Tech, a frat brother sent around an email guide called "luring your rape bait." In 2010, fraternity brothers at prestigious Yale University marched through campus yelling, "No means yes, yes means anal." Women in sororities are 74 percent more likely to experience rape than other college women (Valenti, 2014). A 2009 Violence against Women study reported that sorority women at one university were four times more likely to be sexually assaulted than non-Greeks, and a 2014 University of Oregon study found that nearly one in two sorority members on that campus were victims of nonconsensual sexual contact (Robbins, 2015). The 1996 made-for-television film *She Cried No*, featuring teen stars Candace Cameron Bure and Mark-Paul Gosselaar, tells the story of Melissa, a college freshman eager to be accepted. She and a roommate attend a fraternity party where Scott, a member, rapes her. Scott has a history of date-raping girls at parties. Melissa sees him on campus and he pretends nothing happened, while she suffers from depression and her grades begin to drop. When she is taken to the hospital after a car accident she tells the doctor about the rape and decides to tell the police. Scott is not convicted because Melissa has no physical evidence, and many, including her brother and father, discouraged her from involving the criminal justice system. In the end, the fraternity is shut down and its charter revoked.

John Grisham's *The Associate* tells the story of a young lawyer who is being blackmailed because a videotape depicting a sexual assault involving some of his fraternity buddies has been found. As the story unfolds, the main character Kyle, who was not accused of rape but of witnessing his friends assault an unconscious woman, repeatedly blames the offenses on her sexual promiscuity, noting that "all the guys" had sex with Elaine. He and the others also note that she was always the first person to a party and brought with her alcohol and drugs. They insist that anything that happened was consensual but the videotape suggests that the boys knew she might not be conscious. In addition to being promiscuous, the victim is presented as ambitiously seeking their money, as one of the boys comes from a very affluent family. She and her attorney are not depicted as likeable in the book; they are both aggressive and conniving, while Kyle is the sympathetic character.

MILITARY OFFENDERS

In 2012, the U.S. Department of Defense (DOD) recorded 3,374 incidents of sexual victimization. The number of incidents recorded by the

DOD has nearly doubled since 2004 (DOD, 2013b). A survey conducted by the DOD (2013a) found that approximately 20 percent of women reported experiencing sexual victimization by someone in the military after entering service. It is clear that victims in general, and victims on military bases, face a number of issues with reporting such that these numbers barely scratch the surface. Less than 20 percent of victims report their victimization through official channels (Snyder & Scherer, 2015). Data do show that the perpetrators are almost always fellow members of the military.

An Associated Press report showed that a cause for firing of almost one-third of all military commanders released between 2005 and 2013 was sexual offenses (Baldor, 2013). Cases involving military personnel typically are heard before the military judicial system, which is guided by the Uniform Code of Military Justice (UCMJ). According to the UCMJ, once an incident is reported, the commanding officer (CO) determined whether to open up an investigation or dismiss the report. If the CO moves the case forward, the case will be investigated by the Military Criminal Investigation Organization and findings presented back to the CO who can determine whether to take some sort of administrative action, push for a court-martial, or do nothing (Snyder & Scherer, 2015). Studies have shown that a very low number of cases are referred on by COs and even fewer result in sanctions (Lankford, 2012). Franke-Ruta (2013) explains the problems with the military justice system as it relates to sexual offenses:

> The basic problem with the military justice system in cases of sexual assault—as outlined in horrific detail by the military women and experts featured in *Invisible War* by members of Congress during hearings—is that it combines the dynamics of the workplace with the problems of crime investigation. A woman who is assaulted and wants redress has to report the crime to her commanding officer—her boss—and press charges against one of her colleagues in the military, often someone who also works for her boss, all the while continuing to live near her attacker in a thick soup of overlapping interpersonal and professional relationships between her and his friends.

New York senator Kirsten Gillibrand, a champion for addressing sexual assault in the military, told *PBS NewsHour* in July 2013:

> For those victims who have been courageous enough to report cases, 62 percent have said they have been retaliated against for reporting those cases. Of the tens of thousands who didn't report incidents of sexual assault, rape, and unwanted sexual assault contact, the reason they give us is they

don't trust the chain of command, they think nothing will be done, or that they fear retaliation, or they have seen someone else be retaliated against.

Again, while abuse and assault in the military are significant problems, they have historically received little attention in popular culture. One film that does depict a military rape case is *The General's Daughter*, which is based on the Nelson Demille novel. Although the plot involves some improbable elements, the film does showcase the difficulties with investigating crime on military bases.

The documentary *The Invisible War* focuses on rape in the U.S. military. It includes the stories of women who have been victims as well as their challenges in reporting and obtaining justice. Yet given the prevalence of these problems in the military, it is odd how few examples were found in popular culture.

SEXUAL ABUSE AND RELIGIONS INSTITUTIONS

In recent times, much attention has been paid to sexual abuse by religious leaders, in particular in the Catholic Church. Between 2004 and 2014, 3,400 cases of sexual abuse were reported to the Holy See. More than 2,500 offenders faced some type of sanction while 848 priests were defrocked (Vatican reveals how many priests . . . , 2014). This is also a topic of significant popular culture attention, albeit more in documentaries. For example, *The Boys of St. Vincent* (1992) depicts the abuse of young boys at the Christian Brothers orphanage. The perpetrator is the leader of the orphanage. In *Twist of Faith* (2004), a Toledo firefighter comes to terms with the abuse he endured by a former priest. *Hand of God* (2006), a PBS *Frontline* documentary, chronicles the investigation of Father Joseph Birmingham on rape charges. *Deliver Us from Evil* (2006) is a documentary that reveals the allegations against Oliver O'Grady, a now-defrocked priest who was accused of molesting 25 California boys and girls from the late 1970s to 1991.

FALSE ALLEGATIONS

Although there is a widespread belief that false allegations of abuse and sexual assault are common, in reality, they are not. They are, however, very damaging when they occur, not just to the wrongly accused individuals but to broader efforts to challenge this common myth (which is discussed in more detail in Chapter 3). Yet despite the fact that false allegations are rare, popular culture shows them with great frequency.

Cuklanz (2000) evaluated the depiction of sexual assault in television shows from 1976 to 1990. She found an overrepresentation of false accusations. Brinson (1992) analyzed 26 episodes depicting sexual assault and found that each episode averaged more than five rape myths. The most commonly used myth was "she asked for it," which was featured in 46 percent of the episodes. Parker (2013) describes an episode of *SVU* with the improbable story line of a man falsely arrested for serial rape when it was his twin brother who was the assailant. The man attempted suicide while awaiting trial. Stories like these inevitably result in people overestimating the amount of false accusations.

The popular book *Gone Girl* revolves around false allegations of abuse and assault. The wife, Amy Dunne, is endlessly attention-seeking to the point that she fakes her own death and claims she was raped by the man who actually helped her, whom she brutally murders. Dunne has the entire thing carefully orchestrated such that people who know her and complete strangers believe her story. As Smith (2014) comments, "The characters live in a parallel universe where the immediate reaction to a woman who says she's been assaulted is one of chivalrous concern. Tell that to all the victims, here and in the US, who have had their claims dismissed by skeptical police officers."

In Paula Hawkins's *Girl on the Train*, Rachel reports a missing woman, and as the investigation unfolds and she begins to reflect on her own troubled life, she realizes she was abused by her former husband. But, because she drinks too much and is considered unstable by both her ex and the police officers whom she reports to, she is disbelieved.

HELPING OFFENDERS

In addition to prison time if they are convicted, rapists and abusers are often assigned to attend anger management courses or to undergo a Batterers' Intervention Program. Research has not found either to be tremendously successful, however. Interestingly, my review for this book found almost no depictions of abusers or rapists being helped or treated. The film *The Woodsman* does show the difficulty a person who carries the sex offender label will face in trying to get housing, employment, and other resources, although it also presents the offender in dubious ways that seem to suggest he is constantly thinking about reoffending.

CONCLUSION

There are indeed some examples of popular culture that portray offenders in a realistic way. Some of the young adult fiction described here can help readers understand the dynamics of abuse and get past seeing offenders as simple stereotypes. Likewise, although they are often accused of being "cheesy," *Lifetime* films are more likely to present offenders in more nuanced ways. As was clear, however, popular culture still relies on dangerous stereotypes and easy and titillating tropes that romanticize abuse and discuss sexual assault as if it is a joking matter. The dearth of realistic depictions of female offenders is troubling, as is the overrepresentation of story lines focusing on false accusations. Likewise, when popular culture fails to depict programs or efforts to help perpetrators, it can become easy for consumers to believe there is no hope; that is, these people are incorrigible and not amenable to rehabilitation. While data are clear that Batterers' Intervention Programs and other initiatives are not as effective as we would like, there are indeed abusers and assailants who change their attitudes and do not reoffend after treatment of some sort.

References

Armstrong, E. (2001). Gangsta misogyny: A content analysis of the portrayals of violence against women in rap music, 1987–1993. *Journal of Criminal Justice and Popular Culture, 8*(2), 96–126.

Astig. (2014, September 23). Pro-rape t-shirt at SM Boy's Section used stolen design? Retrieved September 6, 2015, from http://astig.ph/rape-snuggle -struggle-t-shirt-sm-department-store-boys-section/

Baldor, L. (2013, December 27). Reports of sexual assault in the military jumped 50 percent in 2013. *PBS NewsHour.* Retrieved January 8, 2016, from http://www.pbs.org/newshour/rundown/reports-of-sexual-assault-in -the-military-jumped-50-percent-in-2013/

Bancroft, L. (2003). *Why does he do that? Inside the minds of angry and controlling men.* New York: Berkley Books.

Bastenmehr, R. (2013, October 24). Under pressure from activists, Etsy pulls "pro-rape" shirts from site. Alternet. Retrieved September 6, 2015, from http://www.alternet.org/news-amp-politics/under-pressure-activists-etsy -pulls-pro-rape-t-shirts-site

Blay, Z. (2015, August 18). Dr. Dre's ex on why his abusive past isn't in "Straight Outta Compton." *Huffington Post.* Retrieved September 2, 2015, from http://www.huffingtonpost.com/entry/dr-dre-ex-on-abuse-in-straight -outta-compton_55d33b55e4b0ab468d9e580c

Bogle, D. (2001). *Toms, coons, mulattoes, mammies, and bucks: An interpretive history of Blacks in American films,* 4th ed. New York: Continuum.

Brinson, S. L. (1992). The use and opposition of rape myths in prime-time television dramas. *Sex Roles, 27*(7), 359–375.

Bufkin, J., & Eschholz, S. (2000). Images of sex and rape: A content analysis of popular film. *Violence against Women, 6*(12), 1317–1344.

Chesney-Lind, M. (1999). Media misogyny: Demonizing "violent" girls and women. In J. Ferrel & N. Websdale (Eds.). *Making trouble: Cultural constructions of crime, deviance and control* (pp. 115–140). New York: Aldine de Gruyter.

Cecil, D. (2007). Dramatic portrayals of violent women: Female offenders on prime time crime dramas. *Journal of Criminal Justice and Popular Culture, 14*(3), 243–258.

Clark-Flory, T. (2011, August 2). When the rapist is a she. Salon. Retrieved September 14, 2015, from http://www.salon.com/2011/08/03/male_rape/

Cuklanz, L. (2000). *Rape on prime-time: Television, masculinity, and sexual violence*. Philadelphia: University of Philadelphia Press.

Davis, A. (1985). Slavery and the roots of sexual harassment. Retrieved January 8, 2016, from https://law.wustl.edu/faculty_profiles/documents/davis/Slavery%20and%20the%20Roots%20of%20Sexual%20Harrassment.pdf

Durham, M. (2011). Blood, lust and love: Interrogating gender and violence in *Twilight*. Iowa Research Online. Retrieved January 8, 2016, from http://ir.uiowa.edu/cgi/viewcontent.cgi?article=1001&context=jmc_pubs

Edwards, S. (2015, September 6). Damon Wayans defends Bill Cosby, calls women "unrapeable." *Jezebel*. Retrieved September 6, 2015, from http://jezebel.com/damon-wayans-defends-bill-cosby-calls-victims-unrapeab-1729031868?utm_campaign=socialflow_jezebel_facebook&utm_source=jezebel_facebo ok&utm_medium=socialflow

Elsworth, C. (2008, October 11). South Park episode angers viewers with scenes of Hollywood titans raping Indiana Jones. *The Telegraph*. Retrieved January 8, 2016, from http://www.telegraph.co.uk/news/worldnews/northamerica/usa/3179812/South-Park-episode-angers-viewers-with-scenes-of-Hollywood-titans-raping-Indiana-Jones.html

Eschholz, S., Mallard, M., & Flynn, S. (2004). Images of prime-time justice: A content analysis of "NYPD Blue" and "Law & Order." *Journal of Criminal Justice and Popular Culture, 10*(3), 161–180.

Filipovic, J. (2014, September 26). 14 misconceptions about domestic violence. *Cosmopolitan*. Retrieved September 13, 2015, from http://www.cosmopolitan.com/politics/news/a31528/14-misconceptions-about-domestic-violence/

Finley, L. (Ed.). (2013). *Encyclopedia of domestic violence and abuse*. Santa Barbara, CA: ABC-CLIO.

Foshee, V., Linder F., MacDougall J., & Bangdiwala, S. (2001) Gender differences in the longitudinal predictors of adolescent dating violence. *Preventive Medicine, 32*(2), 128–141.

Franke-Ruta, G. (2013, May 9). Ending the culture of impunity on military rape. *The Atlantic*. Retrieved January 8, 2016, from http://www.theatlantic.com/politics/archive/2013/05/ending-the-culture-of-impunity-on-military-rape/275661/

Gajewski, R. (2014, September 28). "Simpsons," "Family Guy" crossover episode criticized for rape joke. *Hollywood Reporter*. Retrieved January 8, 2016, from

http://www.hollywoodreporter.com/news/simpsons-family-guy-crossover
-episode-736244

Gleiberman, O. (1991, February 8). *Sleeping with the enemy. Entertainment Weekly.* Retrieved September 14, 2015, from http://www.ew.com/article/1991/02/08/sleeping-enemy

Goodfriend, W. (2011, November 28). Sexism in "The Girl with the Dragon Tattoo." *Psychology Today.* Retrieved January 8, 2016, from https://www.psychologytoday.com/blog/psychologist-the-movies/201111/sexism-in-the-girl-the-dragon-tattoo

Haggard, N. (2014). The birth of the black rapist: The "brutal black buck" in American culture. In S. Packer & J. Pennington (Eds.). *A history of evil in popular culture*, vol. 1 (pp. 83–94). Santa Barbara, CA: ABC-CLIO.

Hall, J. (1983). "The mind that burns in each body": Women, rape, and racial violence. In A. Snitow, C. Stansell, & S. Thompson (Eds.). *Powers of desire: The politics of sexuality* (pp. 347–361). New York: Monthly Review Press.

hooks, b. (1993). Seduced by violence no more. In E. Buchwald, B. Fletcher, & M. Roth (Eds.). *Transforming rape culture.* Minneapolis: Milkweed Editions.

Hughes, M. (2014, November 21). Review: *Horrible Bosses 2. Forbes.* Retrieved January 8, 2016, from http://www.forbes.com/sites/markhughes/2014/11/21/review-horrible-bosses-2-treats-rape-as-a-punchline/

Kingkade, T. (2014, November 21). "Pitch perfect" keeps making rape jokes. It's not a laughing matter. *Huffington Post.* Retrieved September 14, 2015, from http://www.huffingtonpost.com/tyler-kingkade/pitch-perfect-rape-jokes-its-not-a-laughing-matter_b_6199496.html

Krohn, F., & Suazo, F. (1995, Summer). Contemporary urban music: Controversial messages in hip-hop and rap. *Et Cetera: A Review of General Semantics, 52*(2), 139–154.

Lankford, A. (2012). An analysis of sexual assault in the U.S. military, 2004–09. *Journal of Military and Strategic Studies, 14*(2), 1–21.

Lhooq, M. (2015, April 13). What the "Eat Sleep Rape Repeat" shirt at Coachella says about rape culture at music festivals. Retrieved September 6, 2015, from https://thump.vice.com/en_us/article/what-the-eat-sleep-rape-repeat-shirt-at-coachella-says-about-rape-culture-at-music-festivals

Mierlak, D. (2014, December 4). Why "Sixteen Candles" isn't as charming as you think. *Huffington Post.* Retrieved September 13, 2015, from http://www.huffingtonpost.com/deryn-mierlak/30-years-later-a-16yearol_b_6200986.html

NiCarthy, G. (2004). *Getting free: A handbook for women in abusive relationships.* Berkeley, CA: Seal Press.

Parent, A., & Wallace, S. (1993). Childhood and sexual identity under slavery. *Journal of the History of Sexuality, 3*(3), 363–401.

Parker, S. (2013). The portrayal of the American legal system in prime time television crime dramas. *The Elon Journal of Undergraduate Research in Education, 4*(1), 108–115.

Pennington, L.(2014). *Everyday victim blaming.* London: EVB Press.

Perpetrator risk factors for violence against women. (n.d.). *Futures without Violence*. Retrieved August 20, 2015, from http://www.futureswithout violence.org/userfiles/file/Perpetrator%20Risk%20Factors %20Fact %20Sheet%202013.pdf

Projansky, S. (2001). *Watching rape: Film and television in post-feminist culture.* New York: NYU Press.

Quirk, M. (2013, March 4). Company pulls t-shirts from site because pro-domestic violence slogans are simply awful. *Consumerist.* Retrieved September 6, 2015, from http://consumerist.com/2013/03/04/ company-pulls-t-shirts-from-sale-because-pro-domestic-violence-slogans -are-simply-awful/

Robbins, A. (2015, July 20). Sorority secrets: The dark side of sisterhood that no one's willing to talk about. *Marie Claire.* Retrieved September 14, 2015, from http://www.marieclaire.com/culture/news/a15160/sorority -campus-sexual-assault/

Romano, T. (2012, February 22). Rainn Wilson, "2 Broke Girls," and the rise of the rape joke. *Daily Beast.* Retrieved January 8, 2016, from http://www .thedailybeast.com/articles/2012/02/22/rainn-wilson-2-broke-girls-and -the-rise-of-the-rape-joke.html

Shoos, D. (2003). Representing domestic violence: Ambivalence and difference in *What's Love Got to Do with It. NWSA Journal, 15*(2), 57–77.

Smith, A. (2005). *Conquest: Sexual violence and American Indian genocide.* Boston: South End Press.

Smith, L. (2014, October 6). Liz Smith: David Fincher, Ben Affleck and Rosamund Pike take Gone, Girl to new heights. *Boston Herald.* Retrieved January 8, 2016, from http://www.bostonherald.com/inside_track/ celebrity_news/2014/10/liz_smith_david_fincher_ben_affleck_and _rosamund_pike_take_gone

Snyder, J., & Scherer, H. (2015). Sexual victimization in the U.S. military. In T. Richards & C. Marcum (Eds.). *Sexual victimization: Then and now* (pp. 193–210). Thousand Oaks, CA: Sage.

Soulliere, D. (2003). Prime-time murder: Presentations of murder on popular television justice programs. *Journal of Criminal Justice and Popular Culture, 10*(1), 12–38.

Statistics. (2012). National coalition against violent athletes. Retrieved January 8, 2016, from http://www.ncava.org/statistics.html

Taslitz, A. (1999). *Rape and the culture of the courtroom.* New York: New York University Press.

Travers, P. (2000, April 14.) American Psycho. *Rolling Stone.* Retrieved January 8, 2016, from http://www.rollingstone.com/movies/reviews/american -psycho-20000414

Turner, K. (2014). "Strange Fruit" sounds: The legacy of lynchings in America. In S. Packer & J. Pennington (Eds.). *A history of evil in popular culture*, vol. 1 (pp. 359–370). Santa Barbara, CA: ABC-CLIO.

U.S. Department of Defense. (2013a). 2011 health related behaviors survey of active duty military personnel. Washington, D.C.: Office of the Secretary of Defense, Sexual Assault and Prevention Response Office.

U.S. Department of Defense. (2013b). Department of Defense annual report on sexual assault in the military: Fiscal year 2012. Washington, D.C.: Office of the Secretary of Defense, Sexual Assault and Prevention Response Office.

Valenti, J. (2014, September 24). Frat brothers rape 300% more. *The Guardian*. Retrieved September 14, 2015, from http://www.theguardian.com/commentisfree/2014/sep/24/rape-sexual-assault-ban-frats

Vatican reveals how many priests defrocked for sex abuse since 2004. (2014, May 7). CBS News. Retrieved January 8, 2016, from http://www.cbsnews.com/news/vatican-reveals-how-many-priests-defrocked-for-sex-abuse-since-2004/

Williamson, M. (2005). *The lure of the vampire: Gender, fiction and fandom from Bram Stoker to Buffy*. London: Wallflower Press.

3

Tornados Meeting Volcanos and Asking for It: Myths about Domestic Abuse and Sexual Assault

Myths about victims of rape and domestic violence are so common in popular culture that it is virtually impossible for this chapter to be thorough. An entire area of literature focuses on myths or misconceptions related to rape, called "rape myths." These myths address victims, offenders, and the problem of sexual assault in general. What makes rape myths so prevalent is that the United States is a "rape culture" in which sexualized violence is normalized across many institutions, including popular culture. Likewise, there are many myths about domestic violence, including those that maintain abuse is "mutual," that offenders abuse their partners because they "lose control" or due to mental illness or substance abuse, and that victims stay because they are weak or stupid.

RAPE MYTHS

Burt (1980) defined "rape myths" as "prejudicial, stereotyped, or false beliefs about rape, rape victims, and rapists" that create an environment hostile to rape survivors (p. 217), while Lonsway and Fitzgerald (1994) defined "rape myths" as "attitudes and beliefs that are generally false but are widely and persistently held, and that serve to deny and justify male aggression against women" (p. 134). Those focused on the victim suggest that she is lying or has some ulterior motive for the accusation, or that she was "asking for it" by what she was wearing or how she was behaving.

A common rape myth is that "good" women do not get raped, so victims are presumed to be promiscuous.

Grubb and Turner (2012) explain that "Rape myths vary among societies and cultures. However, they consistently follow a pattern whereby, they *blame the victim for their rape, express a disbelief in claims of rape, exonerate the perpetrator, and allude that only certain types of women are raped*" (emphasis in original). Payne, Lonsway, and Fitzgerald (1999) identified seven categories of U.S. rape myths. They are: (1) she asked for it; (2) it wasn't really rape; (3) he didn't mean to; (4) she wanted it; (5) she lied; (6) rape is a trivial event; and (7) rape is a deviant event.

As should be clear, many of these myths contradict one another. Grubb and Turner (2012) explain, "To believe that rape victims are innocent and not deserving of their fate is incongruous with the general belief in a just world; therefore, in order to avoid cognitive dissonance, rape myths serve to protect an individual's belief in a just world." Harding (2015) offered the following "flow chart" of the seven rape myths, which begins when someone reports a rape.

(1) Did she ask for it? If no, go to 2. If yes, go to 8. (2) Was it really rape? If yes, go to 3. If no, go to 8. (3) Did he mean to do it? If yes, go to 4. If not, got to 8. (4) Did she want to have sex with him? If no, go to 5. If yes, go to 8. (5) Is she lying about whether she consented? If no, go to 6. If yes, go to 8. (6) Was it really such a big effing trauma? If yes, go to 7. If not, go to 8. (7) The kind of rape you're describing is very, very rare. Like, so rare that it's practically nonexistent. Go back over steps 1 through 6, until you find your error and end up at 8. (8) Everything's fine! No need to be upset! (p. 23)

Harding (2015) and many others have debunked each of the seven rape myths. In regard to the myth that "she asked for it," they explain that the very definition of "rape" is that it is unwanted sex. Regarding claims that it wasn't *really* rape, they assert that there aren't categories of rape, there's no "sort-of-rape." Likewise for the myth that "she wanted it," since rape is rape, which means it is unwanted sex, one can't by definition "want" it. Addressing the myth that he didn't mean to do it, they explain that this is suggestive not only that rape is "accidental," but also that men cannot control themselves and in sexual situations can somehow engage in activity without knowing what they are doing. There is plenty of data to debunk the myth that she lied, with FBI statistics suggesting that between 2 and 8 percent of claims may be false, no different than most crimes. It should be obvious that rape is not a trivial event.

That rape is considered a deviant event is, as Harding (2015) explains,

> the myth that props up most of the other six. *Rape hardly ever happens, and it's only committed by mentally ill monsters, not people who resemble—or are—my friends, coworkers, and family members.* As long as you believe this, it makes sense that she must be lying, or he must not have meant it, or it must not have been real rape (see myth #2). As long as this is true, everything is fine, and there's no need to be upset. (p. 25)

Obviously, the statistics about the extent of domestic abuse and sexual assault presented in the Introduction show that these problems are far from rare.

Female victims of sex crimes are often depicted in two contrasting archetypes, the "Madonna" and the "whore" or, as Benedict (1992) calls it, the "virgin" and the "vamp." Virgins/Madonnas are the "good" victims, those whom we have sympathy for, while whores/vamps are "bad" victims who contributed to their own victimization and who are less if not entirely undeserving of our sympathy (Britto et al., 2007). Pennington (2014) notes that media and society at large often blame women for their own victimization, which she refers to as "everyday victim-blaming." She defines victim-blaming as instances when "the victim of a crime or any wrongful act is held entirely or partially responsible for the harm that befell them" (p. 7). Benedict (1992) noted eight factors that influence whether a victim is likely to be punished or blamed for her rape. These are: (1) if she knows the assailant, (2) if no weapon was used, (3) if the victim and perpetrator are of the same race, (4) if the victim and perpetrator are of the same class, (5) if the victim and perpetrator are from the same ethnic group, (6) when the victim is young, (7) if the victim is perceived as pretty, and (8) when the victim in any way deviated from the traditional female role. In sum, rape accusations are far more likely to be taken seriously if the victim is privileged and the assailant is not. "If you must be raped, you should try to be an upper-class white woman attacked by a poor person of color, because that's your best chance of being perceived as credible" (Harding, 2015, p. 142).

Perpetrator-focused myths tend to paint a narrow picture of assailants as strangers and psychopaths. Further, people tend to believe that rape is related to sex, and that men cannot control themselves, as well as that the incident cannot be considered rape if the victim did not fight back or the perpetrator did not have a weapon. Harding (2015) maintains that work from psychologists and linguists focusing on the different communication patterns between men and women has exacerbated the rape culture, as it has led to the notion that it was misunderstandings that resulted in rape, not actual nefarious intent on the part of perpetrators.

One of the most pervasive rape myths is that women frequently lie about sexual assault. Although the fear of false allegations has existed forever, it gained popularity in the 1990s with the publication of Katie Roiphe's *The Morning After: Fear, Sex, and Feminism* (1993). Roiphe maintained that many rape allegations are the result of unfortunate work hookups or poor decisions made when someone is drunk. A 2007 article by Laura Sessions Stepp in *Cosmopolitan* called "A New Kind of Date Rape" introduced the term "gray rape" to describe unwanted sex.

Research has shown that people are more likely to call an incident rape when it meets their predetermined beliefs about sexual assault. If an incident does not meet the criteria people consider a "real rape" (Estrich, 1987), then they are more likely to utilize one or more rape myths to explain what they believe happened. Further, many people want to believe the world is safe and just, and therefore they have a difficult time grappling with the horrors of rape and instead use rape myths to prevent themselves from having disturbing thoughts (Lonsway & Fitzgerald, 1994).

Acceptance of rape myths has been connected to greater blame for victims, lower conviction rates for accused rapists, and shorter sentences for convicted rapists during mock trials (Finch & Munro, 2005; Lonsway & Fitzgerald, 1994). Other studies have found that people who believe rape myths are more likely to commit a rape or report a proclivity to do so when presented with hypothetical scenarios (Bohner, Siebler, & Schmelcher, 2006; Chiroro et al., 2004).

Popular culture is a prominent purveyor of rape myths. As one example of how pervasive rape myths are, Kettrey (2013) analyzed their use in *Playboy* magazine. Of the 174 documents she analyzed, 54.6 percent contained rape myths. Victim-blaming was the most frequently occurring myth, followed by the myth that victims lie.

Kahlor and Morrison's (2007) study of 96 undergraduate college women using the rape myth acceptance scale found a statistically significant correlation between heavier television viewing and acceptance of rape myths. Importantly, the study included general television viewership, not specifically pornographic or misogynistic programming. They also found a statistically significant correlation between television viewing and the belief that rape accusations are likely to be false. Additionally, the respondents who ranked as more conservative were more accepting of rape myths, as were women of color and women born outside the United States.

Franiuk and colleagues (2008) analyzed 156 print media articles about the Kobe Bryant rape case. They coded the articles for use of rape myths, finding that 65 articles used the myth of victim falsification. They also tested media exposure of the rape myths on people's beliefs about the case. Respondents were far more likely to believe Bryant was being falsely accused after they read articles featuring rape myths.

Brinson (1992) analyzed 26 prime-time television story lines that contained references to rape, and found that the average story line contained at least one reference to a rape myth.

Brinson found that 42 percent of the story lines suggested that the rape victim wanted to be raped, 38 percent of the story lines suggested that the victim lied about the assault, and 46 percent of the story lines suggested that the victim had "asked for it" in the way that she dressed or acted (male and female characters were equally likely to make this accusation). On the other hand, only 38 percent of the story lines contained any opposition to the myth that the victim had "asked for it."

The 2012–13 television season saw 109 of 135 scripted dramas featuring a rape or murder. The 2013–14 television season followed with a record number of shows featuring rape scenes. FX's *The Americans*, ITV/PBS's *Downton Abbey*, HBO's *Game of Thrones*, Netflix's *House of Cards*, and ABC's *Scandal* all showed significant female characters being raped, either in the present or depicted in the past through flashbacks (Harding, 2015).

Yet, "The problem with this sudden rapeapalooza" is that it can result in desensitization. Further, when the topic receives so much coverage, writers, directors, and producers must constantly look for new and more interesting depictions. To be both believable and entertaining, according to Bleackley (2004), films typically depict rape using the narratives common in the society, including rape myths. Brinson (1992) found that crime dramas in the 1980s infrequently depicted rape, and when they did, the story lines relied heavily on rape myths.

Women who dare to express their sexuality are often "punished" with rape, as in the iconic scene from *Gone with the Wind* in which Rhett carries Scarlett up the stairs to her bedroom despite her explicit protestations. Often what is clearly rape is presented as though it is not when the victim eventually acquiesces, as does Scarlett (Projansky, 2001). Young (2007) analyzed Ann Petry's *The Street*, Toni Morrison's *The Bluest Eye*, M. F. Beal's *Angel Dance*, Dorothy Allison's *Bastard out of Carolina*, and Margaret Atwood's *The Blind Assassin*. Male rapists in these books used the women's rejection of traditional feminine stereotypes as justification for their assault. Due to their social, racial, and gender status, all of the women were blamed and ostracized for being raped. Women in 1940s' and 1950s' films who contemplated or threatened to leave their marriages often faced rape, which typically led them back to their husbands. Likewise, women who suffered from "nonfeminine" maladies, like excessive sexual behavior such as not wearing panties, or being former or current prostitutes put women in danger of being raped. In *Straw Dogs* (1971), Amy repeatedly flirts with a group of men who are working on her husband's property, including her former lover, who with another man rapes her. Projansky (2001) comments,

> Women are often vulnerable in rape films, but the relationship between rape and women's vulnerability is complex. Specifically, two seemingly antithetical types of narratives are common: those that depict women's vulnerability as leading to rape and those that depict the rape of an independent woman as making her vulnerable. Paradoxically, the first set of texts suggests that women should be more self-sufficient and independent in order to avoid rape, while the second set of texts suggests that independent behavior and sometimes independent sexuality can lead to rape. In both cases, however, most narratives resolve the paradox between vulnerability and independence by providing a conclusion that successfully incorporates the woman into a stable heterosexual family setting. In the films that depict women as innocent, naive, and vulnerable, and as facing rape as a result, the women may lack agency over their own lives or bodies; hence, they lack agency and therefore logically must be rescued from rape. (pp. 30–31)

One such film is *Johnny Belinda* (1948), which shows Belinda as particularly vulnerable since she is deaf and mute. Belinda ends up killing her assailant in self-defense, which renders her even more vulnerable as she must undergo trial with her limited communications. Although she is acquitted when someone else speaks up, "By the end of the film Belinda has become even more silent, vulnerable, and dependent on others than she was at the beginning of the film" (Projansky, 2001, p. 32). In films of the early 1900s, a woman's activity outside the home, perhaps being on a street or train, was enough to make her vulnerable to rape. In the 1910s, it was women who were at work that were at greatest risk as well as those who dared to exert sexuality through flirting, such as in *The Ruse* (1915), *The Cheat* (1915), and *The Talk of the Town* (1918).

Films marketed to teens also utilize rape myths. Long (2013) argues that *Spring Breakers* is more than simply a dumb film. Rather, beginning with an opening montage that is essentially girls-gone-wild (naked chests, scantily covered behinds, and lots of drinking shown in slow motion), the film reinforces the notion that certain "party girls" are "asking for it." Who can blame perpetrators, it suggests, when women act so vampishly?

Robin Thicke's widely popular "Blurred Lines," which reached number one in 14 countries, generated much controversy over the concept implied by the title: that sometimes, men may not know when a woman is really consenting to sex. Critics have said the song objectifies women, trivializes sexual abuse, and reinforces rape myths. Katie Russell, a spokeswoman for the UK group Rape Crisis, explained, "The lyrics of 'Blurred Lines' seem to glamorize violence against women and to reinforce rape myths, which we strive to dispel. Both the lyrics and the video seem to objectify and degrade women, using misogynistic language and imagery that many people would find not only distasteful or offensive but also really quite old fashioned."

The lyrics include: "Nothing like your last guy/He don't smack that ass and pull your hair like that" and "You know you want it," which is repeated 18 times. Russell commented, "More disturbingly, certain lyrics are explicitly sexually violent and appear to reinforce victim-blaming rape myths, for example about women giving 'mixed signals' through their dress or behaviour, saying 'no' when they really mean 'yes' and so on." The video was banned by YouTube as it showed models, wearing nothing but nude colored thongs, dancing with Thicke and his co-collaborators, T. I. and Pharrell Williams. Thicke defended the video in an interview with *GQ magazine*. He nonsensically claimed it did not denigrate women "because all three [artists in the video] are happily married with children" (Wyatt, 2013). When the far older Thicke danced provocatively with Miley Cyrus at the Video Music Awards, he reaffirmed the notion that he was a sexual predator. The song and video did generate many parodies that can be useful in debunking rape myths, such as the one by Law Revue Girls called "Defined Lines," which replaces the chorus with "Yeah we don't want it" and denounces the entire thing as a bigoted, chauvinistic, glorification of sex crime (Lowder, 2013).

In another example of the so-called blurred lines of the consent, the 2006 action movie *Crank,* Jason Statham's character grabs for his girl-friend, played by Amy Smart, right in the middle of Los Angeles's China-town, and demands she have sex with him right then and there. When she says no, Statham's character rapes her. Despite the fact that it is clearly rape, that Smart fights with Statham and yells at him to get off her, Smart's character ends up on the ground saying, "Fuck it, Take me right here" while she moans in pleasure. Conversations about that scene online typi-cally refer to it as "Amy Smart has sex in public." Another film that reframes rape as something open to interpretation is the 2009 comedy *Observe and Report* starring Seth Rogen. Rogen's character rapes a passed out, vomit-covered character played by Anna Faris, who then wakes up and says "Did I tell you to stop, motherfucker?" Harding (2015) explains that this retroactive consent is intended to reassure viewers that she really did want to have sex, regardless of what she said or did, hence it can't really be rape. In an interview, Rogen even expressed concern about that scene but followed it by explaining that the victim's statement made it OK. Similarly, in a 2008 episode of *Mad Men*, secretary Joan Holloway, played by Christina Hendricks, is raped by her fiancé in her boss's office at the end of a workday. Hendricks told *New York Magazine* that some people don't define that instance as rape, that she has heard people call it a "sort of" rape or say rape while making quotation marks with their fingers. Hendricks has referred to it as one of the most disturbing scenes she has filmed because the scene is presented in such a mixed fashion.

Tori Amos addressed the myth that provocative dress is at fault for rape in "Me and a Gun," singing, "Yes I wore a slinky red thing/Does that mean I should spread/For you, your friends your father, Mr. Ed." As Harding (2014) notes, "Contemporary pop culture is still in the business of openly painting rape victims as sluts who deserved what they got" (p. 160). Tyler Perry's *Temptation: Confessions of a Marriage Counselor* was released in spring 2013, earning $21.6 million on its opening weekend. The main character, Judith, is clearly attracted to one of her clients, but has resisted his advances, even fighting him off physically when he persists. He does rape her and Judith says she never wants to see him again, but later Judith flashes back to the incident in a sequence that suggests steamy and consensual sex, and she later begins dating the rapist. Scenes like this reinforce the notion that rape is about lust, and that victims secretly enjoy being sexually violated even when they had clearly said no. It also implies that women don't really know what they want, so what are poor, helpless males to do?

The 2008 Jamie Foxx and T-Pain song "Blame It" also implies that a woman doesn't really mean to say no when she does. "Cause shawty know what she want but she don't wanna seem like she easy." The artists then share the plan to "blame it on the alcohol," implying that the coerced sex is the result of drunkenness and therefore excused. Similarly, rapper Rick Ross features the lines, "Put molly all in her champagne, she ain't even know it/I took her home and I enjoyed that, she ain't even know it," also acknowledging that rapists sometimes ply their victims with drugs or alcohol and use that to excuse their behavior. Such incidents do indeed occur. In 2014, musician Cee Lo Green was charged with slipping ecstasy to a woman, who accused him of sexual assault. While prosecutors did not bring sexual assault charges, Green pled no contest to the drug charge in August 2014. Green then took to Twitter to "refute" the woman's allegations that she woke up naked in bed with him, having no memory of what happened. In doing so, Green, like so many celebrities, drew heavily on rape myths. He wrote "People who have really been raped REMEMBER!!! When someone braked on [*sic*] a home there is broken glass where is your plausible proof that anyone was raped" and "If someone is passed out they're not even WITH you consciously! so WITH implies consent" (in Harding, 2015, pp. 170–71). Green subsequently lost several gigs.

Like Damon Wayans's comments about Bill Cosby's accusers (described in Chapter 2), often rape is depicted as being about lust because only certain women are considered "rapeable." When feminist writer Lindy West challenged comedian Jim Norton on *Totally Biased* with W. Kamau Bell in May 2013, she followed the conversation with a post on *Jezebel* entitled "If Comedy Has No Lady Problems, Why Am I Getting So Many Rape Threats?" in which she described, on video, some of the comments she received via email and Twitter, including "Jim should rape this bitch and teach her a lesson," "No need for you to worry about rape," "Jaba has nothing to worry about, not even a prison escapee would rape her" and "I disagree with her point of view because she's a fat ugly cunt," "fat, ugly, angry, no man wants to rape her" (Harding, 2015, p. 167). These comments again reflect the notion that rape is about sexual lust, because they imply that women who aren't as attractive are not "rapeable." They totally ignore the reality that rape is a crime of opportunity and that perpetrators typically sexually violate those whom they know and to whom they are in close proximity.

One of the most insidious rape myths is that women "cry rape" because they regret having sex with someone or because they are seeking money or fame. As Chapter 2 explains, it is a tragedy when false allegations occur, as they can ruin the lives of the accused. Popular culture would have people believe, however, that virtually all women who claim to be victims of rape or abuse are lying. For instance, Ludacris's "Southern Hospitality" features the lines, "Lie through your teeth you could find your mouth, cold and rip out ya tongue cause of what ya mouth, told."

Some popular culture purposely addresses rape myths and, as such, can be useful in debunking them. In *Rape: A Love Story* (2003), acclaimed author Joyce Carol Oates tells the tragic story of a woman, Teena, who was gang-raped and brutally beaten by a pack of men amped on methamphetamines. Her 12-year-old daughter was with her and suffered injuries before the men forgot about her and she hid in the corner, listening to the attack that she thought had left her mother for dead. In this horrifying tale, Oates addresses the way that rape myths weave themselves into everyday life and, in particular, into the criminal justice system. The story is told from various points of view, so readers learn how the perpetrators see the incident, how law enforcement and attorneys interpret it, and how it impacts the daughter, Bethie. The opening chapter is titled "She Had It Coming," taking on perhaps the most insidious set of myths which assert that women "bring on" rape through their looks and actions. The attack occurred on Fourth of July, and Teena had declined a ride home or the offer to stay with her boyfriend, instead arguing that she and Bethie would enjoy walking home past a park and boathouse in which the men gathered. Teena had a reputation of "liking men." That night, Teena had been drinking, as had most that night, and was dressed in a tank top and denim cutoffs. "Tight sexy clothes showing her bare breasts, her ass, what's she expect?" the book asks (p. 5). Rumors even spread that Teena had allowed her daughter to drink as well "like mother, like daughter" (p. 22). Bethie was able to identify five of the assailants and others were later arrested. During the hearing before the trial, the mother of two of the defendants yelled out "Bitch! Whore! Liar!" at Teena as she entered the courtroom (p. 65). Their defense attorney proceeded to describe an entirely different, and false, set of events for the night of July 4, arguing that Teena had engaged in consensual sex with the men and had been planning on selling her daughter to the men as well. The men are never convicted, but the police officer who was first on the scene takes matters into his own hands and, over the next few years, kills the offenders in ways that allow him not to face legal consequences. The message, then, is that the justice system fails victims of sexual assault.

One TV show that nicely highlighted the nuances of rape is the late 1990s' hit *Felicity*. In one episode, Julie, Felicity's best friend, meets Zach, and they begin dating. He seems generally perfect, albeit a few small signs that he might lose his temper at odd times or get a little too into a make-out session for Julie's comfort, but Julie, Felicity, and others see him as a pretty ideal boyfriend. Several scenes later the two go into her room, kiss, and then Zach shuts the door, implying consensual sex. Yet the next scene shows a despondent Julie, who then tells Felicity and her doctor that the incident wasn't consensual in the end, and despite her wavering, convince that what had happened was rape. As Sposato (2015) explained,

> What's so incredible about the story line is that there's a lot of nuance and ambiguity in these relationships and interactions. Julie and Zach liked and even respected each other; they had a good thing going; they made out for half an hour before she said she didn't want to have sex—but it was *still* rape! Because that's the thing—rape, and especially non-stranger rape (the most common kind)—is rarely black and white; and you don't have to be an entirely bad guy to commit it.

Christa Desir's young adult novel *Fault Line* examines the dramatic effects of victim-blaming in rape cases. At the start of his senior year, Ben meets Ani, the new girl, and the two quickly fall in love. It all falls apart when Ben gets a call saying that Ani is in the hospital. She has no recollection of what happened, but others say that she had attended a party and was very drunk. According to witnesses, she claimed she intended to hook up with other guys, and someone tells Ben they saw Ani being carried up the stairs by a group of young men. Ani suffered from a brutal assault, evidenced by the fact that the doctors had to remove a cigarette lighter from her vagina. Rumors quickly spread that she was actually putting on a show with the lighter and Ani becomes the butt of cruel jokes on top of the sexual assault. Ani refuses to tell her mother about the rape and becomes sullen and promiscuous. Ben tries to support her but struggles to identify the best way. Desir, a rape victim advocate who has worked with victims at the hospital and in the healing process, wrote *Fault Line* to open a dialogue for teens regarding rape and victim-blaming. In an interview, she states:

> I hope I start a discussion about the role people play with survivors. The role they play in victim-blaming, in silencing survivors, in retraumatizing them in a way. I hope to start a discussion about what is the definition of rape, what enthusiastic consent looks like, and how to take care of someone in a situation like Ani is in . . . I want the "messiness" of this book to start a discussion about culpability, about what we can all do to make this look different. (DeYoung, 2013, para. 10)

In addition to pointing out how victims are often judged and blamed, it accurately shows that adolescents rarely tell adults about rape and that they often engage in dangerous behaviors like sexual promiscuity in the aftermath. Further, like many cases, no one identifies the assailants and thus none is ever held accountable.

DOMESTIC VIOLENCE

Several films and television shows portray domestic abuse situations but do not call them such. That it, they describe the relationship as "rocky," "turbulent," "stormy," "passionate," "tempestuous," "volatile," or "acrimonious," all of which imply that both parties are involved in the abuse. Media and popular culture also use words like "domestic dispute," "lovers' quarrel," "tryst," or that the offender was "jilted." As Pennington (2014) notes, "The word 'jilting' stems from 17th-century dialect for '*jillet*,' meaning '*flighty girl*' and as a noun describes a 'woman who jilts a lover.'

Its synonyms include abandon, betray, disappoint and deceive. It is emotive and evokes an idea of a poor, vulnerable man suffering from heartbreak at the hands of a woman who has left him, a '*flighty*' woman, no doubt" (p. 27). Clearly, then, it places the blame on the victim. Pennington (2014) also takes issue with the term "battering," as it suggests that all abuse is physical. Myths like that can result in victims not taking seriously the other types of abuse they may be enduring and may prevent others from believing that they are being abused.

Such language clearly fails to capture the true terror of abusive relationships and can serve to normalize or even romanticize abuse. Similarly, in the 1990s and prior, rapes were often referred to as "bad dates," such as when the main character of the show *Sisters*, Georgie, reveals that she had been raped as a teenager. This is imperative to understanding the dynamics of domestic violence. Many women being controlled and subordinated do not think they fit the "image" of a domestic violence victim. The media are among the primary perpetuators of images and myths of domestic violence (Martin, 2013, p. 3).

For instance, a 2011 episode of *Gossip Girl* showed the character Chuck Bass forcing himself on his girlfriend, Blair Waldorf. When she tries to resist he punches his hand through a window, which shatters the glass, a piece of which cuts Waldorf's face. The two have what is described as a "tumultuous relationship," an understatement to say the least, as in a previous episode Bass pimped his girlfriend out to his uncle. Yet executive producer Josh Safran defended the portrayal, saying:

> They have a volatile relationship, they always have, but I do not believe—or I should say we do not believe—that it is abuse when it's the two of them. Chuck does not try to hurt Blair. He punches the glass because he has rage, but he has never, and will never, hurt Blair. He knows it and she knows it, and I feel it's very important to know that she is not scared—if anything, she is scared for Chuck—and what he might do to himself, but she is never afraid of what he might do to her. Leighton and I were very clear about that. (Is Gossip Girl glamorizing … , 2011)

The term "revenge porn" has become common, in particular as celebrities like Jennifer Lawrence reveal that provocative images were leaked without their consent. While the problem is all too real, Pennington (2014) takes issue with this nomenclature:

> We do not believe that revenge porn is an accurate reflection of the trauma when a video or images of a sexual nature are released into the public sphere

without consent—this includes videos made with the consent of both partners and those images stolen from iCloud and other electronic sources.
These images are released with the sole purpose of humiliating the woman
involved. These are not "pornography." It is sexual assault and should be
dealt with more effectively by the criminal justice system. It also assumes that
men are justified in releasing these videos in "revenge" for some perceived
slight on the part of the woman. There is nothing which justifies the release
of intimate images without consent and we need to stop telling perpetrators
that they are justified in releasing the image because the victim dumped
them/was rude to them/forgot to change her iCloud password (insert as
required). (pp. 22–23)

Rader and Rhineberger-Dunn (2010) conducted an analysis of television shows featuring story lines about domestic violence to assess the
degree to which they blamed the victims. They then developed a typology
of victims which included the following four categories: innocent, innocent with character flaws, unlikable but not culpable, and manipulative
(contributing to or lying about victimization). Offenders were either sympathetic (relatable or having justification for their offenses), unlikeable
(with major personality/character flaws), manipulative (toward victims
and/or the criminal justice system), or predators (engaging in repeated
and particularly vicious offenses). Although some episodes did not feature
enough information to make these categorizations, the majority of victims
were depicted as innocent, followed by unlikeable but not culpable, while
the majority of offenders were depicted as predatory. Victims of intimate
partner violence were portrayed more harshly than were victims of sexual
assault, with 50 percent being characterized as manipulative and none as
innocent. In examining the relationship between offenders and victims,
they found that victims were more likely to be presented as innocent when
their perpetrator was a stranger. Almost 60 percent of victims were characterized as manipulative when the perpetrator was an intimate partner.
Finally, they suggested that "episodes that characterize the victim in a negative light may make the offender more likeable or sympathetic to increase
the viewer's dislike or blame of the victim" (p. 248). It is possible that shows
like these reinforce the myth that victims must be "perfect" (Belknap, 2007).
    Melissa Henson, director of communication and public education for
the Parents Television Council, says that Hollywood often implies that
abusive relationships are not only normal but actually more interesting,
more intense, and more passionate than other romances. As such, teens
seeking excitement and drama may see abusive relationships as more
desirable than others that are based on healthy boundaries and norms.

"To impressionable teens, domestic violence is almost romanticized. We've made great strides in recent years in clearly communicating the message that is never okay to hit a woman," she said. "Today, the hidden message in the entertainment consumed by many impressionable teens is that if he hits you, it is out of love—which is absolutely wrong" (McKay, 2011, para. 6). Another mental health expert, Dr. Jordana Mansbacher, agreed. "Hollywood does what it can to get ratings, so that may include domestic violence scenes. Many adolescents idealize love, especially their first [love]" (McKay, 2011, para. 7).

Eminem and Rihanna's "Love the Way You Lie" perpetuates the myth that abuse is mutual and that victims "like it" with lines like "Just gonna stand there and watch me burn/But that's alright because I like the way it hurts." Later, Eminem raps about the physical violence and threatens to tie her up and set the house on fire. The video for "Love the Way You Lie" in particular depicted physical, sexual, and emotional threats as if they are a normal part of a romantic relationship (Bonomi, Altenburger, & Walton, 2013). It was released not too long after Chris Brown was arrested for the violent attack on his girlfriend at the time, Rihanna, and pictures of her battered face were all over media.

Eminem, too, has been engaged in a long-term abusive relationship with his ex-wife Kim Mathers, of whom he often raps about hurting. Eminem has often addressed domestic violence in his music. In "Kim," Eminem justifies abuse because his wife cheated on him, "Quit crying, bitch, why do you always make me shout at you?"

The singer goes on to threaten her, saying they'll return from a drive with her in the trunk, a theme he picks up in "97 Bonnie and Clyde," as he tells the couple's daughter Hailie that mom "is taking a little nap in the trunk."

Rihanna defended "Love the Way You Lie," arguing that it was realistic.

It just was authentic. It was real . . . It was believable for us to do a record like that, but it was also something that needed to be done and the way he did it was so clever. He pretty much just broke down the cycle of domestic violence and it's something that a lot people don't have a lot of insight on, so this song is a really, really powerful song and it touches a lot of people.

Rihanna later upset many rape advocates with her video for "We Found Love," which depicts a volatile relationship with her costar, Dudley O'Shaughnessy. Critics note that the video features sex, drugs, and abuse, and that O'Shaughnessy even looks like Brown. "Rihanna's new video is a disgrace. It sends the message that she is an object to be possessed by men, which is disturbingly what we see in real violence cases," Eileen Kelly of the Rape Crisis Center in the United Kingdom told Britain's *Daily Star*.

Shoos (2003) notes that the musical score to the Ike and Tina Turner biopic *What's Love Got to Do with It* describes the relationship between the two in ways that can be considered problematic. When young Anna Mae is first rehearsing with Ike Turner's band, they sing "I Wanna Be Made Over," a song that makes "explicit both the power that Ike already exerts over her and her own vulnerability to his obsessive attention" (p. 66). "A Fool in Love," which includes the lines "You know you love him, you can't understand/Why he treat you like he do when he's such a good man." Those lines occur right after a scene of verbal and psychological abuse (Shoos, 2003, p. 66). Another concern is that the repeated portrayals of Ike's cocaine consumption and womanizing may reinforce the misconception that abuse is the result of drug use or that this was just part of the crazy lifestyle of a 1960s' rock star (Shoos, 2003).

Bessie Smith's jazz song "Outside of That" (1923) also features mixed messages about abuse. While it highlights the roller coaster exhibited in such relationships, it seems to suggest that victims are happy to endure the rough times as long as they are occasionally treated decently. "I've got the meanest man in the land/But his love is best, thick and grand." She goes on to say that people call her a fool for staying with this cruel man, but she responds, "outside of that, he's all right with me/Outside of that, he's sweet as he can be."

The popular novel and later film *The Perks of Being a Wallflower* suggests that somehow victims project something that "attracts" to them people who are abusive. When Charlie asks his teacher why it is that the people he is close to (friends and family) are with partners that treat them poorly, Bill responds, "We accept the love we think we deserve." Charlie's sister is slapped and verbally harassed by her boyfriend but she, like so many victims, defends him, claiming that she brought it on and that he is generally a good guy. Later, Sam asks Charlie the same question and he responds the same way. Sam's boyfriend cheats on her, does not value her opinion, and disrespects her, but even though she admits he isn't good for her, she too makes excuses for his poor treatment. Such depictions may lead teens to believe that it is indeed a victim's fault if he or she stay with someone who abuses them and that somehow we can avoid being abused if we simply attract different people. It removes the ownership from abusers for choosing different behaviors.

Stephenie Meyer's *Twilight* saga has frequently been critiqued for glamorizing unhealthy relationships. Edward controls Bella's every action, especially as the series goes on, and he claims that he must do so because he loves her so much. She believes it and even seems to desire the control, while at the same time trying to resist it. Using his vampire "magical powers," Edward can and does easily stalk Bella, even showing up in her bedroom to watch her sleep. He isolates her from others such that Bella is almost exclusively with Edward or his family. He is excessively jealous of her friendship with Jacob, whom he sees as a rival. Bella clearly lacks self-esteem, something many young girls struggle with. That the popular and attractive Edward is interested in her immediately gives him social power over the new girl. Like many girls, Bella is also attracted to Edward's "bad boy" image. Further, the threat of violence seems to excite her and, as was noted earlier in the chapter, imply that this type of relationship is more thrilling than those that do not feature concerns about being killed (Goodfriend, 2011).

The abuse becomes physical in Book Four, where Bella notices her bruised body from Edward's overzealous sexual behavior the night prior. She notes swollen lips, a bruise on one cheek, and bruises all over her arms and shoulders.

McDaniel (2013) noted that the series provides

> evidence of popular social norms that define men's violent behaviors in intimacy as romantic when the woman wants the man, and abusive when she doesn't want him. This subtle but effective victim blaming leaves the determination of what is or isn't abuse mired in the perception of the woman's reciprocation and dependent on her credibility. Twilight in many ways is an ongoing social excusing of men's violence. By situating the partner violence in the form of an old-fashioned but perfect vampire, the story offers Edward's beauty and protectiveness as a justifiable reason for Bella to accept his violence in direct contradiction to the law. (pp. 1–2)

The Crystals' "He Hit Me and It Felt Like a Kiss" (1962), cowritten by Gerry Coffin and Carole King, was seemingly intended to offer a sympathetic telling of the abuse endured by their former babysitter, pop singer Little Eva. The lyrics, however, are easily interpreted as condoning abuse in cases when the partner has not been monogamous. "He couldn't stand to hear me say that I'd been with someone new." The chorus goes on to say, "He hit me and I knew he loved me."

A popular culture example that better captures the dynamics of abusive relationships is Gloria Micklowitz's *Past Forgiving*, which includes both rape and dating violence. Alex is insecure about her looks, her intellect, and her abilities because her older boyfriend Cliff constantly tells her she is worthless. She gives up friends, begins dresses as he wishes, never talks to other boys, and does anything else she can to please Cliff but nothing works. Cliff becomes physically abusive but Alex continues to forgive him. It is only when, during an unwelcome make-out session, Cliff gets "carried away" and rapes her that Alex finally recognizes his abusiveness and decides to close him out of her life. The book documents the difficulties victims face in leaving an abuser who has isolated them from support networks.

In Kathryn Craft's *The Far End of Happy*, Ronnie has just told her husband, Jeff, that she wants a divorce. Jeff is an alcoholic, and Ronnie learns over time that he had lied to her repeatedly about their finances. He spirals into a deep depression and, armed with a cache of weapons, threatens to commit suicide. The book highlights the complex emotions a victim experiences; Ronnie loves Jeff and wants him to be OK, but knows he is not and that he is unwilling to go to therapy or rehab. His mother is an enabler and defends Jeff until the end. Ronnie even learns he had threatened his former wife with a gun and her mother-in-law, Janet, knew about it and never told her.

Pearl Jam's "Better Man" also portrays the difficulties victims have in ending abusive relationships without blaming them or suggesting they are stupid or lack courage. The popular song discusses how a victim waits to tell her abuser she wants to leave, practicing her speech and recalling when she was bolder and stronger. But she grapples with the doubt that she will ever find a "better man," a line that abusers often use to reduce their victim's self-esteem.

Yet another useful tool is the young adult novel *The Lost Marble Notebook of Forgotten Girl & Random Boy*, author Marie Jaskulka tells the stories of two teenagers known only as Forgotten Girl and Random Boy who try escape dysfunctional families. The book is written as a series of free verse poems, and it depicts the two's relationship as Random Boy becomes increasingly controlling and jealous. He then becomes emotionally and physically abusive, demonstrating how these behaviors emerge over time. Lowry (2015) describes the book as "a never preachy depiction of teen dating abuse that is fully humane, complex, avoids victim-blaming and shows compassion for both the victim of violence, and the young perpetrator raised in an incredibly violent home—while never excusing the violence itself" (para 4).

In conclusion, this chapter has documented the many myths and misconceptions that often appear in popular culture that features domestic abuse and sexual assault. While there are indeed realistic and useful examples, mostly in fiction, too often popular culture blames victims and dismisses the severity of these crimes. Consumers of these types of popular culture may do the same, which can lessen the chances that a victim will identify what is or has occurred as problematic behavior, that an abuser or assailant will take responsibility for his or her actions, and that friends, families, and institutions will offer the support and resources needed for victims to heal.

REFERENCES

Belknap. J. (2007). *The invisible woman: Gender, crime and justice*, 3rd ed. Belmont, CA: Wadsworth.

Benedict, H. (1992). *Virgin or vamp: How the press covers sex crimes.* New York: Oxford University Press.

Bleackley, D. (2004). Representing rape: A semiotic analysis of rape myths in three popular films. Master's thesis for the University of British Columbia. Retrieved January 24, 2016, from https://circle.ubc.ca/bitstream/id/37910/ubc_2004-0371.pdf

Bohner, G., Siebler, F., & Schmelcher, J. (2006). Social norms and the likelihood of raping: Perceived rape myth acceptance of others affects men's rape proclivity. *Personality & Social Psychology Bulletin, 32*(3), 286–297.

Bonomi, A., Altenburger, L., & Walton, N. (2013). Double crap! Abuse and harmed identity in *Fifty Shades of Grey. Journal of Women's Health, 22*(9), 733–744.

Britto, S., Hughes, T., Saltzman, K., & Stroh, C. (2007). Does "special" mean young, white and female? Deconstructing the meaning of "special" in *Law & Order: Special Victims Unit. Journal of Criminal Justice and Popular Culture, 14*(1), 40–57.

Burt, M. (1980). Cultural myths and support for rape. *Journal of Personality and Social Psychology, 38*(2), 217–230.

Chiroro, P., Bohner, G., Viki, G., & Jarvis, C. (2004). Rape myth acceptance and rape proclivity: Expected dominance versus expected arousal as mediators in acquaintance-rape situations. *Journal of Interpersonal Violence, 19*(4), 427–442.

DeYoung, A. (2013, November 11). Talking to teens about rape: An interview with YA author Christa Desir. The Stake. Retrieved January 9, 2016, from http://thestake.org/2013/11/11/talking-to-teens-about-rape-an-interview-with-ya-author-christa-desir/

Estrich, S. (1987). *Real rape.* Cambridge, MA: Harvard University Press.

Finch, E., & Munro, V. (2005). Juror stereotypes and blame attribution in rape cases involving intoxicants: The findings of a pilot study. *The British Journal of Criminology, 35*(1), 25–38.

Franiuk, R., Seefelt, J., Cepress, S., & Vandello, J. (2008). Prevalence and effects of rape myths in print journalism: The Kobe Bryant case. *Violence against Women, 14*(3), 287–309.

Goodfriend, W. (2011, November 28). Sexism in "The Girl with the Dragon Tattoo." *Psychology Today*. Retrieved January 8, 2016, from https://www.psychologytoday.com/blog/psychologist-the-movies/201111/sexism-in-the-girl-the-dragon-tattoo

Grubb, A., & Turner, E. (2012). Attribution of blame in rape cases: A review of the impact of rape myth acceptance, gender role conformity and substance abuse on victim blaming. *Aggression & Violent Behavior, 17*(5), 27–68.

Harding, K. (2015). *Asking for it*. New York: Da Capo Lifelong.

Is Gossip Girl glamorizing an abusive relationship? (2011, May 5). Retrieved September 14, 2015, from http://perezhilton.com/2011-05-05-gossip-girl-glamorizes-abuse-between-chuck-and-blair#.VfbiCJdUXeI

Kahlor, L., & Morrison, D. (2007). Television viewing and rape myth acceptance among college women. *Sex Roles, 56*(11), 729–739.

Kettrey, L. (2013). Reading *Playboy* for the articles: The graying of rape myths in black and white text, 1953 to 2003. *Violence against Women, 19*(8), 968–994.

Long, H. (2013, March 28). Spring Breakers isn't just a terrible movie, it reinforces rape culture. *The Guardian*. Retrieved January 9, 2016, from http://www.theguardian.com/commentisfree/2013/mar/28/spring-breakers-movie-wild-girls-rape-culture

Lonsway, K., & Fitzgerald, L. (1994). Rape myths in review. *Psychology of Women Quarterly, 18*(2), 133–164.

Lowder, J. (2013, July 23). Wait, this is the "Blurred Lines" parody we needed. *Slate*. Retrieved January 9, 2016, from http://www.slate.com/blogs/browbeat/2013/07/23/_blurred_lines_gender_swapped_parody_from_mod_carousel_the_best_robin_thicke.html

Lowry, M. (2015, May 27). A chat with Marie Jaskulka about "The Lost Marble Notebook," intense young love and teen dating abuse. *Huffington Post*. Retrieved January 9, 2016, from http://www.huffingtonpost.com/mary-pauline-lowry/a-chat-with-marie-jaskulk_b_7446234.html

Martin, K. (2013). Domestic violence, sexual assault, and sex trafficking in the media: A content analysis. Master's theses and doctoral dissertations. Eastern Michigan University. Retrieved January 6, 2016, from http://commons.emich.edu/cgi/viewcontent.cgi?article=1840&context=theses

McDaniel. D. (2013). Representations of partner violence in young adult literature: Dating violence in Stephenie Meyer's *Twilight* saga. Dissertation submitted to the University of Texas. Retrieved January 7, 2016, from https://repositories.lib.utexas.edu/bitstream/handle/2152/23201/MCDANIEL-DISSERTATION-2013.pdf

McKay, H. (2011, May 31). Hollywood perpetuating dangerous images of domestic violence in teen romances, experts say. *Fox News*. Retrieved January 9, 2016, from http://www.foxnews.com/entertainment/2011/05/31/hollywood-mistaking-domestic-violence-passion-experts-say/

Oates, J. (2003). *Rape: A love story*. Boston, MA: Da Capo Press.

Payne, D., Lonsway, K., & Fitzgerald, L. (1999). Rape myth acceptance: Exploration of its structure and its measurement using the Illinois Rape Myth Acceptance Scale. *Journal of Research in Personality, 33*(1), 27–68.

Pennington, L. (2014). *Everyday victim blaming.* London: EVB Press.

Projansky, S. (2001). *Watching rape: Film and television in post-feminist culture.* New York: NYU Press.

Rader, N., & Rhineberger-Dunn, G. M. (2010). A typology of victim characterization in television crime dramas. *Journal of Criminal Justice and Popular Culture, 17*(1), 231–263.

Roiphe, K. (1993). *The morning after: Sex, fear and feminism.* New York: Back Bay.

Shoos, D. (2003). Representing domestic violence: Ambivalence and difference in *What's Love Got to Do with It. NWSA Journal, 15*(2), 57–77.

Sposato, J. (2015, August 10). How the "Felicity" rape episode was ahead of its time. KQED. Retrieved September 6, 2015, from http://ww2.kqed.org/pop/2015/08/10/how-the-felicity-rape-episode-was-ahead-of-its-time/

Stepp, L. (2007, September 11). A new kind of date rape. *Cosmopolitan.* Retrieved January 9, 2016, from http://www.cosmopolitan.com/sex-love/advice/a1912/new-kind-of-date-rape/

Wyatt, D. (2013, June 21). Robin Thicke's number one single "Blurred lines" accused of reinforcing rape myths. *The Independent.* Retrieved January 9, 2016, from http://www.independent.co.uk/arts-entertainment/music/news/robin-thickes-number-one-single-blurred-lines-accused-of-reinforcing-rape-myths-8667199.html

Young, T. (2007). Rape in contemporary American literature: Writing women as rapeable. Thesis for Florida State University. Retrieved January 9, 2016, from http://diginole.lib.fsu.edu/cgi/viewcontent.cgi?article=5296&context=etd

Evil, Ill, or Controlling: Exploring Depictions of Criminological Theory

Many criminologists have sought to explain domestic violence and rape. From biological to psychological theories, choice-related explanations to learning-focused ones, environmental to macro-level analyses, criminological theory has offered a plethora of explanations for rape and domestic violence. Some of these appear widely in popular culture while others are largely absent from depictions. This chapter begins with a brief review of literature regarding crime theory as presented in popular culture. It then provides descriptions of the categories of crime theory most frequently used to explain rape and domestic violence and includes examples of popular culture depictions utilizing each, where they are available. The following categories of crime theory are included: biological theories, including brain injuries and substance abuse; psychological theories, including mental illness and anger control explanations; learning theories; sociological theories, including strain and techniques of neutralization; and feminist theories.

CRIME THEORY IN POPULAR CULTURE

Crime film plots frequently "draw on general attitudes toward crime, victims, law, and punishment prevalent at the time of their making" (Rafter, 2000, p. 15). Rafter (2000) explains:

> Crime films serve as a cultural resource, creating a reservoir of images and stories on which viewers draw when they think about the causes of crime.

Many crime films also endorse a particular explanation of crime. Whether they merely hint at criminological theory or beat us over the head with one, crime films expose viewers to national (and even international) debates about the causes of crime. (p. 47)

Films typically utilize the theories that are more common in the time period in which they are produced (Rafter, 2000). For instance, conditions in the inner-city were the focus of the 1930s, drawing on popular theories developed in Chicago and centered on social disorganization, while Freudian explanations were popular in the 1940s and 1950s. The 1950s and 1960s saw a focus on crime as an escape from poverty, giving way to an emphasis on strain-related theories, while the 1980s emphasized drug addiction and family violence as causal factors. This era then tended to emphasize individual or micro-level theories, focusing on biology or choice. In the 1990s, films began to examine the media. Further, even while "criminologists drop discredited theories, movies recycle them" (Rafter, 2000, p. 48).

Rafter (2000) maintains that there are three primary sets of explanations for crime offered by films. One focuses on an individual's environment, noting that how one is raised and in what setting shapes a person's behavior. These explanations connect with learning-related theories. Psychological theories emphasizing mental illness or abnormality are also common, and they tend to be used to present the most bizarre and titillating offenders. Third, crime films often depict offenders as merely trying to get a better life, what is typically referred to as the strain theories. Rafter (2000) explains that, "A fourth explanation of crime, bad biology, is favored by neither moviemakers nor criminologists but is nonetheless treated occasionally by both" (pp. 49–50). When biological perspectives are used, it tends to be in the horror genre.

Many have noted that popular explanations for crime and criminality offered in news and entertainment media are overwhelmingly individualistic. Depictions tend to stress that individuals commit crimes because of greed, jealousy, emotional instability, mental pathology, and other individual defects or weaknesses (Barrile, 1986; Cavender & Bond-Maupin, 1993; Estep & MacDonald, 1983). Cavender and Bond-Maupin (1993) report that criminals in media and popular culture are portrayed as dangerous people who often struggle with some degree of mental illness; in essence, they are "crazed killers" and "psychopaths." Maguire (1988) notes that sociological explanations are almost completely absent from popular culture, in particular from crime and police-related dramas. Depictions of gang-related crime, like *Juice* or *Boyz N the Hood*, sometimes show the neighborhood factors that contribute to crime. Fabianic (1997) analyzed the portrayal of homicides in crime dramas and found that they do not use institutional or social-structural explanations. This might be because viewers find it easier to relate to story lines showing micro-level explanations. It is likely also due to the fact that episodes are created such that, while they build on one another, each can also stand alone and thus be attractive to new viewers. As such, it is difficult to fully explore institutions and structures in each episode.

Most research on criminological theory and popular culture has not had a lot to say about the offenses of domestic violence and rape specifically. Most of the focus is on the incidents, but not really on why the offenders perpetrate these crimes. Bancroft (2003) and others note that there are many inappropriate and even dangerous explanations for domestic violence. Among the most common are that mental illness, substance abuse, and anger control problems are the reasons why people abuse their partners. Each of these is addressed in this chapter.

Studies addressing rape and domestic violence more frequently look at the explanations offered in news media accounts. Voumvakis and Ericson's (1984) study of newspaper accounts of attacks on women found heavy victim-blaming, some critique of the criminal justice response, but most frequently, a focus on offender pathology, especially how there is a need to identify and control "dangerous" individuals in society (p. 43). The patriarchal roots of abuse and sexual assault are rarely mentioned or portrayed (Berns, 1999, 2001). In fact, as Berns (1999) showed, popular women's magazines, television shows, and news media instead tend to contribute to the culture of victim-blaming by focusing much of their attention on the victim's behavior and on what she should change in order to avoid further victimization.

Soulliere (2003) analyzed *NYPD Blue*, *Law & Order*, and *The Practice*, all popular prime-time television shows in the early 2000s, for their presentations and explanations of murder. She found that three-quarters of the episodes focused on violent crime, which is out of proportion with reality. Murder or attempted murders were the most commonly depicted crimes, comprising 66 percent of the total crimes portrayed. This is not consistent with official crime reports, which show property crime to be far more common. In the year of the analysis (1999/2000), the Uniform Crime Reports showed only 26.4 percent of the crime in New York City, where *Law & Order* and *NYPD Blue* were to be located, was violent. More than half of the offenders committed their violent crimes due to emotions—generally jealousy, anger, fear, or frustration, which is generally consistent with official statistics. A substantial portion (16 percent) of the offenses were depicted as being due to mental illness, which is an overrepresentation based on crime statistics. Generally, few sociological explanations were provided, although a few episodes grappled with gun control and other more social issues.

BIOLOGICAL THEORIES

There is no evidence of a biological cause for domestic violence or rape, and evidence for biological causation for other forms of violence is inevitably challenged by difficulties ascertaining the effects of biology versus socialization, the classic "nature versus nurture" debate. These theories were popular among criminologists for a long time but went largely out of vogue when it became obvious that alleged biological deficiencies were being used to justify oppressive policies against poor and minorities. The eugenics movement of the early 1900s is a stark example of how belief in crime as biology can result in heinous practices, even forced sterilizations. Biological explanations for crime have reemerged since the 1980s, although most today assert that it is biology in conjunction with environmental factors that causes crime.

Italian criminologist and physician Cesare Lombroso was one of the first to offer a biological theory for crime. Lombroso believed that criminals were genetic anomalies, or evolutionary throwbacks he called "atavists." These people could be identified by physical defects, including sloping foreheads, excessively long arms and large ears, and asymmetrical faces, and Lombroso maintained that they were "born criminals." His research has been critiqued as unethical and not scientifically sound, but nonetheless it has had some degree of lasting power (Finley, 2013).

In 1874, Richard Dugdale began investigating the alleged criminality of an entire family he called the "Jukes." He concluded that the family was born to be criminal when he found that of 29 male immediate relatives, 17 had been arrested and 15 convicted. Henry Goddard (1912) also studied families and determined that those of the lower classes passed along traits that made their children "feeble-minded." Their work helped lay the foundation for the sterilization of those they deemed feeble-minded, what came to be called the eugenics movement, as Goddard and others felt as though reproduction by the poor and minorities would only result in more crime. Forced sterilization laws and policies were upheld in the 1927 Supreme Court case *Buck v. Bell* and lasted until the 1960s, by which time an estimated 60,000 women had been sterilized. It is clear from transcripts of the Nuremberg Trials that Nazi doctors and officials were influenced by this belief in the biology of crime.

Today, some criminologists like Kevin Beaver, an associate professor at Florida State University's College of Criminology and Criminal Justice, using far more sophisticated methods, believe that genetics can account for approximately half of a person's aggressive behavior. Others say it is more like 30 percent, but explain that thousands of genes work together and with the environment to express that aggression. In essence, there is no one "crime gene."

Neurocriminology is the study of the minds of violent criminals using brain imaging. One of the leaders in neurocriminology is Adrian Raine, a professor at the University of Pennsylvania and author the 2013 book *Anatomy of Violence: The Biological Roots of Crime*. Raine explained, "Just as there's a biological basis for schizophrenia and anxiety disorders and depression, I'm saying here there's a biological basis also to recidivistic violent offending." His aim is to improve crime prevention and rehabilitation. He admits, however, that there is danger in presuming that "bad brains" cause bad behavior, as "biology is not destiny." Further, Raine grapples with the question of how to hold accountable offenders, were it possible to determine that biology was a primary factor, as that might imply that the individuals should be held less responsible due to their genetic capacity. Depictions of abusers and rapists in popular culture do not seem to draw heavily on genetic explanations, hopefully because there is no real research that suggests a genetic link to these offenses.

One of the most widely researched explanations for crime and biology has to do with exposure to lead. Lead was commonly used in gas as well as in paint and other products into the 1970s, and particularly in the 1950s. Raine and others have noted a spike in violent crime a generation later as the individuals who were exposed reached their high teens/low adult years. Then crime declined in the 1990s as lead was prohibited and much of it cleaned up. Raine asserts that you can explain 91 percent in the changes in violence over time by mapping lead levels. In 2000, Rick Nevin found that exposure to lead in gasoline between 1879 and 1940 explained approximately 70 percent of the variation in murder rates between 1900 and 1960, while exposure between 1941 and 1986 explained close to 90 percent of the murder rate variance between 1960 and 1998. The effects of lead exposure are more frequently found among urban, poor populations because they were most likely around the substance for longer times and in greater concentrations. Nevin found similar patterns connecting violent crime rates and lead exposure in Australia, Canada, Great Britain, France, New Zealand, Italy, and West Germany. Although films like the comedy *Tommy Boy* make jokes about weird behavior and eating paint chips, lead exposure is not something that appeared in my analysis of depictions of rape and sexual assault.

Another biological explanation for crime focuses on head injuries. A traumatic brain injury (TBI) refers to a specific type of damage to the brain that is not present at birth nor degenerative but rather is caused by external physical force. TBI is typically the result of a blow or repeated blows to head, shaking of the brain, penetration of the brain by an object like a gun or knife, loss of oxygen, or colliding with a stationary object. Further, a person can suffer from a TBI based on the cumulative effect of a combination of traumas to the brain. Annually, an estimated 1.7 million Americans suffer from TBI. Some three-quarters of these are mild forms, generally resulting in concussions. According to the U.S. Department of Health and Human Services (2006), annually "50,000 die; 235,000 are hospitalized with TBI and survive; and 1.1 million people are treated and released from hospital emergency departments." A report by Huw Williams, a professor of psychology at the Centre for Clinical Neuropsychology Research at the University of Exeter, found connections between traumatic brain injuries of children and adolescents and later aggressive and criminal behavior. Such injuries may be sustained through abuse, traffic accidents, sports, or other normal behavior. The most vulnerable groups are children under the age of 4, the elderly, and people in their late teens and twenties: children and the elderly because of falls, while teens and early adults because of car crashes, sports, and other risk-taking behaviors. Military personnel engaged in violent conflicts are also susceptible. Estimates are that some 20 percent of veterans from the wars in Iraq and Afghanistan have a TBI. While TBI itself is not equivalent to permanent brain damage, it can lead to that end. Approximately 26.5 percent of TBIs are caused when the victim's head is struck by or against something, and another 10 percent are caused by assaults.

Rosenbaum and Hoge (1989), Rosenbaum et al. (1994), and Rosenbaum et al. (1997) published a series of studies showing that many abusive men had histories of head trauma and that there could be a causal link between the brain dysfunction and neurological damage. Head trauma may reduce one's impulse control, distort judgment, exacerbate communication difficulties, and create hypersensitivity to alcohol. Given the growing research on this area, it is surprising that popular culture has not utilized more portrayals of head injuries as the cause of crime. The 2015 film *Concussion*, however, focuses on brain injuries among NFL players and may prompt others to include such explanations for changed and even violent behavior. PBS's *Frontline* already focused on this in the episode "League of Denial."

Hormonal explanations for crime are also common. Studies have shown that higher levels of testosterone in the uterus are associated with later aggression. Additionally, while far from conclusive, some point to the fact that crime peaks at the age in which most people are experiencing significant hormonal changes. It is often argued that testosterone rates explain the generally large differences between male and female criminality. It is unclear, however, if there are other factors that explain that gender differences, such as gender role norms, chivalry in the criminal justice system, and more. One study found that increases in testosterone through anabolic steroids increased aggressive feelings among some but not all males in the samples (Pope, Kouri, & Hudson, 2000). Joe Herbert, of the University of Cambridge's Department of Clinical Neurosciences, authored the book *Testosterone: Sex, Power and the Will to Win*. In it, he maintains that testosterone gives men urges to commit behavior that is no longer culturally necessary, such as warding off competing mates. He notes, however, that there is no evidence suggesting rapists have more testosterone (Moss, 2015). Again, although the idea that testosterone is the cause of men's crime is widespread, it does not really appear in popular culture.

Drug and alcohol addictions are also common explanations for domestic violence and sexual assault, at least among the general public. While data are clear that use of alcohol or illicit substances can increase the likelihood and severity of an assault or rape, there remains no causal link. Alcohol impairs neural processing, which might change the way one interacts with others, reduce their inhibitions, and impede their ability to fully consider the consequences of their actions. Brookoff and colleagues (1997) described the characteristics of assailants and victims of domestic violence. Of the responding assailants, 86 percent acknowledged using alcohol on the day of the assault. Victims and family members reported that 92 percent of assailants used drugs or alcohol the day of the assault. Further, 45 percent of victims and family members reported that assailants used alcohol or drugs to the point of intoxication each day during the prior month. A total of 19 percent were classified as alcoholics and 14 percent dually diagnosed as drug addicts and alcoholics. Victims were reported to have been using alcohol or drugs the day of the assault as well, although to a lesser extent (42 percent). Fals-Stewart (2003) studied men who were in batterer's intervention and found that the odds that a man would physically assault his partner were eight times greater on days when he had been drinking. Kyriacou et al. (1999) found that men who used alcohol at the time of a physical assault inflicted greater harm on their partners than did men who had not been drinking. Many abusers blame the abuse on their problem with alcohol, and courts often still mandate attendance in substance abuse programs for abusers. While surely these programs may address the substance abuse problem, they have not been proven to reduce the incidence of domestic violence.

Substance abuse is often an explanation for domestic abuse in popular culture. Nickelback's "Never Again" points to substance abuse as the reason for violence, saying "He's drunk again, it's time to fight" and referring to the living room as a "boxing ring." Demi Lovato's "For the Love of a Daughter" also describes substance abuse as the source of the problem. In it, a little girl implores her father to "put the bottle down." As these examples show, substance abuse tends to be connected to physical violence in popular culture and less so to other forms.

PSYCHOLOGICAL THEORIES

Psychological explanations for domestic abuse and rape are common, both in academic literature and in popular culture depictions. Most of these focus on mental illness specifically. As Rafter (2000) noted, "Films reinforce a close association between mental illness and crime, despite the fact that the mentally ill are more likely to be victimized than to offend" (p. 63). Classic horror films like *Psycho* and the *Halloween* and *Friday the 13th* series, all depict mentally ill mass and serial murderers. Danny Wedding, one of the authors of *Movies and Mental Illness: Using Films to Understand Psychopathology*, notes that horror films like *The Shining* and *Nightmare on Elm Street* often show mentally ill characters violently raping and killing people, including their own families (Suzdaltsev, 2014).

Gleason (2015) noted that while 40 percent of prime-time "normal" characters are violent, 73 percent of characters with a mental illness are violent. One of the most iconic depiction of the rapist and abuser as mentally ill is *American Psycho*, both in the film adaptation released in 2000 and in the original book. Female perpetrators in films like *Fatal Attraction* and *Misery* are shown as suffering from obsessive compulsive disorder, bipolar disorder, or borderline personality disorder.

Female victims are often depicted in ways that suggest mental illness, which is in keeping with reality. Twice as many characters with mental illness on prime-time television are victims of violent crime (Gleason, 2015). Studies have shown that women suffering from mental illness are two to three times more likely to endure domestic abuse, and 69 percent of those with the most severe mental illness had been abused by a partner (Staff Reporter, 2015).Even women who fight back tend to utilize some type of mental illness explanation, most commonly, battered woman's syndrome, which became popularized after the release of the film

The Burning Bed, which depicted the true story of Francine Hughes. For instance, Noh, Lee, and Felty (2010) found that such medicalized explanation for women who kill abusers were included in 39 percent of the articles they analyzed.

In regard to rape, however, popular culture has not taken this approach, generally. This is despite data showing that of women with severe mental disorders, 40 percent had been the victim of rape or an attempted rape, compared to 7 percent of the population in the United Kingdom (Grant, 2014).

Even mental health professionals are often the subject of stereotypical portrayals. Wedding cites movies like *Silence of the Lambs, The Prince of Tides*, and *Tin Cup*, which show psychiatrists as unethical, foolish, or even murderers.

While there are indeed some abusers who struggle with various mental illnesses, as a whole there is no evidence that a particular type of mental illness results in abuse (Sackett & Saunders, 1999), although there have been some studies linking domestic violence to personality disorders such as antisocial, borderline, dependent, depressed, and narcisstic (Hamberger & Hastings, 1986). In fact, advocates argue that it is dangerous to depict abusers as mentally ill, as that may absolve them from taking responsibility for their actions. Likewise, victims who believe that their abuser is mentally ill may justify his or her actions and may consequently remain in unsafe relationships. Taylor Swift's "Dear John" implies that the offender has a sickness, noting his manipulation and "sick need," showing that abusers will use this logic and victims often believe it.

Perhaps the most common explanation for domestic violence is that abusers are unable to control their anger. Many people mistakenly believe that domestic abuse is caused by anger. That is, abusers must have problems with anger control and thus need to develop anger management strategies. Courts often operate on this premise, assigning abusers to attend anger management courses as a condition of their sentence. Given that domestic violence is not really an anger control issue, however, this intervention has had limited effectiveness in changing abusers' behavior. Advocates argue that abusers very much control their anger; that is, they select whom they will "take it out on," in what ways, under what circumstances, and who will witness it. As evidence of the fact that abusers generally can control their anger in other settings, advocates point out that most do not get in trouble for acting out at work, with peers, or in other situations. In fact, many people find it hard to believe that abusers are really hurting their partners because they often put on public a "nice guy" face. As Lundy Bancroft and many others have noted, while victims are often not believed or supported, abusers tend to receive a lot of support, both in real life and in popular culture.

CHOICE THEORIES

Choice-related theories remain among the most popular in criminology. These perspectives emerged during the Enlightenment era as a challenge to previous explanations of crime that focused on demonic possession. Philosophers and others began to see that individuals have free will and consequently developed theories that focused on the idea that people choose to commit offenses much like they choose to engage in other behaviors. Philosophers Cesare Beccaria (1738–1794) and Jeremy Bentham (1748–1832) are largely credited with founding the classical school of criminology.

Rational choice theory was offered first by Derek Cornish and Ronald Clarke. It is based on the idea that people are self-interested and seek to maximize benefits and minimize costs. They thus make a conscious decision to engage in crime after weighing out what they perceive to be the costs and benefits. Similarly, routine activity theory by Lawrence Cohen and Marcus Felson, focuses on crime as a choice, but it adds the element of opportunity. Specifically, routine activity theory maintains that crime occurs when three conditions are met: (1) a motivated offender, (2) a suitable target, and (3) the absence of capable guardians. Cohen and Felson described a suitable target as something of value to the offender that he or she is physically capable of acquiring or attacking. Security guards, police, or guard dogs might be capable guardians, but it could also be a physical device like a lock, security system, alarm, or something else. Seductions of crime theory, promoted by Jack Katz, maintained that the thrill or rush of crime has to be considered when one discusses what an offender perceives as benefits. Studies tend to lend support for rational choice explanations for property crimes and for explaining white-collar offenses, as numerous studies have found that these largely educated, middle- or upper-class offenders clearly have the capacity to make rational choices. Research in the 1980s by Sherman and Berk (1984) seemed to support a rational choice perspective. As such, it was concluded that the threat of legal sanctions would deter men from committing potential offences, which lead to mandatory arrest laws in 15 states in the United States (O'Grady, 2007), despite the fact that other researchers could not replicate the original findings and later studies in the United States actually contradicted them. Sherman (1992) concluded that arrests had no impact on reducing crime in repeat domestic offences. In fact, in some cases, in particular among unemployed and/or unmarried offenders, or those who generally lack a stake in conformity, arrests increased incidences of re-offending (O'Grady, 2007).

Another type of choice theory is seductions of crime. Jack Katz maintains that, when determining whether the benefits of a particular crime outweigh the costs, offenders also consider the risk and excitement, what he called the "sneaky thrill" of committing the act. He studied property and violent offenders and found most got a rush out of their actions. This could well be the case with domestic abusers, who feel more powerful as they continue to control their victims. And it surely is the case with some rapists, mostly strangers, who select victims who appear vulnerable.

These individual explanations sometimes result in the ownership for crime prevention being placed on the potential victims, in particular in the cases of domestic violence and rape. As has been previously discussed, victims are often told that they should take any number of measures so as not to be victimized. Women should avoid saying, doing, or wearing certain things, and if they are victimized, they should struggle violently or it won't be perceived as "real rape" or "real domestic violence."

While choice theories do not seem to be dominant in coverage of domestic violence, they do sometimes appear in popular culture depictions of rape. For instance, TV shows and films may show rapists purposely plying their victims with excessive quantities of alcohol, which in some ways implies their offending is a deliberate choice. Depictions of stranger rapists are most likely to use routine activity theory, as they emphasize that victims are selected because they were viewed as an "opportunity" without sufficient guardianship. Women walking alone, for instance, are depicted as making themselves vulnerable to the possibility of rape.

LEARNING THEORIES

As the title would suggest, learning theories focus on the fact that crime, like any other behavior, is learned from one's environment. Edwin Sutherland's differential association theory argues that crime is learned from people with whom we have frequent, intense, and priority relationships. The primary source of this learning, then, is our family, followed by peers (in particular in adolescence). Sutherland asserted that offenders learn not only the motivation to commit a particular crime but also how to do so. These ideas gained popularity in the 1960s with the experiments conducted by Albert Bandura. Bandura showed that children exposed to violent modeling were prone to engage in violent behavior, in particular when it was reinforced or not sanctioned.

Daniel Glaser's differential identification theory added an important element to the notion that crime is learned. Glaser maintained that offenders may learn crime not only from those with whom they are in physical proximity but also from persons with whom they identify. That might include historical or fictional characters.

Advocates generally promote the notion that domestic violence and rape are learned behaviors. They note the studies, many of which were included in Chapter 1, showing the increased risk of offending for those who grow up in abusive homes. For instance, in his study of 25 male domestic violence offenders, Rahmatian (2009) found that 16, or 64 percent, had a family member who had been a victim of domestic violence. The same percentage of female victims cited having a family member who had been a victim. Wareham, Boots, and Chavez (2009) studied 204 male batterers in a court-appointed program. They found that the men were more likely to engage in verbal or physical abuse the more that they observed their close friends and family doing so. Moreover, the men who were more frequent media consumers were more likely to engage in verbally abusive behaviors.

As noted in Chapter 1, popular culture often focuses on what child witnesses to domestic violence learn and how it might shape their future behavior. Lucinda Williams's "He Never Got Enough Love" uses learning theory, claiming that being abandoned and neglected, and constantly told he was no good was what created a criminal. The song begins with mama running off and daddy drinking. Dad tells his son, "You'll never do anything right." Williams laments that the boy "never got enough love" so the things he understood were "the screams and the bruises and the broken bottles." He ultimately proved his daddy right by shooting and killing someone during a robbery.

SOCIOLOGICAL THEORIES

Sociological explanations for crime look past individuals to describe the institutional and societal factors that may be important. Berns (1999) calls this "the cultural/structural frame of responsibility," which focuses on social factors that encourage or tolerate violence. One category of sociological theories focuses on strain, or the disjuncture between the measures of success in the United States and one's actual ability to obtain it. Merton's strain theory posits that people in the United States are "marketed" the American Dream but not all equally are situated to achieve it. People will then respond using one of five adaptations. Conformists simply stay the course, doing the right thing although perhaps never becoming successful. Ritualists often end up overworked and emotionally drained from trying to achieve an impossible dream. Entrepreneurs look for innovative, often illegal, means to obtain monetary or other forms of success, while rebels reject the goal completely. Finally, retreatists are societal dropouts, often hardcore addicts or entrenched homeless. They no longer try to achieve success. A more recent theory offered by Agnew (1992) called general strain theory "argues that strains or stressors increase the likelihood of negative emotions like anger and frustration. These emotions create pressure for corrective action, and crime is one possible response" (p. 319). The more noxious stimuli one is exposed to, the more likely it is that he or she will feel strain that may prompt criminal behavior. Noxious stimuli include people, odors, sounds, and much more.

While a lot of dramas focus on these depictions, showing poverty as a source of strain that might induce illegal activity, it is not very common in depictions of domestic violence and rape. As has been noted, in large part, the focus is on the victim's precipitating behaviors and not on presenting the background of abusers and assailants. This is a bit odd, given that studies have indicated that economic stressors dramatically escalate abuse. The National Institute of Justice cites studies identifying that violence was more than three times higher for couples experiencing high levels of financial strain compared to those experience lower levels of financial strain. Abuser unemployment also increases the risk of abuse (Economic Distress and Intimate Partner Violence, 2009).

Sykes and Matza's techniques of neutralization theory says that offenders use mental techniques to rationalize or justify their behavior. They do this both in advance of perpetrating and to assuage any sense of guilt or accountability thereafter. Common techniques of neutralization include denying responsibility, denying the victim, denying injury, appealing to higher loyalties, and condemning the condemners. This explanation is promoted widely in popular culture, as it is perhaps the most connected to victim-blaming. Abusers and rapists claim they are not to be blamed when a woman acted flirtatiously, or when their wife said something that upset them and they subsequently attacked her. As described in the Introduction, one of the types of popular culture that clearly presents offenders as rationalizing or neutralizing their behavior is professional wrestling, what has been called the "soap opera for men." Male characters tell audiences that "she had it coming" and "she deserved it" before they appear to violently assault female characters. Announcers accuse the women of "liking it" when a male character violently kisses them.

FEMINIST THEORIES

Freedman (2003) defines "feminism" as "a belief that women and men are inherently of equal worth" (p. 7), while sociologist Michael Kimmel (2008) explains feminism more boldly, proclaiming that it "dares to imagine that women can be whole people, embracing and expressing ambition and kindness, competence and compassion. And feminism dares to expect more from men. Feminism expects a man to be ethical, emotionally present, and accountable to his values in his actions with women—as well as with other men" (p. 264). Although there are multiple types of feminists, most are critical of patriarchal societies, or those that are male-dominated.

Before the 1970s, domestic violence and rape were not a real focus for criminologists. It was, as some have said, a "virtual conspiracy of silence" around these issues (Clark & Lewis, 1977, p. 26). Feminist sociology and criminology emerged as a challenge to the androcentrism of the field (Shantz, 2012). Historically, scholars and researchers were almost exclusively male, studied male offenders, and tried to explain male criminality. As such, they paid little attention to crimes like domestic violence and rape, which disproportionately impact women and girls. Even critical theorists from the Marxist tradition did little to address domestic violence and rape, although their focus on macro-level political and economic structures provides some framework for understanding the devaluing of women that feminist theorists propose as a root cause for abuse and assault. Anarchist theories, which generally condemn the state, typically view the domestic realm as private and thus ignore abuse and assault as well. Anarchist feminist Emma Goldman did make connections between moral regulations imposed by the state and by religion and the oppression of women and domestic violence. Goldman also identified economic inequality for women and the dependent relationship of many marriages as important factors in explaining domestic violence (Shantz, 2012). Critical feminist theorists today continue to see domestic violence and rape as being related to the social and economic exclusion of women. Further, societal patriarchy results in males having security at home as well as outside of it. Male dominance is reinforced by societal structures, institutions, and ideologies that remain deeply pervasive. Johnson (2005) defines "patriarchy" as "a social system in which men disproportionately occupy positions of power and authority, central norms and values are associated with manhood and masculinity (which in turn are defined in terms of dominance and control), and men are the primary focus of attention in most cultural spaces" (p. 4).

Feminist thought helped usher in efforts to help victims. In the 1980s, the Duluth Model was created by feminists in Minnesota to help explain abuse, protect victims, and hold batterers accountable. It still serves as the template for most domestic violence shelters and services and for many batterer intervention programs. The Duluth Model emphasizes that abuse is about power and control and, in its original iteration particularly, reflected feminist understanding of the ways that men in a patriarchal society use their privilege to obtain and maintain it.

Feminists are concerned with gender role norms that are binary in nature. That is, the narrow definition of masculinity as something powerful, controlling, and aggressive while femininity is perceived as soft, nurturing, and emotional. Such dichotomies serve to reinforce men's superiority with women, and are thus clearly connected with violence against them. Cuklanz (2000) argues that rape depictions generally serve to reinforce these gender role norms, as they often feature a hypermasculine offender, a somehow weak woman, and a heroic male savior or avenger. Most often, it is a male detective who triumphs, meaning finds the assailant. The revictimization of the trial and the victim's healing are rarely shown, as is documented in Chapters 5 and 6.

The 1993 biopic *What's Love Got to Do with It* tells the story of musician Ike Turner's abuse of his wife, fellow musician Tina Turner, born Anna Mae. Shoos (2003) maintains that the film does better than most at capturing the complexities of abusive relationships. It shows battering "not as an involuntary or aberrant reaction to stress or anger, but as one point along an extended continuum of male dominance. Similarly, the film does not focus solely on instances of physical violence but situates these along an ever-escalating trajectory of abuse that includes a broad range of controlling behaviors that exert their own psychological damage" (p. 65). Further, "What's Love counters the myth that domestic violence is an individual pathology and identifies it instead as the product of a set of culturally sanctioned attitudes about men and women, attitudes supported on multiples levels by a range of institutions, including popular culture" (Shoos, 2003, p. 67). In sum, though, few examples of a feminist explanation for domestic violence and rape can be found in popular culture.

REFERENCES

Agnew, R. (1992). Foundation for a General Strain Theory of crime and delinquency. *Criminology, 30*(1), 47–87.

Bancroft, L. (2003). *Why does he do that? Inside the minds of angry and controlling men*. New York: Berkley.

Barrile, L. (1986). Television's "bogeyclass"? Status, motives and violence in crime drama characters. *Sociological Viewpoints, 2*(1), 39–56.

Berns, N. (2001). Degendering the problem and gendering the blame: Political discourse on women's violence. *Gender & Society, 15*(2), 262–281.

Berns, N. (1999). My problem and how I solved it: Domestic violence in women's magazines. *Sociological Quarterly, 40*(1), 85–108.

Brookoff, D., O'Brien, K., Cook, C., Thompson, T., & Williams, C. (1997). Characteristics of participants in domestic violence: Assessment at the scene of domestic assault. *JAMA: The Journal of the American Medical Association, 277*(17), 1369–1373.

Cavender, G., & Bond-Maupin, L. (1993). Fear and loathing in reality television: An analysis of *America's Most Wanted* and *Unsolved Mysteries. Sociological Inquiry, 63*(1), 305–316.

Clark, L., & Lewis, D. (1977). Rape: The price of coercive sexuality. Toronto: Women's Press.

Cuklanz, L. (2000). *Rape on prime-time: Television, masculinity and sexual violence.* Philadelphia: University of Pennsylvania Press.

Economic distress and intimate partner violence. (2009). National Institute of Justice. Retrieved January 24, 2016, from http://www.nij.gov/topics/crime/intimate-partner-violence/pages/economic-distress.aspx

Estep, R., & MacDonald, P. (1983). How prime-time crime evolved on TV, 1976 to 1981. *Journalism Quarterly, 60*(2), 293–330.

Fabianic, D. (1997). Television dramas and homicide causation. *Journal of Criminal Justice, 25*(3), 195–203.

Fals Stewart, W. (2003). The occurrence of partner physical aggression on days of alcohol consumption: A longitudinal diary study. *Journal of Consulting and Clinical Psychology, 71*(1), 41–52.

Finley, L. (Ed.). (2013). *Encyclopedia of domestic violence and abuse.* Santa Barbara, CA: ABC-CLIO.

Freedman, E. (2003). *No turning back: The history of feminism and the future of women.* New York: Ballantine.

Gleason, M. (2015). "Crazy eyes" and how pop culture portrays mental illness. Mental Health Association of Oklahoma. Retrieved October 25, 2015, from http://mhaok.org/how-pop-culture-portrays-mental-illness/

Goddard, H. (1912). *The Kallikak family: A study in the heredity of feeble mindedness.* New York: Macmillan.

Grant, P. (2014). Mental illness and sexual abuse: The shocking link. *The Guardian.* Retrieved October 25, 2015, from http://www.theguardian.com/science/occams-corner/2014/sep/04/mental-illness-sexual-abuse-rape-victim

Hamberger, L., & Hastings, J. (1986). Personality correlates of men who abuse their partners: A cross validation study. *Journal of Family Violence, 63*(1), 232–241.

Johnson, A. (2005). *The gender knot: Unraveling our patriarchal legacy,* 2nd ed. Philadelphia: Temple University Press.

Kimmel, M. (2008). *Guyland: The perilous world where boys become men.* New York: HarperCollins.

Kyriacou, D., Anglin, D., Taliaferro, E., Stone, S., Tubb, T., Linden, J. A., Muelleman, R., Barton, E., & Kraus, J. F. (1999). Risk factors for injury to women from domestic violence. *New England Journal of Medicine, 341*(25), 1892–1898.

Moss, C. (2015, June 29). Are men's lives ruled by testosterone? *The Telegraph.* Retrieved September 14, 2015, from http://www.telegraph.co.uk/men/thinking-man/11701933/Are-mens-lives-ruled-by-testosterone.html

Noh, M., Lee., M., & Felty, K. (2010). Mad, bad or reasonable? Newspaper portrayals of the battered woman who kills. *Gender Issues, 27*(3), 110–130.

O'Grady, W. (2007). *Crime in Canadian context: Debates and controversies.* Toronto: Oxford University Press.

Pope, H., Kouri, E., & Hudson, J. (2000). Effects of supraphysiological doses of testosterone on mood and aggression in normal men: A randomized controlled trial. *Archives of General Psychiatry, 57*(2), 155–156.

Rafter, N. (2000). *Shots in the mirror: Crime films and society.* New York: Oxford.

Rahmatian, A. (2009). Breaking down the social learning of domestic violence. *Iranian Journal of Psychiatry and Behavioral Sciences, 3*(1), 62–66.

Raine, A. (2013). *The anatomy of violence: The biological roots of crime.* New York: Vintage.

Rosenbaum, A., Abend, S., Gearan, P., Fletcher, K., Raine, A., Brennan, P., et al. (1997). *Biosocial bases of violence.* New York: Plenum Press.

Rosenbaum, A., & Hoge, S. (1989). Head injury and marital aggression. *American Journal of Psychiatry, 146*(8), 1048–1051.

Rosenbaum, A., Hoge, S., Adelman, S. A., Warnken, W., Fletcher, K., & Kane, R. (1994). Head injury in partner-abusive men. *Journal of Consulting and Clinical Psychology, 62*(6), 1187–1193.

Sackett, L., & Saunders, D. (1999). The impact of different forms of psychological abuse on battered women. *Violence and Victims, 14*(1), 105–117.

Shantz, J. (2012). *Crime/punishment/power: Sociological explanations.* Dubuque: Kendall Hunt.

Sherman, L. (1992). *Policing domestic violence: Experiments and dilemmas.* New York: Free Press.

Sherman, L., & Berk, S. (1984). The specific deterrent effects of arrest for domestic assault. *American Sociological Review, 49,* 261–272.

Shoos, D. (2003). Representing domestic violence: Ambivalence and difference in *What's Love Got to Do with It. NWSA Journal, 15*(2), 57–77.

Soulliere, D. (2003). Prime-time murder: Presentations of murder on popular television justice programs. *Journal of Criminal Justice and Popular Culture, 10*(1), 12–38.

Staff Reporter. (2014). Study finds link between mental illness and sexual assault. *Nature World News.* Retrieved October 25, 2015, from http://www

.natureworldnews.com/articles/8889/20140905/study-finds-link-between
-mental-illness-sexual-assault.htm

Suzdaltsev, J. (2014). We spoke to a psychologist about Hollywood's depiction of mental illness. *Vice*. Retrieved October 25, 2015, from http://www.vice .com/read/hollywood-sucks-at-portraying-mental-illness

U.S. Department of Health and Human Services. (2006, August). Traumatic brain injury screening: An introduction. Retrieved June 23, 2012, from https://tbitac.norc.org/download/screeninginstruments.pdf

Voumvakis, S., & Ericson, R. (1984). *News accounts of attacks on women: A comparison of three Toronto newspapers.* Toronto: Centre of Criminology.

Wareham, J., Boots, D., & Chavez, J. (2009). Test of social learning and intergenerational transmission among batterers. *Journal of Criminal Justice, 37*(2), 163–173.

Calling the Cops and a Day in Court: Depictions of Criminal Justice Responses

One of the main problems related to criminal justice responses is the fact that laws and public policies continue to reflect myths and misconceptions about abuse and assault. This chapter begins from that framework. It then addresses how victims of sexual assault and domestic violence are typically encouraged to contact law enforcement and thus to allow the criminal justice system to hold perpetrators accountable. Victims often report that the system is not very helpful and, in actuality, may be a source of revictimization. Much of popular culture is devoted to showing the responses by the criminal justice system, from police to prosecutors, judges, and juries, as well as occasionally the correctional system. While sometimes these depictions critique the system, more often than not they present it as still the best, if not only, choice for victims. Noh, Lee, and Felty (2010) argue that certain stereotypes of battered women, some of which are disseminated by the media, can affect how they are treated by the criminal justice system and by other social service agencies. Such treatment is a result of the expectations that are held about the behavior of battered women. Noh et al. (2010) also argue that secondary claims makers, such as newspapers, have more influence over what details of the situation are accepted as truth than primary claims makers (the battered woman; Martin, 2013).

Harding (2015) points out several recent examples in which policies were based on rape myths. Sadly, this is just a smattering of the many examples. On August 12, 2014, Missouri representative Todd Akin made a name for himself by making one of the most asinine comments ever.

Akin claimed that "If it's a legitimate rape, the female body has a way of shutting that whole thing down." But, as Harding (2015) notes, Akin is far from the only politicians to make such ridiculous claims. In 2011, 214 Republicans sponsored a bill called the No Taxpayer Funding for Abortion Act, which specified that exceptions would only be allowed for victims of "forcible rape," as opposed to those "gray" rapes. Similarly, Indiana Republican senate candidate Richard Mourdock claimed that God intended for rapes to happen, while former GOP presidential candidate Rick Santorum told Piers Morgan that he believes that pregnancies resulting from rape are still a gift from God. Eventually President Obama made a statement acknowledging that rape is rape and it's a crime, but not before all of these blowhards were given ample opportunity to spew such nonsense.

RESTRAINING ORDERS

One legal option for victims of domestic violence, sexual assault, and, in some states, dating violence is to apply for restraining or orders of protection against their abusers or assailants. While this is often encouraged as a way to create documentation of abuse and to hopefully deter abusers or assailants, in reality the results are mixed. Research suggests that abusers with stakes in the community—generally those who are middle class at least and who are employed—are inclined to comply with the restraining orders while others who perceive little to lose often do not. Klein and colleagues (2013) examined the effectiveness of orders of protection against juvenile perpetrators of dating violence. They found that in the first two full years after New York's Order of Protection (OP) expansion, only 1,200 teens petitioned New York family courts for civil orders for dating violence against 1,205 different respondents. Given even the lowest estimates of the extent of teen dating violence, this represents a very small portion of the teen dating violence victims across New York. Surveys of at-risk youth about their knowledge of the new law allowing juveniles to petition for dating violence OPs revealed that most were not very aware of this possibility. Less than 10 percent of the youth who petitioned for protection orders had been involved with police, although research is clear that police referrals are a major source of OPs for adults. Focus group data did not reveal that schools were filling in the gaps. More than 90 percent of the petitioners were females against males, and two-thirds were younger than their assailants. The mean age difference was 2.92 years, resulting in most of the petitioners being teens while the abusers were on average 20.9 years old.

Harassment and assault were the two most commonly cited reasons for the OP petition. A smaller number involved sexual allegations, most of which were repeated. Youth who petitioned were moved to do so based on repeated and escalating violence. While some had parents or other caring adults who encouraged them to seek the OP, most lacked such an individual, and most domestic violence or youth-focused agencies did not provide support during the OP petition process. Youth reported being overwhelmed by the court processes and finding them not well-structured to support youth petitioners.

The reabuse rate for those against whom someone had an OP was 27–28 percent, although less than 10 percent were charged with violating the OP. That is a much lower rate than among domestic violence OPs. Those who were older, had a child in common, and had a prior criminal history were more likely to reabuse.

Youth identified a number of barriers to obtaining OPs. Many are fearful of their effectiveness, whether it would affect their friends' perceptions of them (including the risk of being branded a snitch), and their accessibility. Youth who had obtained an OP expressed that they lost far more than just their boyfriend; they tended to lose friends as well. In general, studies have found that 30 to 77 percent of OPs for domestic violence are not violated (Logan & Walker, 2011), and victims report less fear after they have obtained an OP.

Logan and Walker (2011) studied the effectiveness of civil protection orders in rural areas. They note that while overall rates of domestic violence may be similar between rural and urban areas, homicide rates among intimate partners are higher among rural couples. This is likely related to poverty, unemployment, lack of educational and social service resources, and more conservative gender roles and policies, among other factors. Research suggests that rural women may face a host of barriers in seeking to obtain OPs, including bureaucracy, physical distance, and negative, blaming attitudes. In their study of rural Central Appalachia, Kentucky, they found that victims were more likely to be unemployed than were urban victims, and had longer relationships and more children with their abusers. A total of 213 women were interviewed approximately three weeks after having received their OP. Only half indicated that the order was not violated, a rate similar to that of the comparable urban women. Even among those whose orders were violated, however, there appeared to be a reduction in the violence and harassment they endured. In all, 86 percent of the rural and 87 percent of the urban women felt the OP was effective. Rural women reported a far lesser decline in their feelings of fear of future harm than did the urban women, however. Logan and Walker found data to indicate that urban police are more likely to arrest those who violate the OP, as 56 percent of the urban offenders had a specific domestic violence charge after violation compared to just 6 percent of the rural offenders.

Data are clear that sometimes the restraining order or protection order makes matters worse. Abusers who are committed to controlling victims by any means possible don't always appreciate being served with paperwork telling them they can have no contact. Some become enraged, which is why it is not unusual to read about violent attacks and even homicides immediately after a victim files for an OP.

Popular culture does not focus much on the option of restraining orders, although for a time in the mid-2000s there was a show with that title. The 1989 Lifetime movie *A Cry for Help: The Tracey Thurman Story* shows an abuser who is enraged when his wife obtains a restraining order against him. It was based on the real story of Tracey Thurman, who won a lawsuit against Connecticut police for their inadequate response to the physical abuse she endured from her husband, Buck. At one point Buck kidnaps their son and the police tell Tracey she can get him back if she agrees to return to her husband. He stabs her multiple times, with neighbors and police as witness, and no one intervenes. Tracey was awarded $2,300,000, and the case prompted greater attention to police response to domestic violence.

In 1994, Lifetime aired *Cries Unheard: The Donna Yaklich Story*. Donna's husband Dennis is a handsome and charming police officer, but he has a much darker side. As he gets deeper into steroid use and weightlifting, he becomes increasingly aggressive toward Donna, who is unsure where to turn because of Dennis's work. Even though he promises never to hurt her after Donna tells him she is pregnant, the abuse continues. When she tries to leave with their child, Dennis rapes her. She escapes to a domestic violence shelter but he finds her there as well and threatens to kill her. Donna sees no way out and ends up paying someone to murder Dennis. She is convicted of conspiracy to commit first-degree murder and is sentenced to 40 years in prison. The real Donna was released in 2009 after serving 18 years. Although the film was widely criticized for sensationalizing the issue, it did help call attention to police-perpetrated abuse.

Less than a decade later, the courts were again grappling with the issue of police refusal to enforce restraining orders. After years of abuse, on May 21, 1999, Jessica Gonzales obtained a temporary restraining order that restricted Simon Gonzales from her home and her three daughters and ordered him to remain at least 100 yards from it at all times unless in a supervised visit. Simon continued to harass Jessica and the girls so the temporary order was made permanent in June 1999. On June 22, 1999, in violation of the restraining order, Simon Gonzales abducted his three daughters and their friend from the street outside of Jessica's home. Over the next 10 hours she called and visited the Castle Rock police, growing increasingly frantic that Simon would do something horrible to the girls. At approximately 3:15 a.m., Simon Gonzales drove up and parked outside of the police station. After sitting for approximately 15 minutes, he began shooting at the station. Police returned fire and Simon was killed. They then discovered the bodies of Leslie, Katheryn, and Rebecca in the back of Simon's truck. All had been shot to death. Jessica filed suit, alleging that the police violated her rights. In 2005, the U.S. Supreme Court ruled that they did not, explaining that the wording of the law in Colorado did not compel the police to enforce restraining orders. Jessica and her lawyers then took the case before the Inter-American Commission on Human Rights, which ruled that the U.S. Supreme Court erred and that Jessica's human rights had been violated.

More recently, several television shows have depicted victims obtaining restraining orders, although they do not focus on the process or the enforcement. Tyler Perry's *For Better or Worse* and *Samantha Who* both included restraining orders in their plots. The Eels (2003) song "Restraining Order Blues" is from the perspective of the man served, who claims "Everybody knows that I'm not a violent man," and "I made mistakes. Everyone does." Alex Flinn's *Breathing Underwater* begins when Caitlyn is before a judge, seeking a restraining order against her boyfriend, Nick. As he attends a court-mandated family violence class he writes in a journal, describing how he came to abuse Caitlyn. He also violates the order by contacting her several times, which is typical.

POLICE RESPONSE

Prior to the 1970s, the common response of officers called to domestic violence situations was to avoid arrests. Most states had laws that made it impossible to arrest offenders if the officer did not witness the assault. The Victim's Rights Movement of the 1970s called for stronger responses and, coupled with a study by Sherman and Berk (1984) that suggested arrest would be a deterrent for abusers, led to the passage of mandatory arrest policies. It was believed that the mandates would help standardize responses to domestic violence and ensure protection of female victims. Mandatory arrest laws state that an officer must take action and make an arrest if there is probable cause to believe that an offense has been committed, per the state statute that defines domestic violence.

Advocates of mandatory arrest argue that victims of domestic violence are afraid to cooperate with police or are too helpless to make an appropriate decision at a time of great stress. Proponents aimed to remove police discretion in the arrest decision since police were often reluctant to make arrests for domestic violence because it was considered a private matter and because many officers felt as though responding to these calls was a waste of time since the abusers often reoffend. Those opposed to mandatory arrest policies believed that mandatory arrest policies put victims in great danger of retaliation from their partners and disempower victims. Sometimes officers are faced with an ambiguous situation in terms of who is the offender and who is the victim, and thus the officer may be forced to make a dual arrest. While the intent of these new mandates was out of concern for the victim, mandatory arrest policies have inadvertently produced an increase in the number of victims arrested in domestic violence cases. An unintended consequence of mandatory arrest policies has been an increase in the number of women arrested for domestic violence when their behavior is defensive rather than aggressive. Sherman and Harris (2015) found that victims were 64 percent more likely to have died of all causes if their partners were arrested and jailed than if warned and allowed to remain at home, suggesting that arrest is not an effective deterrent but instead may escalate the abuse.

There are many reasons why women who are subjected to abuse choose not to engage the police to intervene on their behalf. First, women may not want to subject their partners to automatic arrest and prosecution. Women also choose not to engage the police because their opinion as to what would be the safest option for them and what would lead to the best outcome for them is often ignored. In some instances, separating from the abuser can be extremely dangerous. Women will choose not to engage the police because they believe it is the best way to ensure their safety. Another reason women may not want involve the criminal justice system is because such an action could result in diminishing the family income, loss of a parenting partner, and loss of an intimate partner. When women who are subjected to abuse are able to make their own decisions about how to respond to the abuse, they may be more satisfied with the results and the violence to which they are subjected is likely to decrease (Filipovic, 2014).

Further, despite decades of attention to the issue, training of officers, and resources provided, police still sometimes fail to respond to domestic violence situations appropriately. They may arrive far too slowly to a situation and thus allow the abuse to escalate, or upon arrival may fail to separate the parties or to investigate thoroughly. Given that abusers are controlling and manipulative, police officers must take care not to allow the offender to talk his or her way out of the situation.

Rape stories in TV and films of the 1970s and 1980s generally depicted crazy offenders with hero police officers. Detectives were avengers against rape, which was typically stranger-perpetrated and especially violent (Cuklanz & Moorti, 2006). This made the victims themselves little more than bit players. Later shows like *The Wire* and *The Shield* present a more complex view of rape, yet still focus more on detectives than on victims. Critics note that TV still does this poorly. Ray McKinnon, creator of Sundance's *Rectify*, which focuses on the aftermath of various traumas, has commented that victims' stories are often told backward, as investigators begin with a dead body or an assault victim and weave pieces together to identify what happened. McKinnon explained, "It takes away from the individuality of the victim, and a lot of it came on the edge of questionable titillation."

Although NBC's *Law & Order: Special Victims Unit* (*SVU*) is supposed to be devoted to sexual crimes, Cuklanz and Moorti (2006) found that the story lines of episodes often condemn the actions of female victims, and they do so typically through the police characters. Similarly, Alcid (2013) commented that while some people are happy to see a show like *SVU* devoted to this important topic, the experience of rape victims in reality is far different from the glorified version presented on the show. The show features far more than the estimated 2 to 8 percent of false accusations and overrepresents stranger-perpetrated rape. Harding (2015) notes that Ice-T's character Tutuola is perhaps the worst, but the other three male detectives also blunder often. In one 2010 episode, named "Gray," the four detectives, who are all allegedly experienced and specialized in sex crimes, are discussing a college student who reported rape and whether it was her fault because she was so drunk and then blame her because she went to his apartment, In another episode called "Closure," Stabler, Tutuola, and Captain Donald Cragen noted that a rape victim's story is open for interpretation because she was drunk and had been flirting, therefore it was likely "a case of buyer's remorse." Detectives on primetime often make comments like "She went and got herself raped."

Tracy Chapman's "Behind the Wall" is haunting, both in its lyrics and in the performance, which features only Chapman's soulful voice with no instrumentals. It tells the story of a neighbor who hears the abuse and sees the police do nothing. It also depicts the failure of police to respond, noting

> The police always come late
> If they come at all
> And when they arrive
> They say they can't interfere
> With domestic affairs
> Between a man and his wife.

The system's responses tend to be even more problematic for marginalized groups like those in the lesbian, gay, bisexual, and transgender (LGBT) community. As Kramer (1998) explained, "any discussion of how the criminal justice system can best cope with cases of same-sex rape must take into anti-gay bias into consideration" (p. 311). One study by the National Coalition of Anti-Violence Projects (2011) found that in 55 percent of cases, LGBT victims of domestic violence and sexual violence were denied OPs, a rate far higher than for non-LGBT victims. Studies have also found that people are more likely to attribute blame to gay survivors than to heterosexual male survivors. The same is true for lesbians, although to a lesser degree (Wakelin & Long, 2003). Following this, Guadalupe-Diaz (2015) notes, "Homophobic stereotyping may lead lawyers, judges, and juries to attribute much more responsibility to victims of same-sex violence by assuming that the victim wanted or deserved the assault" (pp. 186–87).

In cases of LBGT domestic violence, the police may struggle with determining which individual is the victim. Due to their contentious history with law enforcement and other governmental institutions, gay and lesbian individuals may avoid reporting victimization or minimize the seriousness of an incident when police are called. Same-sex couples experience intimate partner violence at a more frequent rate than heterosexual couples, and face unique challenges when reporting incidents to responding officers. One reason for not reporting is that the batterer may tell the police that either the victim was also abusive or the victim instigated the altercation.

An episode of *SVU* called "Gray" features a campus rape, a topic that has garnered a lot of attention in recent years as the Department of Education is investigating 143 campuses for their inadequate response to sexual assault allegations as of May 19, 2015 (Kingkade, 2015). That episode irked a number of sexual assault advocates, who noted that campus officials gave police confidential information and that a prosecutor actually used the term "gray rape" to describe the situation. Not once did anyone in the episode mention a sexual assault crisis center or counselor to the victim (REACTION to "Law & Order: SVU" titled "Gray," n.d.)

In 2013, *SVU* aired an episode called "Girl Dishonored" about a woman who was gang-raped at a fraternity party. *SVU* producers uncovered the fact that the school had been covering up sexual assault reports and claimed to have been inspired by the Department of Education's investigations.

Anderson (2010) comments about the show *SVU*:

> Not only are *SVU*'s cases strange anomalies, but often the detectives' handling of the cases are rather absurd. In New York City, hospitals are legally

prohibited from reporting a sexual assault to the police against the victim's wishes (unless a weapon was used in the attack). Yet time and again on *SVU*, the detectives are called in without the victim's permission. What is worse, even after a victim has turned them away, Detectives Olivia Benson (Mariska Hargitay) and Elliot Stabler (Christopher Meloni) will open an investigation, follow the victim to her home, park outside her front door and refuse to leave until she agrees to cooperate (such was their conduct in "Behave," a Season Twelve episode featuring Jennifer Love Hewitt). This would be a gross breach of protocol in real life, and this misrepresentation of reality is dangerous. How many victims will opt to stay home rather than seek medical treatment or counseling because television has them convinced that seeking help means having to report?

Harding (2015) explains that police are often not only poor resources for victims but actually part of the problem. When three women who had been assaulted by Pittsburgh Steelers quarterback Ben Roethlisberger at a club left, they encountered Sergeant Jerry Blash, who, according to Harding (2015), actually posed for a picture with the star earlier that night. Blash evidently went straight to a party Roethlisberger was attending and told him the women had accused him, describing them in crude and dismissive terms. Studies have clearly shown that officers do indeed believe many rape myths, in particular the idea that victims can prevent rape if they try hard enough and that women falsely report rape (Harding, 2015).

NiCarthy (2004) offered the following suggestions for victims in regard to getting the most effective response from police:

- Be as calm as you possibly can be.
- Don't be afraid to ask the police to make a report.
- Tell them about the assault in detail.
- Show them any injuries or bruises or damaged property.
- Let them know if there were witnesses.
- Tell them about other violent incidents.
- Show them any court documents you have such as "no contact" or "restraining" orders.
- Ask them for community resources such as shelters, hot lines, counseling, and advocacy.
- Ask for the case number of the report and a phone number if you want to follow up on the case (p. 76).

These are indeed good ideas, and ones that are not typically depicted in popular culture.

POLICE AS PERPETRATORS

Police officers are overrepresented as abusers. While there is no precise source of data on police-perpetrated abuse, it is clear that when a law enforcement officer is involved the situation becomes far more complex. Two different studies did find that at least 40 percent of police officer families experience domestic violence, a rate more than four times higher than that of families in the general population (Friedersdorf, 2014). Often the offending officers face no sanction at all, not even a notice in their personnel file. PBS's *Frontline* featured an episode called "Death in St. Augustine" that focused on police-perpetrated domestic violence. Anna Quindlen's *Black and Blue* also highlights the unique challenges faced by victims whose abusers are police officers. Frannie knows she cannot turn to the police for help because they are all her husband's buddies. Further, she knows he has at his disposal resources that other offenders lack and thus is easily able to find her and their son when they flee and try to adopt new identities.

Additionally, research suggests that the culture of policing often contributes more to rape myths to justify sexual assault committed by officers (Eschholz & Vaughn, 2001). Eschholz and Vaughn (2001) found that police officers, particularly in jails and prisons, use rape myths and gender stereotypes to justify their actions against inmates (Martin, 2013).

PROSECUTING DOMESTIC VIOLENCE AND RAPE

The White House Council on Women and Girls (2014) explained that almost two-thirds of rape survivors had their legal cases dismissed; 80 percent of the time this was against the survivor's wishes. Prosecutors were most likely to continue cases in which there was physical evidence, if the suspect had a prior criminal record, and if there were no questions about the survivor's background or character. Harding (2015) notes that only 6 percent of rape cases in Salt Lake County, Utah, were prosecuted.

One reason for the low prosecution rates is lack of physical evidence. Sometimes the system is at fault for that, however. In 2009, a *CBS News* investigation found 12 cities had no idea how many rape kits were stored and untested. That same year in Detroit, prosecutor Kym Worthy found more than 11,000 rape kits in a warehouse, only 1,600 of which had still been tested by early 2014 (Harding, 2015).

SVU aired an episode in 2010 based on the rape kit backlog. A woman is repeatedly raped and there is concern that the rapist will go free because the physical evidence has either been misplaced, improperly stored, or destroyed. Not only did the assailant rape the victim, played by Jennifer Love Hewitt, but he is identified as having raped other women as well.

Richards and Restivo (2015) note that

> evidence suggests that sexual violence between intimates is rarely treated as seriously as sexual victimization perpetrated by a stranger. Specifically, research reveals that sexual assaults perpetrated by strangers are more likely to be investigated thoroughly and are less likely to be treated as unfounded by law enforcement than are cases including intimates. Such differential treatment is most likely related to stereotypical notions held by officers regarding what constitutes a "real rape." (p. 75)

Further, since officers are often interested in clearance rates, or the rates in which an arrest can be made in a case, they may not investigate marital or dating rape situations as seriously, believing there will be no evidence to apprehend a suspect. Lord and Rassel (2000) found that in nine North Carolina counties, police still use polygraph tests to assess victims' truthfulness. Likewise, research shows that prosecutors are more likely to pursue cases in which the alleged rapist was a stranger rather than an intimate partner (Richards & Restivo, 2015).

Even in cases when a perpetrator is held accountable, victims still endure victim-blaming. *Lucky* is Alice Sebold's memoir, describing the rape she endured at the end of her first year at Syracuse University. The title refers to a comment made by a police officer who investigated the rape, as he commented that another girl had been killed at the same location, so Sebold was "lucky" to have survived. Alice screams, resists, even tells her rapist to spare her virginity, to no avail. Athough her rapist, Gregory Madison, a black man, is eventually found guilty, Alice suffers from victim-blaming by her parents, friends, and the justice system. Questioning by police focuses on what she did and did not do to fend off her assailant.

Too often, judges, juries, politicians, and the general public disregard victims' experiences as anecdotal. But as Pennington (2014) explains,

> When we hear men's anecdotal evidence from their experience of war, it is not met with disbelief or questions of validity; we look for commonalities in these experiences and accept them as truth. We do not always do the same with women's experiences. When we hear women's experiences of sexual and domestic violence, we look for the disparities, not the commonalities. (p. 12)

Popular culture contributes to this perception, as it has repeatedly shown that it is everyone else's story BUT the victims' that receive the most attention.

Some jurisdictions have established specialized courts that only hear cases involving domestic violence. Advocates maintain that this sends a powerful message to the community about the importance of the issue and helps victims obtain justice by allocating judges who are most knowledgeable about the complexities of abuse. Further, these courts can help streamline the process, which can be cumbersome, intimidating, and time-consuming. Critics maintain that such courts may be biased against offenders or victims, in particular when the individuals involved have appeared numerous times before the same judge. Proponents note that when offenders are less likely to encounter the same judge, the percentage rate of repeat domestic violence offences is typically around 20 percent. In Erie County, New York, under the integrated system, the percentage of repeat offences dropped to only 10 percent.

The film *The Accused* does show a largely accurate depiction of the prosecutor's key role in rape cases. As is often true, the prosecutor Kathryn Murphy, played by Kelly McGillis, does not want to take the case because she believes it to be unwinnable, despite Sarah's identification of the suspects and the physical evidence of her assault. That is, because of her flirtatious behavior at the bar, her seductive dress, and her alcohol and drug use, Murphy does not see Sarah as an "ideal" victim. Subsequently, Kathryn seeks a deal with the defendants that essentially makes it look as though Sarah was never violently victimized but instead put on a show for their enjoyment. After Sarah's continual pressure, Kathryn feels bad and realizes that her failure to prosecute the case has revictimized Sarah, so she proceeds with charges of solicitation against the persons who witnessed the incident and whose actions she and Sarah argue kept it going. Finally, despite Sarah repeatedly being shown as a "rotten witness," Ken Joyce, one of the men who was at the bar that night, confirms her story and the audience begins to see what really happened. We learn that Ken was the one who called 911 about the incident but that he has been reluctant to participate in the trials because his friend, Bob Joiner, was one of the rapists.

While popular culture isn't fantastic at depicting the criminal justice response to abuse and assault, there are some great resources available in real life. Human Rights Watch (2013) listed 40 pages of recommendations for police, sexual assault nurse examiners, prosecutors, forensic lab chiefs, and rape crisis advocates, all using a victim-centered approach that involves collecting the facts while assuring victims they will be believed and not judged. It includes being thoughtful about how many times a victim is asked to tell her story and when and how interviews are conducted.

REFERENCES

Alcid, S. (2013, October 1). Law & Order: SVU v. reality: Offensively different. *Jezebel*. Retrieved September 15, 2015, from http://everydayfeminism.com /2013/10/law-order-vs-reality/

Anderson, K. (2010, December 1). The rape survivors SVU doesn't show. *Jezebel*. Retrieved September 14, 2015, from http://msmagazine.com/blog/2010/12/01/the-rape-survivors-svu-doesnt-show/

Cuklanz, L., & Moorti, S. (2006). Television's "new" feminism: Prime-time representations of women and victimization. *Critical Studies in Media Communication, 23*(4), 302–321.

Eschholz, S., & Vaughn, M. S. (2001). Police sexual violence and rape myths: Civil liability under Section 1983. *Journal of Criminal Justice, 29*(5), 389–405.

Filipovic, J. (2014). Why is an anti-feminist website impersonating a domestic violence organization? *Cosmopolitan*. Retrieved January 6, 2016, from http://www.cosmopolitan.com/politics/news/a32452/antifeminist-site-white-ribbon/

Friedersdorf, C. (2014, September 19). Police have a much bigger domestic abuse problem than the NFL does. *The Atlantic*. Retrieved September 15, 2015, from http://www.theatlantic.com/national/archive/2014/09/police-officers-who-hit-their-wives-or-girlfriends/380329/

Guadalupe-Diaz, X. (2015). Disclosure of same-sex intimate partner violence to police among lesbians, gays and bisexuals. *Social Currents*, 1–12. Retrieved January 6, 2016, from http://www.academia.edu/19566904/Disclosure_of_Same-Sex_Intimate_Partner_Violence_to_Police_among_Lesbians_Gays_and_Bisexuals

Harding, K. (2015). *Asking for it: The alarming rise of rape culture—And what we can do about it*. Boston: Da Capo Lifelong Books.

Human Rights Watch. (2013). Improving police responses to sexual assault. Retrieved January 6, 2016, from https://www.hrw.org/sites/default/files/reports/improvingSAInvest_0.pdf

Kingkade, T. (2015, July 24). 124 colleges, 40 school districts under investigation for handling of sexual assault. *Huffington Post*. Retrieved January 6, 2016, from http://www.huffingtonpost.com/entry/schools-investigation-sexual-assault_55b19b43e4b0074ba5a40b77

Klein, A., Salomon, A., Elwyn, L., Barrasch, A., Powers, J., Maley, M., Gilmer, J., Pirchner, M., Harris, J., Tiffany, J., & Exner-Cortens, D. (2013). An exploratory study of juvenile orders of protection as a remedy for dating violence. U.S. Department of Justice. Retrieved January 6, 2016, from https://www.ncjrs.gov/pdffiles1/nij/grants/242131.pdf

Kramer, E. (1998). When men are victims: Applying rape shield laws to male same-sex rape. *New York University Law Review, 73*(10), 293–332.

Logan, T., & Walker, R. (2011). Civil protective orders effective in stopping or reducing partner violence. Retrieved January 6, 2016, from http://scholars.unh.edu/cgi/viewcontent.cgi?article=1130&context=carsey

Lord, V., & Rassel, G. (2000). Law enforcement's response to sexual assault: A comparative study of nine counties in North Carolina. *Women & Criminal Justice, 11*(1), 67–88.

Martin, K. (2013). Domestic violence, sexual assault, and sex trafficking in the media: A content analysis. Master's theses and doctoral dissertations. Eastern

Michigan University. Retrieved January 6, 2016, from http://commons
.emich.edu/cgi/viewcontent.cgi?article=1840&context=theses

National Coalition of Anti-Violence Projects. (2011). Lesbian, gay, bisexual, transgender, queer, and HIV-affected intimate partner violence 2010. Retrieved September 6, 2015, from http://www.avp.org/storage/documents/2012_NCAVP_IPV_Report_Final.pdf.pdf

NiCarthy, G. (2004). *Getting free: A handbook for women in abusive relationships.* Berkeley, CA: Seal Press.

Noh, M., Lee., M., & Felty, K. (2010). Mad, bad or reasonable? Newspaper portrayals of the battered woman who kills. *Gender Issues, 27*(3), 110–130.

Pennington, L. (2014). *Everyday victim blaming.* London: EVB Press.

REACTION to Law & Order: SVU titled "Gray." (n.d.). Date Safe Project. Retrieved January 6, 2016, from http://www.datesafeproject.org/svu-reaction/

Richards, T., & Restivo, M. (2015). Gender and crime. In W. Jennings (Ed.). *The encyclopedia of crime and punishment.* Malden, MA: Wiley-Blackwell.

Sherman, L., & Berk, R. (1984). The specific deterrent effects of arrest for domestic assault. *American Sociological Review, 49*(2), 261–272.

Sherman, L., & Harris, H. (2015). Increased death rates of domestic violence victims from arresting vs. warning suspects in the Milwaukee Domestic Violence Experiment (MilDVE). *Journal of Experimental Criminology, 11*(1), 1–20.

Wakelin, A., & Long, K. (2003). Effects of victim gender and sexuality on attributions of blame to rape victims. *Sex Roles, 49*(9–10), 477–87.

The White House Council on Women and Girls. (2014, January). Rape and sexual assault: A renewed call to action. Retrieved January 24, 2016, from https://www.whitehouse.gov/sites/default/files/docs/sexual_assault_report_1-21-14.pdf

Getting over It or Taking Matters into Your Own Hands: Victim and Other Responses

As noted in Chapter 5, many times the criminal justice response is inadequate or not one that a victim prefers. As such, sometimes victims seek help from family members, friends, shelters, or therapists. These individuals may provide invaluable support, yet in other cases they join in on the judging and victim-blaming. Sometimes victims see none of these as viable options and instead feel as though they must take matters in their own hands. Popular culture rarely depicts any of the above, with the exception of the self-defense or "rape revenge" portrayal that is widely popular across all types and genres.

Unfortunately, even when people know that others are experiencing abuse or assault, they often fail to intervene. One explanation for this is the notion of "groupthink," an idea that gained attention after the brutal rape of Kitty Genovese in a New York public housing complex. Many people heard or saw Genovese being assaulted and did nothing; her assailant even left her there bleeding and then came back after a couple of minutes to finish his attack. Suzanne Vega's "Luka" discusses a situation when neighbors know what is happening and refuse to intervene. Luka, a little girl, narrates the song, imploring her neighbors to do something when they hear the sounds late at night. She lists the excuses she will make, is making to herself—that she is clumsy, talks too loud, acts too proud.

Those who speak out about abuse and assault often face repercussions at school, home, and work, and in their relationships with others.

Friends may blame the victim for being in the situation at all, family member may not believe that it's happening, and therapists are likely to ask what the woman did to provoke it. Although none of these people state in so many words that they approve of the violence, denial of the battering or the implication that the victim is at fault has the effect of giving the man a "hitting license," especially if the batterer is the victim's husband. (NiCarthy, 2004, pp. 5–6)

The film *Enough* accurately shows how people in a victim's life are often not very helpful when they are told about the abuse. At one point Slim tells her mother-in-law about Mitch's behavior, but all she does is ask what Slim did to set him off. When Mitch finds out that Slim confided in his mother, the abuse escalates, as it so often does in real life. Similarly, the film accurately depicts the financial control exerted by many perpetrators. When Slim flees with Gracie, Mitch freezes all of their accounts so that she has no access to money (Martin, 2013).

Halbrook's young adult novel *Every Last Promise* starts out with two sentences: "This is a story about heroes. I am not one of them." It is the story of Kayla, a popular girl who was driving the car when two boys are killed. The narrative alternates back and forth between that spring and the fall of senior year, when Kayla, who is now a social outcast, struggles to piece together what happened during that party. It turns out Kayla saw a classmate's sexual assault, and if she remains silent, she stands a chance of getting her old life back.

Halbrook commented about what prompted her to write her novel:

Something I researched a lot about as I wrote *Every Last Promise* was the array of reasons victims remain silent after sexual assault. For Kayla, in my story, her home, family, friendships and safety are on the line. For a student at the University of Oregon, her personal medical records were on the line. For numerous women, physical threats and public release of their personal information, in the form of doxxing, is on the line. It was recently announced that the rapist from Columbia University is suing the school. Universities are going to be even more wary to believe and support victims effectively if it means it's going to cost them time and money with lawsuits. Women of color watch their whole lives as their communities are attacked by racist law enforcement agencies in violent, reactionary ways. Teenagers today see this. They're seeing how the attack against rape victims isn't only a subversive, shaming culture, but it's head-on, active attacks against the time, safety, finances, education, and personal lives of those who speak up. That's terrifying. (Kuehnert, 2015, para. 17)

Courtney Summers's *All the Rage* tells the story of Romy, a girl from the "wrong side of town" who agrees to go on a date with Kellan, the sheriff's son. Kellan rapes Romy, but because he is the town's golden boy and she is nothing, no one believes her. She's ostracized and taunted by her old group of friends. She seeks refuge at a diner outside of town where no one knows her, but when it is revealed that Kellan raped another girl Romy is conflicted about what to do.

Sarah Dessen's young adult novel *Just Listen* reminds readers of how judgmental of their peers teens can be. We don't know why Annabel is out of favor with her former best friend and super-popular Sophie until deep into the book; all that is revealed is that something happened at a party and now Annabel is ostracized as a slut. She is suffering from the isolation as well as getting physically ill, all of which improves as she becomes friends with another outcast, Owen Armstrong. It is through his support as well as learning that Sophie's boyfriend Will had done the same thing to other girls that Annabel feels comfortable telling what really happened. She had kept it all in, never telling her parents or anyone else. When Sophie walked in on her and Will at a party, it wasn't Annabel who initiated the contact. Rather, Will was trying to hold her down and rape her when Sophie interrupted his assault. The book highlights how difficult it is for teen victims to tell anyone about abuse and assault. It is also consistent with data showing that most perpetrators of sexual assault commit multiple offenses before they are caught.

Korn's song "Daddy" was written by lead singer Jonathan Davis, whose neighbor abused him. When he told his parents they thought he was lying or joking and never did anything about it. The song vividly describes being tied down and hurt by the assailant and questioning why he was chosen as the victim. In the song, his mom watches and does nothing.

"Daddy's Girl" by the Scorpions also comments on cases in which family members deny abuse, noting that they always look away because, "She don't wanna hear you cry/She will pray that it's over for a while."

Laurie Halse Anderson's popular young adult novel *Speak* tells the story of Melinda, who enters her first year of high school as an outcast because she called the police at a party after eighth grade. The bulk of the book highlights the difficulties Melinda faces as she tries to navigate the high school social scene. She grows increasingly reluctant to speak to anyone, and while readers know that something horrible must have happened, it is not clear until close to the end precisely what occurred at the party. We eventually learn that Melinda, like most of her classmates, was drunk when she was raped by popular Andy Evans. When she tries to warn her former best friend, Rachel, about Evans, he assaults her, which leads to the unveiling of the entire story. The book offers important insight into the ways that victims internalize their trauma.

Jessica Knoll's *Luckiest Girl Alive* is the deeply disturbing story of a high school freshman who is sexually assaulted by three boys from her school. Desperate to be accepted by the "in" crowd, TifAni goes to one of the boys' houses, drinks too much, and then wakes up during one of the assaults. She tells a close friend and a teacher but refuses to report it through official channels. The boys tell everyone that they "scored" with TifAni, resulting in her being labeled as a slut and ostracized by almost everyone. The friend she told, Arthur, has also suffered verbal abuse at the hands of these boys and tells TifAni about other horrifying harassment they perpetrated on another boy, Ben. Unbeknownst to TifAni, Arthur and Ben plot their revenge and, armed with weapons, attack the school, killing some of the most popular kids and wounding several others. The story weaves back and forth from her experience as a teen and her life as an adult who now goes by Ani but is still deeply troubled, although she tries very hard to put on a facade of confidence. As the story unfolds, we learn that Ani's mother blamed her for the assault, telling her that she should never have gone to the house with those boys or drank so much.

SHELTERS, THERAPISTS, AND THE HEALING PROCESS

Rarely does popular culture present the healing process. In fact, some depictions have been criticized because they focus on the impact on husbands and their healing when they learn their wives have been abused. One exception to this is in popular fiction books, which, because the medium allows for more extensive coverage, sometimes present victims in the healing process. This typically involves therapy versus shelter. Therapists are thus depicted as the key component of healing, although in reality many victims do not seek therapeutic assistance. Victims often do participate in some type of support group but this rarely if ever appears in popular culture. Poore, Shulruff, and Bein (2013) discuss the importance of holistic healing efforts, noting that while therapy and crisis intervention can help, they often fail to address the physiological and nonverbal aspects of the victimization. This may be especially true for victims from different cultures. Sarah Dessen's *Dreamland* tells the story of Caitlin O'Keron, who until her older sister Cass ran away with her boyfriend was always second fiddle. Caitlin gets lost as her family worries incessantly about Cass, and she is an easy target for Rogerson Biscoe, an attractive and mysterious "bad boy" in town. Caitlin at first appreciates his all-consuming focus on her, until he needs to always know where she is, has an obsession with her being on time to meet him, and begins to alienate all her friends so that she eventually spends virtually all her time with him. When Rogerson first hits her, Caitlin feels bad for him, as she has seen that his father hits him. And she knows he is sorry, because he says so. As he introduces her to drugs and becomes more demanding, Caitlin begins to struggle at school and with her friends, but her family still barely notices. She feels like she is in too deep to tell anyone, and besides, she knows she is now confirmed as the "loser sister," since Cass was too put together ever to have an abusive boyfriend. Caitlin hides the bruises behind long sleeves and pants and "fell on the ice" the time her face was injured from Rogerson's punches. Her best friend Rina suspects something is wrong but Caitlin is too embarrassed and scared to say what it is. The abuse finally ends when a neighbor sees Rogerson beating her outside of her house and calls Caitlin's parents and the police. Even still, Caitlin screams for Rogerson, because as flawed as he was, she felt he was the only one who really cared about her. While she is healing at a mental health facility she comes to realize she is not to blame and begins to reconnect with her family and friends.

In *Sleeping with the Enemy*, Julia Roberts's character Laura (who took on the name Sarah when she fled from her husband) befriends and later develops a romantic interest in a man named Ben. When he first attempts to kiss her, however, she demands he stop, demonstrating the difficulties victims often have in engaging in new relationships after enduring unhealthy ones. Laura/Sarah also has an intense fear of strangers and a difficult time trusting anyone, even Ben, which is true of many victims.

Neither Laura in *Sleeping with the Enemy* nor Slim in *Enough* utilizes shelters or social service agencies. Slim even comments that they would not keep her and Gracie safe and that living in one would traumatize her daughter (Martin, 2013). Shelters and service providers have been critiqued for their lack of attention to class, race, and cultural differences, to their interactions with police and courts, and because of their hierarchical nature that is individual, not collective, focused (Bhattacharjee, 1997; Projansky, 2001). NiCarthy (2004) commented on the role of professionals in helping victims acquire safety: "Professionals can also make things worse for you. Some of them are not competent in their work, regardless of formal training. Others are competent but their social attitudes and ways of relating to clients have dangerous effects that sometimes outweigh the good they do in the operating room, courthouse, or counselor's office" (p. 69).

Abuse and assault are hard on family members and friends as well. In her first book, *The Lovely Bones*, which was made into a movie, Alice Sebold tells the fictional story of a girl who was raped and murdered by her neighbor. Teenager Susie Solomon narrates the story from heaven, struggling as she watches her family and friends go on without her. Although critics contend that the movie version sanitizes the offenses, the story does highlight how difficult it is for all around to heal when someone is violently victimized.

Many songs have been written from a child witness's perspective and focus on the trauma children experience while watching a parent get abused. As noted in Chapter 1, some also note the increased likelihood that the child will become a perpetrator, which in reality is two to four times more likely than for children who do not witness abuse. Films, songs, and TV shows generally end with either the victim surviving or even killing her abuser or living in a continual state of fear. Research is clear, however, that enduring domestic violence or sexual assault generates both short- and long-term effects. Richards and Restivo (2015) note that sexual violence in intimate partner relationships has been linked to a host of physical and mental problems that can require extensive healing. Studies indicate that domestic violence victims whose abuser rapes them typically suffer from greater physical injury than do women who were only physically abused (McFarlane et al., 2005). "A woman who is raped by a stranger lives with a memory of a horrible attack; a woman who is raped by her husband lives with her rapist." Common effects include depression, posttraumatic stress disorder, bladder infections, vaginal and anal tearing, pelvic pain, urinary tract infections, sexually transmitted diseases, unintended pregnancies, and sexual dysfunction (Richards & Restivo, 2015).

Joni Mitchell's "Not to Blame" describes a girl who commits suicide after being abused. Rumors were that the song was about Mitchell's ex-boyfriend, Jackson Browne, who allegedly beat his girlfriend, actor Daryl Hannah. "They said you beat the girl You loved the most" and notes the fist marks left on her face. Browne defended himself, asserting that Mitchell was the violent one who attacked him.

The TV series *Veronica Mars*, which aired for only three seasons, is perhaps one of the best to focus on date rape. Mars loses her virginity when she is raped by a classmate who drugged her at a party. Her attempts to uncover her assailant's identity and bring him to justice drive the remainder of the series. In the final episode she does this, and, as Duhaime-Ross (2013) explains,

> Unlike most televised rape accounts, Veronica was no damsel in distress waiting to be rescued. She had agency and was given a voice that went deeper and was more honest than any of its predecessors. Throughout the television show, Veronica has nightmares about the night she was assaulted. Viewers also find out in the second season that Veronica has an STI as a

result of her rape, making the assault all the more realistic. Needless to say, the teenager ends up developing a keen distrust of the men around her, affecting all her future relationships throughout the show. But despite getting laughed out of the police chief's office when she comes forward about her ordeal, Veronica never loses sight of the fact that she is not to blame for her rape—and neither do the show's viewers, who are treated to a dramatic story-line that is both realistic and empowering.

Anna Klein's *Rape Girl* focuses on the aftermath of being a rape victim. Valerie had long wished to be popular and pretty. But now she is known as the Rape Girl. She feels guilty and responsible because she made out with Adam while drunk the night prior, and when he came by the next day she said no but feels as though she led him on by her previous decisions. Valerie is, like so many other teen girls, eager to please and dying for attention from her crush.

Shania Twain's "Black Eyes Blue Tears" focuses on a woman trying to get it out of an abusive situation. After describing the black eyes and frequent tears, Twain explains, "I won't live where things are so out of whack/No more rollin' with the punches." Similarly, Pink's "18 Wheeler" shows a victim's resiliency, noting that even being pushed out a window or run over by a truck won't keep her down.

Lauryn Hill's "I Get Out" is considered by many to be an anthem for those seeking to leave abusers or even to simply shed something in their lives that is oppressive. Hill explains that she will "get out of all your boxes," and will no longer be held in chains. She pronounces that, "I won't support your lie no more/I won't even try no more/If I have to die, oh Lord/That's how I choose to live." She is a victor, not a victim.

Some have applauded *Orange Is the New Black* for its handling of the revelation that popular character Pennsatucky was raped as a teen. As Yuan (2015) notes, "When Big Boo, like any good friend would, concocts an elaborate revenge scheme and drugs Coates unconscious so Pennsatucky can shove a broomstick up his ass, Pennsatucky opts out. 'I'm not angry,' she tells Big Boo. 'I'm just sad.'"

An episode of *House of Cards* took it further, depicting a rape survivor who becomes an outspoken advocate. Claire, played by Robin Wright, encounters General Dalton McGinnis, who had raped her in college but who had the audacity when meeting her husband Frank to say "Claire and I dated in college." Frank is outraged, not least of which is because he is supposed to honor McGinnis with an award. She later talks to Frank about the pain and emotional scars left by rape, and she actually speaks out publicly as an advocate for victims.

SELF-DEFENSE AND OTHER RECOMMENDATIONS

Women are often encouraged to take actions to minimize the likelihood that they will be victimized. One recommendation is that women limit their alcohol consumption, which Pennington (2014) says is another form of victim-blaming, as the focus is on the victim, not on the offender, to make changes. It also reinforces the notion that rape and abuse are the result of intoxication, which is a dangerous misconception.

> It leads us again to the myth of the stranger, preying on intoxicated women, the "accidental rapist" (who didn't understand consent), or the "opportunist rapist" (who saw an intoxicated woman and decided to rape her). These myths are pervasive in our society, and unless we take the time to unpick them, and really look at the message we are sending, it is easy to contribute to victim blaming of this type. It is damaging to survivors of sexual violence, it contributes to self-blame and it suggests that men should not be trusted— if we are to keep our wits about us all of the time, what does this say to men? It says—we think you are unsafe. We think you might rape us, or attempt to do so. Men, you should be outraged at the message this safety advice implies about you, and your fellow men. (pp. 8–9)

Pennington (2014) comments on how ludicrous it is to ask women to change as a way to prevent rape.

> When we see safety messages about the dangers of drink-driving [*sic*], they are not aimed at the pedestrian walking home after an evening out. We don't tell citizens to stay home, in case a driver who has been drinking may be travelling the same route home as them. We tell drink drivers [*sic*] not to consume alcohol and drive—focusing wholly on their choices, their behaviour, and their responsibility for avoiding the harm they may cause if they choose to drink and drive. (p. 9)

In addressing the self-defense "tips" commonly given to women, Harding (2015) explains that women are too often told that they must change their daily activities to avoid getting assaulted by a stranger while little if any attention is paid to what rapists can do to NOT rape. And, even though these suggestions may be asinine, the typical response is "Better safe than sorry!"

Gender role expectations and media representations insist that domestic violence is a personal problem that a woman has to solve on her own (Noh, Lee, & Felty, 2010). However, many women cannot simply "escape" their batterer by themselves. With the complications of finance, children, and the very real threat of retaliatory violence, it could be argued that an abused woman may view killing the abuser as the only realistic way to end the violence (Martin, 2013, p. 4). When they do, however, the criminal justice system does not necessarily see their actions as justified.

One study of female inmates in a California prison found that 93 percent who were incarcerated for killing their significant other had endured abuse from that individual, and 97 percent of those women reported that they wounded or killed their partner while trying to defend themselves or their children. Another study in New York found that 67 of the women who were imprisoned for killing someone had been abused by that individual (Law, 2014). Law (2014) interviewed several domestic violence survivors who were imprisoned for defending themselves. Each woman reported that she had defended herself only after repeatedly trying to seeking help. These women called police, shelters, and other resources and none was helpful. One woman recalled seeing police drive by as her boyfriend beat her on the street. When she called them the police did nothing except arrest him once for having drug paraphernalia—he was released the next day only to continue his abuse. Each woman that Law (2014) interviewed expressed that they knew at some point they would be killed or would have to kill. "You know that this is the end," said one woman, "You see it in their eyes that they're going to kill you" (Law, 2014). Sociologist Elizabeth Leonard explains that a battered woman is 75 percent more at risk of being killed after she leaves, an increased risk that remains for two years after.

Although there is huge risk in fighting back, Hollywood loves these story lines. In fact, Hollywood loves vigilantes in general, although more often they are men. As has been described elsewhere in this book, women are far more likely to be portrayed as helpless victims than as persons with agency who make decisions, either good or bad, about their own survival. *The Girl with the Dragon Tattoo* book series and later movies were a huge success with viewers perhaps because they challenged these stereotypes. As Chemaly (2013) explains, "Every permutation of gender-based violence accurately and graphically featured in that trilogy thrives in the real world justice systems that fail women." The criminal justice system, however, seems to almost criminalize the very survival strategies these women are using, as many are unsuccessful in their attempts to claim that their retaliatory violence was actually self-defense or the result of battered woman syndrome (BWS). Even when they are in imminent danger, women cannot always count on the criminal justice system for help nor for understanding when they do what is needed. Marissa Alexander, who had long suffered abuse at the hands of her boyfriend (with whom she had a young child), received a 20-year sentence for firing a warning shot into the ceiling. No one was hurt, and Alexander thought her actions would be protected by Florida's Stand Your Ground law. Other reports show that most of the women who are incarcerated for killing their partners or having them killed by someone else were prohibited from introducing all the evidence of their abuse at trial. Interestingly, while more men are in prison for murdering their spouses, women who kill abusive husbands receive disproportionately long sentences. The Michigan Women's Justice and Clemency Project has reported that while men who kill intimate partners receive an average sentence of two to six years, the average sentence for women who do so is fifteen years.

Women of color are both at greater risk for abuse and even more marginalized within the criminal justice system. In some Native American communities, women are killed by intimate partners at rates 10 times the national average. Yet few cases are reported to police, and when they are, few result in arrest, prosecution, and conviction (Chemaly, 2013).

In 1977, Lenore E. A. Walker studied data from 400 battered women survivors. Walker identified a cycle of violence that characterized many of the relationships. She also noted that many women coped with and remained in the situation through learned helplessness, a concept that describes how women come to believe that the abuse is their fault and are fearful for their lives and the lives of their children. Walker also identified gender-role socialization as an important factor in what she named the battered woman syndrome. She asserted that men are socialized to be more powerful than women, and that this socialization can manifest in men's need to control women.

Walker's cycle of violence involved four stages. The first she described as tension-building, in which the victim was exposed to verbal and/or emotional abuse, as well as possibly occasional physical abuse. In this phase, Walker said that victims often attempt to pacify their abusers by using placating verbal techniques. Such approaches may actually escalate the abuse, as perpetrators use this perceived passivity to their advantage. In stage two, the abuser uses more severe forms of violence, heightening the risk of injury for the victim. The discharge of tension in stage two, according to Walker, result in a "honeymoon stage" or stage three in which the perpetrator exhibits conciliatory behaviors intended to win back the victim. Walker's thesis was that women stayed in abusive relationships because they were deceived by the "honeymoon phase" of the cycle, in which abusers apologize and attempt to be nice. This is followed by a generally calm phase, until tensions build again. Further, according to the BWS, women believe that they can change their abusers and so stay in dangerous situations far too long. Walker's work is said to have helped dispel some myths about abuse, such as that women can easily leave abusers but do not want to.

BWS has been used in court cases to explain why battered women use violent means to defend themselves against their battering partners. Most studies have shown that when women use violence in their intimate relationships they are acting either in self-defense or are retaliating for abuse they have endured. In 70–80 percent of intimate partner homicides, the man physically abused the woman before the murder. While legal definitions of self-defense vary slightly from state to state, most criminal laws state that physical force upon another person is justified when such force is necessary to protect oneself from imminent harm. Also included is the element of proportionality, which specifics that force used during self-defense should not be out of proportion to that which is necessary to protect oneself from imminent harm. This can pose a challenge for victims who kill their partners, as deadly force may be construed as "out of proportion" by judges and juries. Most states now instruct juries and judges to consider self-defense if the male partner has a history of abuse and if the female is in reasonable fear of imminent harm—hence BWS. BWS can help others understand that the abuse that battered women experience may cause her to re-experience previous trauma to the current battering incident. Perhaps the most notable case, and the one that first popularized BWS, was that of Francine Hughes, who killed her abusive husband while he slept. Hughes was acquitted of the murder. The case was depicted in the 1984 film *The Burning Bed*, in which Farrah Fawcett starred as Francine Hughes. The film version of *The Burning Bed* helped bring the issue of domestic violence to mainstream audiences. The late Farrah Fawcett, a beauty best known for portraying one of Charlie's Angels, played Francine Hughes, and seeing her bloodied and beaten "mobilized people," said Susan Shoultz, executive director of EVE Inc., a Michigan nonprofit that serves domestic violence victims. "The movie was so graphic, and that moved things forward. . . . Public awareness jumped leaps and bounds at that moment" (Ahern, 2009).

Critics like Lee Bowker have expressed concern that BWS paints a picture of victims as helpless and as having victim-prone personalities. Walker herself has responded to these criticisms, maintaining that the "battered woman is not helpless at all but rather skilled in staying alive and minimizing her physical and psychological injuries in a brutal environment" (Walker, 2009, p. 8). BWS is not always effective as part of a legal defense, though. Mary Ann Franks of the University of Miami Law School has argued that it forces women to plead for mercy and, when used it court, subjects women to tremendous scrutiny and judgment of their behaviors. This is in contrast to Stand Your Ground laws, which can be invoked by men to provoke arguments and justify their violent behavior. She refers to this as a "two-track system of self-defense." Many women are incarcerated for hurting or killing their abusers. Shirley Lute was freed after serving 33 years in prison for her husband's murder. She was convicted before evidence of BWS was allowed in court.

Enough (2002) stars singer and actor Jennifer Lopez as Slim Hiller. She is swept off her feet by Mitch, a handsome man who seems only to want to romance her, until he turns verbally and physically violent. Slim eventually takes their daughter and runs, with both changing their appearance and taking on new identities. But Mitch is determined to find them and he does. She decides that the only way out is to defend herself and to kill Mitch when he attacks, which she does. The comments about the film on the IMDB site indicate widespread support for this approach. "Classical-Bookworm" (2004) posted:

> This is a great movie for women to watch because it shows that size is no disadvantage in a fight, and that wit and preparation are half the battle. So many women are in exactly this situation and end up being killed because they can't stop it early. This movie could have gone into more detail on her physical preparation, and also on the emotional trauma of abuse and her gradual transition to a fighting mentality, but there is only so much you can pack into one movie. But it sure is nice to see a non-helpless female for a change. It is a sad comment on the world that a woman who fights back is so unusual that it makes a dramatic movie. This movies [*sic*] has a great message: no on [*sic*] is going to rescue us, so we'd better take matters into our own hands.

In *Sleeping with the Enemy*, Laura's husband Martin tries to control everything, believing he knows better than she does what is best for her. This is a hallmark of abusive relationships. The film ends with Laura and Ben, her new boyfriend, embracing after she shot Martin, suggesting that all is done. In reality, victims often take years or even decades working through what they experienced with therapists and other supporters.

As is typical in domestic violence situations, Ike's abusive behavior in *What's Love Got to Do with It* is camouflaged as affection and concern. Also typical is that fact that a particularly brutal incident serves as Tina's catalyst to leave the relationship. The scene occurs in Ike and Tina's home, where she is recording her song "Nutbush City Limits." Ike brutally rapes her, and even when she leaves, as is often the case with abusers, the story does not end. As Shoos (2003) explains,

> At the point when Anna Mae escapes from Ike in their hotel room and runs to a nearby Ramada Inn, it would have been narratively convenient to

abandon the domestic violence plot for the more upbeat rock star success story. Instead, in tacit response to the question "Why doesn't she just leave?" the film relates the experience of not only Tina Turner, but many abused women who find themselves more than less endangered when they finally break away from their abusers. (p. 68)

At the same time, this scene sends a dangerous message, one that popular culture likes: the rebellious victim taunting her abusers. When Ike threatens her, Anna Mae dares him to shoot her. Like *Enough* and *Sleeping with the Enemy*, the implication is that standing up to the abuser is the best, maybe even only, way to end it, rather than to plan for one's safety or to seek help from an agency or organization.

> Furthermore, in spite of the fact that, through the character of Jackie, the film acknowledges the importance of informal support systems for abused women, it fails to address the role that institutions such as the police and the legal system play in either intervening in, or in some cases, facilitating and perpetuating domestic violence. Thus, just as its star narrative and performance numbers foreground Turner's phenomenal talent and her superstar potential, the film's portrayal of Turner as a fighter, who through her newfound religious faith succeeds in saving herself, comes perilously close to suggesting that the responsibility for the abused woman's fate beings and ends with her. (Shoos, 2003, p. 69)

As has been noted throughout the book, rape victims are often not believed unless they fight back. *Such a Pretty Girl* tells the story of a young girl's self-defense from rape. Meredith's father, Charles, is in jail for sexually abusing her and other children when she learns that he is to be released after only three years. Meredith is scared but her mother, Sharon, is happy because she forgives him and wants the family to reconnect. Meredith tries to run away multiple times and receives a lot of support from her boyfriend, Andy, who is paralyzed. Meredith and friends eventually confront her father, who tries to attack her. She defends herself by hitting him on the head and knocks him unconscious. Her mother is then charged with negligence for leaving her daughter alone with a known pedophile. Charles is eventually sent back to jail for life.

REVENGE

Much has been written about rape-revenge films, which cross virtually all genres. Victims seeking revenge against their perpetrators and others doing so on their behalf are common fixtures in television programming, fiction books, and music lyrics. Several texts have been devoted to the topic, including Heller-Nicholas's *Rape-Revenge Films* (2011) and Projansky's *Watching Rape: Film and Television in Postfeminist Culture* (2001).

Portrayals of rape victims' revenge can be found as early as the 1930s. In *Shanghai Express* (1932), Hue Fei kills her perpetrator, Cheng. Rape-revenge films became very popular in the 1970s. "In these films, sometimes the revenge is taken by a man who loses his wife or daughter to a rape/murder, and sometimes the revenge is taken by women who have faced rape themselves." The films in the latter category can be understood as feminist narratives in which women face rape, recognize that the law will neither protect nor avenge them, and then take the law into their own hands. Heller-Nicholas maintains that one of the first rape-revenge films was *Safe in Hell* (1931). In a fight with her rapist who is her ex-boss, Gilda kills him and then is hidden by her boyfriend on an exotic island so that she cannot be extradited and tried for the offense. *Anatomy of a Murder* (1959) received (but did not win) seven Oscar nominations. It focuses on how the legal system responds to rape, telling the story of a soldier on trial for murdering the man who raped his wife. Some maintain that the film *Lipstick* mainstreamed rape-revenge. It was the launch of supermodel Margaux Hemingway and brought attention to her younger sister, Mariel. The rapist is Kathy's (the younger Hemingway) music teacher, and he is not depicted as entirely repulsive. When he rapes the older sister, Chris, and Kathy walks in on it, her face appears confused, suggesting the situation could be consensual. Further, the film can be viewed as problematic in that it repeatedly references and shows Chris's involvement as a model and seems to suggest that Gordon cannot resist himself due to the fact that she is positioned as a sexual commodity.

Ms. 45 (1980) is, like *Lipstick*, set in the fashion world, but the victim is a seamstress, not a model or executive. Thana is harassed by males at work and then raped by a masked male stranger on the way home. When she arrives home, a burglar also attacks her, and she kills him with an iron. Thana then becomes a vigilante, roaming the streets shooting men who harass and assault women. In *Straw Dogs*, David Sumner (played by Dustin Hoffman) is an academic who receives funding to work on a project and thus moves to a house on the Cornish coast. Immediately a group of local roughs begin harassing David, who ultimately protects the village idiot (and suspected pedophile) Henry Niles, with whom he drives off at the end of the film. One of the harassers, wife Amy's ex-boyfriend Charlie, holds her down while another character sodomizes her and then also rapes her. Susan George admits that she was scared of filming the rape scene in

Straw Dogs, concerned about how it would impact her, and at one point quit the film only to return after she convinced director Sam Peckinpah to film it to her liking.

In *Extremities*, Farrah Fawcett follows her portrayal of an abused woman who kills her spouse in *The Burning Bed* with the story of a woman who endures an attempted rape on her way home from work. She escapes and receives no assistance from the police while realizing that the assailant, Joe, has stolen her wallet with all of her personal information in it. He attacks her at home when her roommates are gone and she fights him off, but again realizes her only recourse is not the police but to kill Joe. Her roommates return, however, and convince her to contact police after all.

The re-emergence of the violent female-avenger was not well received in the 1970s, despite the multiple depictions. *I Spit on Your Grave* is perhaps the goriest. Professional writer Jennifer is repeatedly gang-raped by four men near a country house she rented for the summer. Instead of going to the police, Jennifer decides to seek vengeance against the men by murdering them viciously one at a time. The violence includes a bathtub castration scene where she first plies the man to her home with sexual promises and then leaves him to bleed to death in the bathroom as she listens to music downstairs. Critics of the film were astounded at the level of violence, with Gene Siskel and Roger Ebert "warn[ing] that the film inspired violence against women" (Schubart, 2007). Ebert (1980) further proselytized in his article in the *Chicago Sun-Times* that the film was "sick, reprehensible and contemptible" (para. 1) and condemned those that may have enjoyed watching the film as having "suffered a fundamental loss of decent human feelings" (para. 8). He cites not only the violence of Jennifer's vengeance, but "also more specifically the violent representations of the repeated (there are three) gang-rape scenes leading up to the revenge" (Stache, 2013, pp. 49–50).

Thelma and Louise (1991) is perhaps the most analyzed film that depicts rape. It was featured on the cover of *Time* on June 24, 1991, and in the editorial pages of the *New York Times*, discussed at the 1991 Academy Award ceremony, and the topic of subsequent conversations in and out of popular culture. Some painted the film as male-bashing and an example of "toxic feminism," noting that the males in the film were portrayed stereotypically and that it is actually a masculine "buddy film" with female protagonists and therefore not progressive (Projansky, 2001). Discussions broadly asserted that the film empowered women and threatened men, despite a lack of actual evidence to support that. It does, however, bring the rape-revenge plot to the mainstream.

From newspapers to talk shows to scholarly articles and book chapters, much has been said about whether the film is a feminist depiction. Projansky (2001) notes that the film offers at least four possible responses victims may take to sexual assault: (1) run from it, (2) ignore it, (3) defend oneself and get revenge, and (4) learn from and about it. "Thelma and Louise's climactic flight into/over the Grand Canyon is both utopic, because it evokes women's freedom and pleasure, and dystopic, because it suggest that the assaultive male-dominated social order is so powerful the only way to escape it is to die" (p. 123).

The rape scene takes place in a parking lot, and like so many other films, while it is not the first scene, it drives the narrative thereafter. Before the actual rape, the film offers a critique of the male gaze, as it shows Harlan at first complimenting the women. Interestingly, Thelma initially enjoys the attention; the camera shifts to Louise who clearly sees the danger and who comments that "I haven't seen a bar like this since I left Texas," where viewers learn she was raped. Louise ultimately shoots Harlan, connecting all of his behaviors to the rape when she says "You watch your mouth, buddy." The film continues to show the women fighting rape culture, as later they encounter a truck driver who has naked women on his mud flaps and who makes obscene comments and gestures, showing that male gaze and sexualized language are a part of daily life for women.

The women utilize a variety of techniques to respond to the male sexualized gaze and none is privileged in the film. For instance, Louise clearly "ran from rape" in Texas and even refuses to drive through the state on their way to Mexico. Several scenes show the women discussing when or if to ignore the problem, such as when they encounter the lewd trucker for the second time and Louise tells Thelma to ignore him. Both use self-defense and revenge, as Louise does (albeit defense of her friend) when she shoots Harlan and both use their guns to destroy the trucker's vehicle the third time they encounter him. Finally, Thelma and Louise learn about and criticize rape and rape law. Thelma especially articulates that the law will not believe them nor work in their favor, which she has learned from Louise's experiences. While in one scene Louise takes responsibility, noting that she should have gone to the police earlier, it is Thelma who tells her that they wouldn't be believed.

Death Wish is the ultimate rape-revenge-savior film, showing how Kersey becomes a vigilante, hunting down bad guys after his wife is murdered and his daughter raped. Some have argued that the film was critical in shifting public attention from the liberal policies about crime control of the 1960s to the more conservative approaches of the 1970s and 1980s, as it seemed to strike a chord with white, middle-class men who felt threatened and believed they must take matters in their own hands (Heller-Nicholas, 2011). *Rob Roy* (1995) is a historical drama in which Mary is raped because her husband Robert Roy McGregor challenged the aristocracy. The film shows Robert assuring Mary she will be safe while she is home alone, which proves to be anything but true. When she is raped, Mary becomes decisive and her actions control the narrative. She controls the circumstances leading up to a final sword fight between her husband and her assailant, and when Robert wins, he not only escapes his debts but also avenges Mary's rape. Yet she had previously avenged it herself, having killed the man who watched.

In *A Mother's Revenge* (1993) Wendy is a smart and successful suburban high school girl. A school janitor, Frank, who has been watching her, rapes Wendy when she stays after school to work on a project. While Wendy is hospitalized, her mother, Carol, receives a call from Frank, who threatens to hurt Wendy again if she talks to the police. Carol wants Wendy to help the police but begins carrying a gun with her wherever she goes. Police find evidence of the assault and turn it over to a prosecutor, but Frank's mother has hired a highly acclaimed lawyer for her son. The case ends up being dismissed, and in a rage, Carol grabs the gun from her purse and shoots him several times in open court. Carol is arrested and faces trial, but Wendy finally emerges from her coma. Frank dies from his wounds, though, and the public and media are divided on Carol's fate. At the trial Carol describes simply losing it when she saw that Frank was to be released. Carol is found guilty of manslaughter (Martin, 2013).

Fear (1998) tells the story of a father's revenge. Nicole, played by Reese Witherspoon, lives with her father, stepmother, and stepbrother in a small town. Her rebellious behavior has resulted in a strained relationship with her parents. She meets David at a local pool hall while skipping class. He is good-looking and mysterious. David is polite when he meets her parents and things seem to go well at first. David proves to be insanely jealous, however, and brutally attacks a male friend he sees walking with Nicole at school. Nicole is mad and tries to intervene and David hits her as well. She vows never to see him again, but he apologizes. Nicole's parents are concerned but David still claims to be sorry. Her father conducts a background check on David and finds he had a troubled childhood but no criminal record. He confronts David and the situation escalates. Nicole vows to keep seeing David, if for no other reason than to bother her parents. She sneaks off to his house and witnesses him raping her friend. Again, David pursues Nicole and apologizes. Her father learns about the incident and forbids Nicole from seeing David and warns school security about his behavior. In a rage, David carves "Nicole 4 eva" on his chest with a razor and continues stalking Nicole. He assaults one of her friends and vandalizes Nicole's father's car. Her dad tries to confront David at his home and ends up seeing that he has a creepy shrine to Nicole, replete with pictures, her jewelry and even her underwear. David realizes her father has ransacked his home and gets his friends to help him cut the phone lines and ambush Nicole's home. David eventually takes Nicole's father as a hostage, with Nicole begging him not to kill her dad. In the end, Nicole stabs David in the back with a sharp implement she found in her room, and her father eventually is able to throw him out of the second story window where David falls to his death (Martin, 2013). This film's presentation of stalking definitely aligns with reality, and, like *Enough*, when the police are contacted they claim they cannot assist.

A popular trope is the white avenger in the rape of a black woman. One example comes from a December 12, 1992, episode of *The Commish*, in which Stacey Winchester, an attractive woman, is raped by a white man. While the white folks figure out how to save the day, Stacey is depicted in stereotypical angry black woman fashion, which culminates in her revenge-seeking behavior.

Male avengers are also depicted in story lines about domestic abuse. For instance, in the book and film *Water for Elephants*, Jacob falls in love with Marlena, who is married to the abusive circus owner August. August tries to kill her when he (rightly) suspects she and Jacob are having an affair. Jacob plots to kill August but in the moment finds it impossible to do so. The elephant, Rosie, takes care of it for him.

Sudden Impact (1983) features Clint Eastwood as "Dirty" Harry Callahan, who struggles as a policeman who sees the limitations of the criminal justice system in responding to crime. Callahan is punished for stepping outside the appropriate boundaries of his job and is sent to another town to investigate the murder of George Wilburn, who we learn has raped Jennifer Spencer and her sister. Callahan and Spencer begin a sexual relationship while Spencer pursues the others who have raped her and her sister. Callahan rescues Spencer as the man, Mick, attempts to rape her, and, surprising to her, frames him instead of calling police on her. "*Sudden Impact* pitches the two types of rape-revenge—the male-lead vengeance trope, where a man takes revenge as an agent for the female victim, and the female-lead vengeance trope where a woman is the agent of her own revenge—directly against each other" (p. 57).

In the 2001 episode of *The Sopranos* called "Employee of the Month," Tony Soprano's (James Gandolfini) therapist Dr. Melfi (Lorraine Bracco) is raped in a parking garage. As she struggles to recover from the experience she considers enlisting Tony's help in obtaining justice outside the law because she does not believe the law will help.

Several Lady Gaga videos feature rape-revenge themes. In "Paparazzi," the star is raped by her boyfriend, played by actor Alexander Skarsgard, who refuses to stop their consensual activity when she asks him to because she has seen the paparazzi watching. The video concludes with Gaga poisoning him. "Telephone" follows this, showing Gaga serving time for the offence and then her escape, with artist Beyoncé, in the model of Quentin Tarantino's *Kill Bill Vol. 1*.

The 1980's *Demented* begins with the violent gang rape of a woman named Linda. Although her rapists are convicted and incarcerated, Linda continues to have hallucinations about them assaulting her. When some teens break into her house and one tries to rape her, Linda kills him with a meat cleaver. The title and depictions clearly show Linda as demented and emphasizes gore over nuance, as do most horror/slasher films.

The 1990s saw rape-revenge in *Eye for an Eye* (1996), *No One Could Protect Her* (1995), and *The Rape of Dr. Willis* (1991). Sally Field is Karen McCann in *Eye for an Eye*. Her daughter was raped by Robert Doob, played by Keifer Sutherland, and she begins to stalk him and then lures him to her house to kill him. Although her husband and others are aware of the truth, McCann is not punished for the murder. In *No One Could Protect Her*, Joanna Kerns is Jessica, who is raped by a home invader. Her husband is committed to avenging her rape, but she'd rather have a supporter during her trauma.

Rape-revenge films cross genres, from serious dramas to action films, screwball comedies to western, horror/slasher films to supernatural stories. And, while they may be more common in the United States, they can be found across the world (Heller-Nicholas, 2011).The 2000s saw a resurgence of the rape-revenge film, especially among blockbusters, including *Law-Abiding Citizen* (2009) and *The Girl with the Dragon Tattoo* (2009). *The Girl with the Dragon Tattoo* series reveals that androgynous Lisbeth Salander is seeking revenge for the rape she endured at the hands of her guardian, corrupt and sadistic Nils Bjurman. After using her impressive intellect and technology skills to invade his home, she rapes him with a dildo and then tattoos "I am a rapist and a sadistic pig" on his stomach after making him watch the DVD he made when he raped her. While the books and films could be seen as an indictment of systemic abuse and the failure, even complicity of officials in gender-based violence, Heller-Nicholas (2011) maintains that because Salander is so extreme, the violence she endures and her subsequent revenge appear as little more than a one-off.

Stache (2013) contends that the brutal depiction of Lisbeth Salander's rape is intended to set the stage for audience approval of revenge violence. Because the audience vicariously experience her victimization, it is poised not to question her violent vengeance, which she pursues in lieu of contacting police or other resources.

TV shows frequently featured rape-revenge, including but not limited to *Beverly Hills 90210*, *Home and Away*, *Law & Order: Special Victims Unit*, *The Bold and the Beautiful*, *Coronation Street*, *Battlestar Galactica*, *Star Trek: The Next Generation*, *The Sopranos*, *The Shield*, *Dexter*, *Game of Thrones*, and *Downton Abbey*.

Some films, like Quentin Tarantino's *Kill Bill Vol. 1* (2003) and *Death Proof* (2007), don't actually depict rape but the story line makes it clear that the revenge depicted is due to a rape. In *Descent* (2007), Rosario Dawson plays university student Maya, who is date-raped. She initially becomes depressed and withdrawn, but later encourages a male friend to rape her assailant, Jared.

Music also features revenge themes. In their 1946 song "Stone Cold Dead in the Market (He Had It Coming)," Ella Fitzgerald and Louis Jordan tell the story of a woman who publicly kills her abusive husband. The duet features Fitzgerald as the woman who claims she "So I tell you that I doesn't care if I was to die in the 'lectric chair. Mon!," while Jordan is the man who announces "Hey, child, I'm coming back and bash you on yo head one more time." The song is to a bouncy, Caribbean beat and was very popular at a time in which abuse in the home was not discussed publicly.

Pop singer Rihanna, herself a victim of domestic violence, offered to refilm the video to her single "Man Down," which generated much controversy because it features the artist hunting down the man who raped her and shooting him. Media watchdog groups like Mothers against Violence and the Parents Television Council have called for the video to be banned. Some maintain that the controversy is not about what is being called gratuitous violence but rather about the fact that the depiction dares to show a survivor responding in a "nonfeminine" fashion (McRobie, 2011). Further, McRobie (2011) explains that the video also showed the emotional trauma that victims endure, with the singer crying, "momma, momma, momma" and "what happened to me?"

Country singer Martina McBride's (1994) "Independence Day" also features the revenge theme, as the victim burns the house down while her abuser sleeps, stating, "Now I ain't sayin' it's right or it's wrong, but maybe it's the only way." While the song leaves the woman's fate unclear, the video shows her also perishing in the fire. Narrated by an 8-year-old girl, "Independence Day" also condemns the townspeople, noting that the while many gossiped about it, they never did anything to help.

Nickelback's "Never Again" (2001) shares the perspective of a son who hears and sees the abuse committed by his dad against his mom. While the song features some important insights, such as that victims often want to but don't disclose their abuse to medical professionals and that children always know that something is wrong, it also ends with the predictable "fight back" situation in which the mother kills her husband (evidently before the child can).

Aerosmith's "Janie's Got a Gun" is about a girl who shoots her father because he was sexually abusing her. Steven Tyler, who wrote the lyrics, explained "That song is about a girl getting raped and pillaged by her father. It's about incest, something that happens to a lot of kids who don't even find out about it until they find themselves trying to work through some major f—king neuroses." The video showed the girl killing her father.

The Dixie Chicks' "Goodbye Earl" (1999) tells the story of best friends Mary Anne and Wanda as they plot how to kill Wanda's abusive ex-husband Earl, who attacked her, landing Wanda in intensive care. In this case, her friends come quickly to help Wanda get back at Earl. The girls take little time deciding Earl must die, then discuss poisoning him and disposing of his body.

Although revenge films suggest that the action is empowering, Rebecca Stringer (2011) suggests that the lone female vigilante is actually anti-feminist due to the focus on individualism over community. Stringer argues "lone vigilantism is the very opposite of the actual strategies advocated in feminist anti-violence efforts, which have primarily assumed the form of collective political struggle" (in Stache, 2013, p. 93).

Stache (2013) conducted an analysis of the depiction of avenging women in popular TV and film. While the typical narrative is that these depictions empower women, at the same time Stache (2013) maintains that they also represent a cautionary tale to women about the dangers of subverting traditional gender roles. "One consistent theme within avenging-woman narratives is violence," where "women appropriate male power in the forms of weaponry and physical prowess" (Dole, 2001, p. 78). Traditionally, violence has been culturally viewed as a form of active male power, while women are encouraged to deal with anger passively (Heinecken, 2004). The avenging woman reifies an individual explanation of abuse and assault. She may have the agency to act, but only individually, not collectively (Stache, 2013).

Stringer (2011) explains:

> The avenging-woman is first disempowered through a type of physical,
> financial, social and/or legal victimization, and then re-empowered through
> the act of revenge. However, instead of finding a support group, or joining a
> march to raise her voice against the violence inflicted against her, she doles
> out a vigilante punishment to her attackers. The avenging-women are
> "strong female lead characters who actively disobey the patriarchal culture
> of disarmament, in an apparently feminist display of empowerment and re-
> sistance." (p. 269)

Stringer (2011) elaborates on the ways that revenge themes are actually
disempowering.

> The avenging-woman's act of revenge is presented sympathetically to the
> viewing audience because of the initial depiction of injustice. After witness-
> ing her rape or victimization, and understanding the limited options avail-
> able to her if she wants justice for the crimes against her, the text
> rhetorically constructs her turn to vengeance in a way that persuades the
> audience to root for her success. But, this contingency presents a problem-
> atic depiction of female empowerment by perpetuating a rhetoric of
> misogyny. Although the avenging-woman "disrupts the sexist script of femi-
> nine victimhood, articulating instead female agency and the capacity to fight
> back against male violence" at the same time she is also "figured a[s] a griev-
> ous misrepresentation of feminism." (Stringer, 2011, p. 280)

Ultimately, Stache (2013) comments that "The narrative storyline first
disempowers the woman so that she can then be empowered. This rhetorical move creates a troubling construction of an empowered woman where
victimization is required before strength, and conveys a problematic depiction of women and power when an audience is persuaded rhetorically that
her turn to vengeance is a sign of empowerment" (p. 21). Lehman (1993)
asserts that "female rape-revenge films are a licensed form of violence in
which a woman acts out male desires for the erotic satisfaction of a pre-
dominately male mass audience." Schubart maintains that, in film, "rape
is the initiation rite that pushes women from being 'soft' victims to becoming 'hard' avengers." Many authors question the alleged "victory" of
female victim-heroes, asserting that merely not dying is far from reason
to celebrate (Heller-Nicholas, 2011).

In sum, the most common depiction of the aftermath of abuse or assault
is revenge. In reality, however, victims mostly want to be safe and free,

never to encounter their assailants again. Additional portrayals of their healing would be far more realistic.

References

Ahern, L. (2009, October 21). "The Burning Bed": A turning point in fight against domestic violence. *Lansing State Journal*. Retrieved August 5, 2015, from http://archive.lansingstatejournal.com/article/99999999/NEWS01/909270304/-Burning-Bed-turning-point-fight-against-domestic-violence

Bhattacharjee, A. (1997). The public/private mirage: Mapping homes an undomesticating violence work in the South Asian immigrant community. In M. Alexander & C. Mohanty (Eds.). *Feminist genealogies, colonial legacies, democratic futures* (pp. 308–329). New York: Routledge.

Chemaly, S. (2013, October 3). "I'm an instrument that will avenge": The stories of women who fight back. Salon. Retrieved September 14, 2015, from http://www.salon.com/2013/10/03/im_an_instrument_that_will_avenge_the_stories_of_women_who_fight_back/

ClassicalBookworm. (2004, February 21). Brutality is no match for wit and skill: Review of *Enough*. IMDB. Retrieved January 6, 2016, from http://www.imdb.com/title/tt0278435/reviews?start=10

Dole, C. (2001). The gun and the badge: Hollywood and the female lawman. In M. McCaughey and N. King (Eds.). *Reel knockouts: Violent women in the movies* (pp. 78–105). Austin, TX: University of Texas Press.

Duhaime-Ross, A. (2013, March 14). "Veronica Mars," TV's realest depiction of rape, is going to be a movie. *The Atlantic*. Retrieved September 14, 2015, from http://www.theatlantic.com/sexes/archive/2013/03/veronica-mars-tvs-realest-depiction-of-rape-is-going-to-be-a-movie/274028/

Ebert, R. (1980). *Irreversible*. Retrieved January 6, 2016, from http://www.imdb.com/title/tt0278435/reviews?start=10

Harding, K. (2015). *Asking for it: The alarming rise of rape culture—And what we can do about it*. Boston: Da Capo Lifelong Books.

Heinecken, D. (2004). No cage can hold her rage? Gender, transgression, and the World Wrestling Federation's Chyna. In S. A. Inness (Ed.). *Action chicks: New images of tough women in popular culture* (pp. 181–206). New York: Palgrave Macmillan.

Heller-Nicholas, A. (2011). *Rape-revenge films*. Jefferson, NC: McFarland & Company.

Kuehnert, S. (2015, June 1). Three YA novelists discuss rape culture in fiction: A chat. *Jezebel*. Retrieved January 10, 2016, from http://themuse.jezebel.com/three-ya-novelists-discuss-rape-culture-in-teen-fiction-1701059484

Law, V. (2014, September 16). How many women are in prison for defending themselves against domestic violence? *Bitch Magazine*. Retrieved September 14, 2015, from http://bitchmagazine.org/post/women-in-prison-for-fighting-back-against-domestic-abuse-ray-rice

Lehman, P. (1993). "Don't blame this on a girl": Female rape-revenge films. In S. Cohen and I. R. Hark (Eds.). *Screening the male: Exploring masculinities in Hollywood cinema* (pp. 103–117). New York: Routledge.

Martin, K. (2013). Domestic violence, sexual assault, and sex trafficking in the media: A content analysis. Master's theses and doctoral dissertations. Eastern Michigan University. Retrieved January 6, 2016, from http://commons.emich.edu/cgi/viewcontent.cgi?article=1840&context=theses

McFarlane, J., Malecha, A., Watson, K., Gist, J., Batten, E., Hall, I., & Smith, S. (2005). Intimate partner sexual assault against women: Frequency, health consequences, and treatment outcomes. *Obstetrics & Gynecology, 105*(1), 99–108.

McRobie, H. (2011, June 20). Mamma I just shot a man down: Rihanna's response to violence against women. Retrieved January 10, 2016, https://www.opendemocracy.net/ourkingdom/heather-mcrobie/mamma-i-just-shot-man-down-rihanna%E2%80%99s-response-to-violence-against-women

NiCarthy, G. (2004). *Getting free: A handbook for women in abusive relationships.* Berkeley, CA: Seal Press.

Noh, M., Lee., M., & Felty, K. (2010). Mad, bad or reasonable? Newspaper portrayals of the battered woman who kills. *Gender Issues, 27*(3), 110–130.

Poore, T., Shulruff, T., & Bein, K. (2013). Holistic healing services for survivors. National Sexual Assault Coalition Resource Sharing Project. Retrieved January 10, 2016, from http://www.vawnet.org/domestic-violence/summary.php?doc_id=4144&find_type=web_desc_GC

Projansky, S. (2001). *Watching rape: Film and television in post-feminist culture.* New York: NYU Press.

Richards, T., & Restivo, M. (2015). Gender and crime. In W. Jennings (Ed.). *The encyclopedia of crime and punishment.* Malden, MA: Wiley-Blackwell.

Schubart, R. (2007). *Super bitches and action babes.* New York: McFarland.

Shoos, D. (2003). Representing domestic violence: Ambivalence and difference in *What's Love Got to Do with It. NWSA Journal, 15*(2), 57–77.

Stache, L. (2013). The rhetorical construction of female empowerment: The avenging-woman narrative in popular television and film. Theses and dissertation, University of Wisconsin, Milwaukee. Retrieved January 6, 2016, from http://dc.uwm.edu/cgi/viewcontent.cgi?article=1167&context=etd

Stringer, R. (2011). Vulnerability after wounding: Feminism, rape law, and the differend. *Substance, 42*(3), 148–168.

Walker, L. (1977). Battered women and learned helplessness. *Victimology, 2*(3–4), 525–534.

Walker, L. (2009). *The battered woman syndrome*, 3rd ed. New York: Springer Publishing.

Yuan, J. (2015). Orange Is the New Black is the only TV show that understands rape. *Vulture.* Retrieved October 26, 2015, from http://www.vulture.com/2015/07/orange-is-the-new-black-is-the-only-tv-show-that-understands-rape.html

Conclusion

As should be clear from this book, there are many problems with the way that domestic violence and rape are depicted in popular culture. Myths about victims, offenders, and the dynamics of these crimes abound across all types and genres. These shape the responses we see as appropriate, from victims themselves to family and friends, to the criminal justice system. While there is no simple or quick solution, this chapter provides some ideas for improvement. These include teaching media literacy, engaging in prevention initiatives that overtly address the myths and misconceptions, and educational programming and training. The chapter concludes with a call to return to the feminist origins of the women's rights movement that first called attention to rape and sexual assault in the 1970s. Reframing abuse and assault as collective, not individual, problems can not only assist victims more effectively but also begin to dismantle our culture of misogyny.

Although many of the films, TV shows, music videos, video games, and other forms of popular culture discussed in this book are deeply disturbing, I do not recommend censorship. Some have argued that films which involve sexual assault, no matter how it is depicted, should automatically receive "R" ratings by the Motion Picture Association of America. Many rape advocates, as well as some feminist groups, maintain that the decision should be more nuanced, as films like *Trust*, which includes the sexual assault of a 14-year-old girl who is pressured into having sex by a man she met online but features no nudity, can help educate teenagers about these issues were they given a PG-13 rating (McCarthy, 2011).

Harding (2015) concurs that censorship is not the answer, explaining,

> Relax. I'm not about to tell you to stop watching TV—or seeing Seth Rogen or Jason Statham or Tyler Perry movies or listening to misogynistic hip-hop. I'm not especially interested in censoring entertainment media, either. (When an Eminem might inspire an Angel Haze, who would ever be qualified to determine what stays and what goes?) I am keen on criticizing it, in hopes that people will stop writing and producing stereotypical bullshit of their own volition, because they realize it's wrong, harmful, and above all, not entertaining. But while we're wishing and waiting, the least we can do is connect some dots. A culture that thinks Joan Holloway was only "sort of" raped is also a culture that believes a victim must be bruised and torn apart to be believed. A culture where "Took her home and enjoyed that, she ain't even know it" is something a grown man would sing in public without a second thought is also one where a jury can listen to police officers describe going back to a drunk woman's house three times to "snuggle" and think, "Yeah, that sounds reasonable." The entertainment we consume both reflects and reifies the rape myths we cherish. We owe it to ourselves to take it seriously and expect better. (Harding, 2015, p. 179)

Instead of censoring media that are violent or that depict myths and misconceptions about abuse and sexual assault, we should engage viewers in general, and youth in particular, in critical conversations about those depictions and what they say about our culture.

MEDIA LITERACY

As is clear, young people are constantly bombarded with violent media. Most school curricula do not include critical media studies, however. Thus young people are typically left to their own devices to make sense of the messages they receive. Adults, too, may lack the skills to sift through the array of representations and messages received through popular culture daily.

Media literacy involves "the ability to access, analyze, evaluate, and create media. Media literate youth and adults are better able to understand the complex messages we receive from television, radio, Internet, newspapers, magazines, books, billboards, video games, music, and all other forms of media" (What is media literacy?, n.d.).

Fingar and Jolls (2013) examined the use of a media literacy program called Beyond Blame in a number of California schools. They found that this program decreased aggressive behaviors and threats while also decreasing their overall media use. In 2010, the New Jersey Coalition against Sexual Assault partnered with the Media Literacy Project to create a curriculum using media literacy as a tool for sexual violence prevention. The coalition commented that "Media literacy skills teach people to identify and comment on negative sexualized mass media and understand the impact of such damaging messages."

Holbrook and Summers, authors of young adult books about rape and relationship violence, advocate media literacy. Summers explained:

> I think it's so critical, when exploring topics like sexual violence and rape culture, to ask yourself what your work is adding to the larger conversation *about* sexual violence and rape culture. Are you undermining it? Are you doing more harm than good? I believe those questions should put a very necessary pressure on a creator to treat the materially thoughtfully, carefully, respectfully, and to do the best by it that they can. If you're not asking yourself these questions or feeling that pressure when you write about these things, that's a huge problem and it's going to show in the work. It's offensive. It's lazy writing. (Kuehnert, 2015, para. 10)

Halbrook noted that we can teach people to consume different media. She explained:

> I get to choose what to consume. I get to turn off my TV, close a book, not buy a product that is lazily marketed. My one opinion isn't going to matter to the creators of those products. They don't care about my disapproval. But that's not my point. My point is that it matters to me. It matters that I don't let the normalization of rape as a plot point—a way of making men, usually, a villain or a hero on the literal backs of women's bodies— enter my own life. And that makes for more internal peace, which is something I need when there is so much rape culture surrounding me that I can't turn off. Which means, as I wrote Kayla's story, I wanted to be thorough. I wanted to create something real, human, complex and meaningful. There is no shock value in this story. (Kuehnert, 2015, para. 12)

Teens can be encouraged to explore the mediums that they use most frequently and taught to critically analyze the messages presented. For instance, instead of prohibiting youth from watching horror/slasher films, these can be a component of a media literacy project in which they are asked to assess how female victims are sexualized. Likewise, the many great documentaries by the Media Education Foundation (included in Appendix A) can be used in school and other settings to critique how popular culture presents gender roles and violence against women. Other documentaries like *Miss Representation* and

The Mask We Live In (also listed in Appendix A) can help viewers see the connections between gender roles, gender inequality, and domestic abuse and sexual assault. Many of these even come with curricular guides or discussion recommendations. Malo-Juvera (2014) conducted an experiment examining the effect of literary instructional activities about Laurie Halse Anderson's *Speak* on middle school students. He found significantly reduced rape myth acceptance among both boys and girls who completed the unit.

Given that teen girls often use magazines as a source of information about relationships, they too can be a tool for media literacy. Kettrey and Emery (2010) studied the presentation of dating violence in popular teen magazines. The review included 35 articles distributed from *Teen* (12), *Seventeen* (6), *YM* (5), *Teen People* (5), *Cosmo Girl* (4), *Girls' Life* (2), and *Teen Vogue* (1). These publications typically used case studies or stories in their coverage of dating violence. Most added statistics or other information to highlight the scope of the problem. Few articles linked gender roles to victimization, although one did, stating "when we're little girls, we're taught not to get angry, not to fight. But this is a case [when a victim of dating violence] where you have every right to be angry, and to fight back" (Karlsberg, 1991, p. 16). Another article mentioned gender stereotypes that result in people believing abuse is somewhat normal. Many also noted that males can be victims and were careful to point out that abuse is not acceptable no matter the perpetrator. Another common theme was that people learn abuse from their home and thus efforts must be taken to break the cycle. Several articles noted that law enforcement is not always the best answer, noting in particular the limitations of restraining orders, and most provided hotline numbers or other listings of resources for victims in need of help. A large percentage of the articles discussed sexual violence within abusive dating relationships, and many were quick to note the victim's virginity. This portrayal is potentially problematic as it may reinforce the notion that only "good" victims are worthy of being believed and supported. Consistent with Berns's (2004) findings, most of the recommendations for teens in need of help emphasized individual responsibility. Articles provided checklists on how to "avoid getting abused," recommended psychological counseling, or resulted in fairytale endings. The latter involved either a new boyfriend or friend "rescuing" the victim or described changed abusers. In sum, while these depictions offer a lot of useful information, they too can reinforce myths and thus are ripe for analysis by critical readers.

The BBC has started a controversial series called, *Is This Rape? Sex on Trial* in which it features fictional rape scenarios and then ask the audience to vote as to whether the female gave her consent. While some see the show as a way to engage young people in difficult conversations, critics are concerned about how the audience votes will be handled and to what degree the show will be a trigger for victims.

PREVENTION PROGRAMS

It is imperative that prevention programs be in place in schools and on campuses to prevent abuse and sexual assault. Ideal programs focus on primary prevention, which emphasize preventing abuse or assault from ever occurring. This is done by changing social norms and societal conditions. Most primary prevention programs are school-based, such as the Safe Dates curriculum for 8th and 9th grade students and ExpectRespect, a school-based program developed by SafePlace: Domestic Violence and Sexual Assault Survival Center.

One of the most important elements of curtailing abuse and assault is the role played by bystanders. In most cases, at least one other person suspects or knows what is happening, but oftentimes those individuals are passive, not active, bystanders. Many times, bystanders are actively involved in encouraging the incident. Research has found that men in general are less likely to intervene than are women (Banyard, Moynihan, & Plante, 2007; McMahon, Postmus, & Koenick, 2011). Those most immersed in hegemonic masculinity—the conception that males must be tough, aggressive, and in control—are least likely to challenge violence against women for fear of being seen as weak or gay, according to research by Fabiano and colleagues (2004) and Carlson (2008).

The Centers for Disease Control and Prevention released a report in 2014 (DeGue, 2014) reviewing the effectiveness of campus rape prevention programs. Only two were found to work. Both were sustained educational initiatives that focused on consent, gender stereotypes, healthy relationships, and bystander support. The report noted that one-off presentations, which are typical on campuses, do nothing to change risk factors of behaviors in the long term. Bystander intervention programs do not approach participants as would-be victims or would-be offenders but rather as people who must be empowered to disrupt incidents of abuse, bullying, and assault. Multiple studies have found Foubert's "The Men's Program" (2000) to decrease men's acceptance in rape myths, increase empathy toward rape victims, and increase men's willingness to speak out when others are making sexist comments (Foubert, 2000; Foubert & La Voy, 2000; Foubert & Perry, 2007). Banyard, Moynihan, and Plante (2007) found that a sexual violence bystander intervention program increased prosocial attitudes among diverse groups of participants. The group included athletes, sorority and fraternity members, student leaders, and the general student population. Similarly, Jackson Katz's Mentors in Violence Prevention, which has been used with athletes, military members, and numerous other groups, has been found to increase participants' willingness to intervene.

Prevention programming should also include policies regarding victim assistance and offender accountability. Many expressed concern when campuses began to adopt affirmative consent policies, worrying that it will kill the sexual moment. As Harding (2015) argues, if people are enjoying one another sexually, having a conversation about what each person is comfortable with will add to, not diminish, the experience.

EDUCATION AND TRAINING

It is more than just youth who must be taught about abuse and assault. Rather, education and training for professionals in fields who are likely to encounter victims and offenders as well as for people employed in the entertainment and media industries must begin to receive more accurate information about domestic violence and sexual assault. Everyday Victim Blaming, a UK-based organization, has four specific aims: (1) provide mandatory specialist training for lawyers, police, judges, and juries about domestic and sexual assault and abuse; (2) increase funding for victim services that use a gendered understanding of domestic and sexual violence and abuse; (3) provide specialist courses for journalists and others in media on how to accurately and appropriately report about these issues; and (4) provide mandatory sex and relationships education.

As pre-professionals in criminal justice, students should receive extensive information about domestic violence and sexual assault. Yet studies have found that this is not always the case. Sciarabba and Eterno (2008) analyzed 60 of the most frequently adopted introductory to criminology and criminal justice textbooks for their coverage of domestic violence. They found that the criminology books contained more coverage than did the criminal justice books, and that the criminal justice books covered largely the legal and policy aspects of domestic violence, not the scope, extent, and dynamics of the problem. Further, none of the books addressed same-sex domestic violence. Thus these future police officers, lawyers, correctional officials, and other employees of the criminal justice system may be receiving little in terms of how to actually understand and appropriately deal with abuse and assault.

Even advocates who work with victims of abuse and assault are not immune from believing the many myths and misconceptions that are so widely disseminated in popular culture. When I worked at a domestic violence agency, I routinely heard advocates make comments suggesting that they didn't believe victims or that the victim in some way precipitated her abuse. Even the prevailing philosophy used in most domestic violence shelters contributes to the notion that abuse is an individual problem and thus requires individual solutions (Finley & Esposito, 2012). Berns (2004) notes that the individual "frame" for the domestic violence movement is "empowerment-based." It emphasizes that abusers robbed victims of their power and that service providers will help them to "take their power back." As Finley and Esposito (2012) note, "While this mantra may be an improvement on the previous medicalized emphasis, it still aims exclusively on the individual, not on social or systemic issues, and the onus for change lies squarely on the victim." Bumiller (2008) explains that domestic violence advocates are charged with guiding victims to make "better" relationship choices, which diminishes their personal agency in much the same way as did their abusers. Power is being defined as the ability to make personal choices, not harnessing broader social or structural power to effect meaningful social change (Morgen & Bookman, 1988). True empowerment, however, involves, "an understanding that powerlessness is a result of structural and institutional forces that allow for inequality in power and control over resources. Therefore, empowerment should be a process that aims to identify and change the distribution of power within a culture to achieve social justice" (Berns, 2004, p. 154). Berns (2004) explains that this understanding of empowerment as solely a personal issue " may help build support for programs that help victims of domestic violence. However, it does little to develop public understanding of the social context of violence and may impede social change that could prevent violence" (p. 3). Pennington (2014) comments similarly, explaining,

> Empowerment is the new go-to word to hold those facing structural oppressions, whether this be race, class, gender, sexuality, faith etc, responsible for failure to "succeed." It erases any political analysis of oppression and makes failure to success the fault of an individual, not the system. Increasingly, we have seen "empowerment" used to denigrate victims of sexual violence: if x would only take responsibility for drinking alcohol/wearing a short skirt/ being out at night/and then being raped, they would be empowered to defend themselves. We don't quite have the vocabulary to express the particular level of rage that this piece of victim blaming causes. Holding women responsible for being the victim of a violence crime in order to empower them is pretty much the essence of victim blaming culture. (p. 23)

In essence, female empowerment is little more than empty rhetoric that can in no way result in political or social change. Critical scholars suggest that the problem with contemporary conceptualizations of female empowerment is that they utilize an empty rhetoric with no political potential or goal to change the system. It is collective action that is needed (Stache, 2013).

Studies seem to suggest that training professionals is effective. For instance, Ryan, Anastario, and DaCunha (2006) studied the changes in print news coverage of domestic violence murders before the introduction of a handbook for journalists by the Rhode Island Coalition against Domestic Violence. The handbook was introduced in June 2000, so the analysis compared pre-handbook coverage from 1996 to 1999, and coverage between June 2000 and 2002. Although they determined that it was not exclusively the handbook that was responsible for the results, the researchers found that journalists more frequently labeled murders as domestic violence murders than pre-handbook. Further, journalists dramatically increased their use of domestic violence advocates as sources for stories.

FEMINIST FRAMEWORK, REVISITED

The movements to end domestic violence and rape in the 1970s were deeply informed by feminist conceptualization of patriarchy, of understanding the connections between gender roles and gender inequality, and of collectively challenging these ideologies. With the ushering in of the conservative Reagan era and what Susan Faludi (1991) described as a backlash against feminism, these movements eventually became more conservative and lost a lot of those feminist connections. I argue here and elsewhere (see Finley, 2010; Finley & Esposito, 2012), as have Bumiller (2008), Ferraro (1996) and others, that it is essential to reframe these issues through a feminist lens.

Television plays an important role in framing what feminists are and what they look like (Projansky, 2001; Rabinowitz, 1999). Too often, feminists are portrayed as stereotypical "feminazis," aggressive man-haters, or what Gay (2014) describes as "essentialist" depictions. These overly simplistic and negative portrayals suggest that feminism is no longer necessary or is so trivial it cannot make a difference in creating greater gender equality. Stache (2013) notes that "third wave feminism's embrace of the 'girlie' model and simultaneously its emphasis on individual action has resulted in a depiction of the empowered woman who is beautiful/sexy as the one with the power . . . not that different from previous depictions focusing on a female's looks over other features" (p. 27). As was noted multiple times in this book, depictions of rape and domestic violence rarely utilize a feminist stance. This can and should be changed.

Feminism is obviously far more than feeling comfortable dressing how one wants or making one's own choices. It is the notion that our gender should not define our worth, whether we identify as male, female, or neither. As such, it is not just helpful in addressing abuse and assault of women and girls but of anyone. Feminism recognizes that abuse and assault harm more than just victims; they hurt families and communities and, ultimately, must be addressed on structural and institutional levels.

Surely there is much more to be fleshed out in these recommendations and far more to be done to ensure that domestic violence and rape become things of the past. It is my hope, however, that these suggestions, coupled with the material provided throughout this book, can help facilitate important dialogue and consideration of how that can be done.

REFERENCES

Banyard, V., Moynihan, M., & Plante, E. (2007). Sexual violence prevention through bystander education: An experimental evaluation. *Journal of Community Psychology, 35*(4), 463–481.

Berns, N. (2004). *Framing the victim: Domestic violence, media, and social problems.* New York: Aldine de Gruyter.

Bumiller, K. (2008). *In an abusive state: How neoliberalism appropriated the feminist movement against sexual violence.* Durham: Duke University Press.

Carlson, M. (2008). I'd rather go along and be considered a man: Masculinity and bystander intervention. *Journal of Men's Studies, 16*(1), 3–17.

DeGue, S. (2014). Preventing sexual violence on college campuses: Lessons from research and practice. CDC. Retrieved January 7, 2016, from https://www.notalone.gov/assets/evidence-based-strategies-for-the-prevention-of-sv-perpetration.pdf

Fabiano, P., Perkins, H. W., Berkowitz, A., Linkenbach, J., & Stark, C. (2004). Engaging men as social justice allies in ending violence against women: Evidence for a social norms approach. *Journal of American College Health, 52*(3), 105–112.

Faludi, S. (1991). *Backlash: The undeclared war against American women.* New York: Broadway Books.

Ferraro, K. (1996, fall). The dance of dependency: A genealogy of domestic violence discourse. *Hypatia, 11*(4), 77–92.

Fingar, K., & Jolls, T. (2013). Evaluation of a school-based violence prevention media literacy curriculum, *Injury Prevention, 19*, 225–233. Retrieved January 10, 2016, from http://injuryprevention.bmj.com/content/19/4.toc

Finley, L. (2010). Where's the peace in this movement? A domestic violence advocate's reflections on the movement. *Contemporary Justice Review, 13*(1), 57–69.

Finley, L., & Esposito, E. (2012). Neoliberalism and the non-profit industrial complex: The limits of a market approach to service delivery. *Peace Studies Journal, 5*(3), 4–26.

Foubert, J. (2000). The longitudinal effects of a rape-prevention program on fraternity members' attitudes, behavioral intent, and behavior. *Journal of American College Health, 48*(4), 158–163.

Foubert, J., & La Voy, S. (2000). A qualitative assessment of "The Men's Program": The impact of a rape prevention program on fraternity men. *NASPA, 30*(1), 18–30.

Foubert, J., & Perry, B. (2007). Creating lasting attitude and behavior changes in fraternity members and male student athletes. *Violence against Women, 13*(1), 70–86.

Gay, R. (2014). *Bad feminist: Essays.* New York: Harper Perennial.

Harding, K. (2015). *Asking for it: The alarming rise of rape culture—And what we can do about it.* Boston: Da Capo Lifelong Books.

Karlsberg, E. (1991, November). Acquaintance rape: What you should know. *Teen, 35*(11), 14–15.

Kettrey, H., & Emery, B. (2010). Teen magazines as educational texts on dating violence: The $2.99 approach. *Violence against Women, 16*(11), 1270–1294.

Kuehnert, S. (2015, June 1). Three YA novelists discuss rape culture in fiction: A chat. *Jezebel.* Retrieved January 10, 2016, from http://themuse.jezebel.com/three-ya-novelists-discuss-rape-culture-in-teen-fiction-1701059484

Malo-Juvera, V. (2014). Speak: The effect of literary instruction on adolescents' rape myth acceptance. *Research in the Teaching of English, 48*(4), 404–427.

McCarthy, A. (2011, April 4). *Trust:* Should rape be "R" rated? *Ms.* Retrieved January 24, 2016, from http://msmagazine.com/blog/2011/04/04/should-rape-mean-r/

McMahon, S., Postmus, J. L., & Koenick, R. A. (2011). Conceptualizing the engaging bystander approach to sexual violence prevention on college campuses. *Journal of College Student Development, 52*(1), 115–130.

Morgen, S., & Bookman, A. (1988). *Women and the politics of empowerment.* Philadelphia: Temple University Press.

Pennington, L. (2014). *Everyday victim blaming.* London: EVB Press.

Projansky, S. (2001). *Watching rape: Film and television in post-feminist culture.* New York: NYU Press.

Rabinowitz, N. (1999). Changing lenses: The politics and discourse of feminism in classics. Retrieved January 7, 2016, from http://www.stoa.org/diotima/essays/fc04/Rabinowitz.html

Ryan, C., Anastario, M., & DaCunha, A. (2006). Changing coverage of domestic violence murders: A longitudinal experiment in participatory communication. *Journal of Interpersonal Violence, 21*(2), 209–228.

Sciarabba, A., & Eterno, J. (2008). Analyzing domestic abuse coverage in introductory criminal justice and criminology textbooks. *Journal of Criminal Justice and Popular Culture, 15*(2), 217–237.

Stache, L. (2013). The rhetorical construction of female empowerment: The avenging-woman narrative in popular television and film. Theses and dissertation, University of Wisconsin, Milwaukee. Retrieved January 6, 2016, from http://dc.uwm.edu/cgi/viewcontent.cgi?article=1167&context=etd

What is media literacy? (n.d.). Media Literacy Project. Retrieved September 14, 2015, from https://medialiteracyproject.org/learn/media-literacy/

Appendix A: Films, Documentaries, Songs, and Popular Books Featuring Domestic Abuse and Sexual Assault

Note: Many other films, television shows, books, and song lyrics discuss rape and domestic violence. This list represents a sampling of those in which these social problems are central to the plot or story line. For compilations of other examples in various forms of popular culture, please see the recommended reading list in Appendix B.

FILMS

The Accused (1988)
A woman is gang-raped in a local bar and fights for justice in court.

Affliction (1999)
A small-town cop, who is investigating a mysterious death, is deeply troubled by his own history of family abuse.

Boys Don't Cry (1999)
A transgender man in Nebraska is horribly raped, assaulted, and murdered once it is discovered that he is biologically female. This is based on the true story of Tina Brandon.

The Color Purple (1985)
Based on the 1982 novel by Alice Walker, an adolescent, uneducated African American woman in rural Georgia suffers from serious abuse and incest.

Cries Unheard: The Donna Yaklich Story (1994)
A woman is abused and threatened by her husband, who is a police officer and steroids user. After being rebuffed in her attempts to seek help, she pays to have her husband killed.

Crimes of the Heart (1986)
The story of three sisters, the youngest of whom shoots her abusive husband.

A Cry for Help: The Tracey Thurmond Story (1989)
A woman attempts to flee her abusive husband but is stalked, beaten, and seriously injured with police officers standing by.

Dangerous Intentions (1995)
A woman leaves her abusive husband and takes their child to her parents' house and eventually to a protective shelter, but he continues to stalk and abuse her.

Deliverance (1972)
A group of men take a camping and canoeing trip that turns disastrous when one is raped by a group of men.

Double Jeopardy (1999)
A woman is framed for her husband's murder and finds out that he is still alive and that she cannot be convicted of the same crime twice if she kills him.

Enough (2002)
A woman marries the man of her dreams, has a child with him, and then discovers that he is unfaithful. When she confronts him, he becomes physically abusive. When she leaves him, he uses his wealth and power to pursue her.

Fried Green Tomatoes (1991)
A housewife befriends an old woman in a nursing home and hears a story about domestic abuse.

The Fugitive (1993)
A doctor comes home to find a man attacking his wife and fights him off. His wife dies as a result of the attack, and he is forced to clear his name and solve the case.

The Girl with the Dragon Tattoo (2011)
An intrepid Swedish investigative reporter teams up with a young computer hacker with a long history of abuse to uncover the truth behind the disappearance of a young woman, whose case is tied to several grisly murders of women.

I Spit on Your Grave (1978, remade in 2010)
Graphic depiction of the gang-rape of a woman who then seeks revenge against the perpetrators.

Precious (2010)
An adolescent African American woman is physically and psychologically abused by her mother and has two children as a result of being raped by her father. She struggles to overcome the odds and build a future.

The Promise (1999)
A woman leaves her abusive husband with the help of her sister. He then pursues her and kills her, leaving the sister to take care of her kids.

Shattered Dreams (1990)
The story of a woman in a long marriage with a physically and psychologically abusive husband.

Shutter Island (2010)
A U.S. marshal investigates the disappearance of a patient at an insane asylum before realizing that he is actually a patient himself committed for murdering his wife after she murdered their children.

Sleeping with the Devil (1997)
A woman who was raped in the past falls in love with a billionaire who physically assaults her and uses his wealth and the legal system as a means of control.

Sleeping with the Enemy (1991)
A woman fakes her own death and starts a new life in an attempt to escape her abusive husband, but he finds her and stalks her.

Slumdog Millionaire (2008)
Depicts abuse and trafficking in India.

The Twilight Saga (2008–2012)
A young woman, who is attracted to danger and the forbidden, is engaged in an other-worldly love triangle involving a vampire and a werewolf.

The relationship dynamics that result are harmful and abusive, if not explicitly so.

What's Love Got to Do with It? (1993)
The true story of singer Tina Turner's rise to fame and how she broke free of her abusive husband, Ike Turner.

When No One Would Listen (1992)
A woman with two kids seeks support from her long-time abusive husband.

The Woodsman (2004)
A convicted child molester comes home and attempts to reform himself in the face of threats and ostracism from family, coworkers, and police.

DOCUMENTARIES

Breaking Our Silence (2002)
A 11-minute glimpse of a group of male activists in Massachusetts speaking out against domestic violence.

The Bro Code: How Contemporary Culture Creates Sexist Men (2011)
Addresses multiple forms of contemporary popular culture that glorify misogyny and promotes men's control and subordination of women.

Defending Our Lives (1993)
This film reveals the story of Battered Women Fighting Back!, a grassroots organization that developed out of a prison support group for battered women who killed their attackers.

Every F—ing Day of My Life/One Minute to Nine (2007)
This film documents the story of Wendy Maldonado, a mother of four from Oregon who goes to prison for killing her abusive husband.

Generation M: Misogyny in Media and Culture (2008)
An assessment of misogyny and sexism in mainstream American media.

Hip Hop: Beyond Beats and Rhymes (2006)
Shows how hip-hop and the culture surrounding it promote destructive gender stereotypes. Also highlights hip-hop artists who have and are challenging this culture of exploitation.

The Hunting Ground (2015)
This film uncovers the epidemic of sexual violence on college campuses and the institutional cover-ups that ensue.

The Invisible War (2012)
This film examines the epidemic of sexual violence within the military and the difficulty for survivors to get help due to the command structure.

Killing Us Softly 4 (2010)
The latest update from Jean Kilbourne exploring how advertisements promote dangerous conceptions about female bodies.

The Mask You Live In (2015)
Addresses the unrealistic and unhealthy expectations faced by men and boys as they navigate a world that promotes aggressive hypermasculinity.

My Girlfriend Did It (1995)
This film explores sexual and domestic violence within lesbian relationships.

Not Just a Game: Power, Politics & American Sports (2010)
This film explores how American sports have glamorized militarism, racism, sexism, and homophobia. It also profiles the many athletes who have fought for social justice, both on and off the field of play.

Power and Control: Domestic Violence in America (2010)
This film explores physical and emotional abuse in the United States through the eyes of survivors and antiviolence activists.

Romeo (2009)
This film tracks the work of a domestic violence counselor in Massachusetts, Antonio Arrendel, to reform batterers.

Sex Crimes Unit (2011)
This film looks into the New York district attorney's unit that prosecutes sex crimes and exposes the injustice experienced by rape survivors.

Sin by Silence (2009)
This film reveals the lives of women incarcerated at the California Institution for Women who have formed the group Convicted Women against Abuse in order to confront domestic violence.

Telling Amy's Story (2010)
This film examines the life and death of a victim of domestic violence, Amy Homan McGee.

V-Day: Until the Violence Stops (2003)
This film documents how the Broadway show *The Vagina Monologues*, written by Eve Ensler, became a global movement to combat violence against women and girls.

Wrestling with Manhood: Boys, Bullying and Battering (2002)
An in-depth analysis of sexism, homophobia, and violence presented in professional wrestling.

SONGS

"Ain't So Easy," David & David (1990)
From the perspective of a batterer who is trying to convince his partner that he will change his ways.

"Amy in the White Coat," Bright Eyes (2006)
About a father sexually abusing his daughter from the perspective of two bystanders.

"Animal," Pearl Jam (1993)
About a woman being abducted on the street and raped. Key line: "I'd rather be with an animal."

"Behind the Wall," Tracy Chapman (1988)
About law enforcement's reluctance to intervene in domestic violence cases. Key line: "It won't do no good to call/The police always come late/If they come at all."

"Black Eyes Blue Tears," Shania Twain (1997)
About a survivor of domestic violence who is full of resolve. Key line: "I'd rather die standing/Than live on my knees, begging please."

"Cocaine Blues," Johnny Cash (1968)
About a drug user who kills his girlfriend and attempts to escape justice. Key line: "I took a shot of cocaine, and I shot my woman down."

"Crack in the Mirror," Betty Elders (1993)
About a child who is sexually abused by a "hired hand" in her house for years while her family remains in denial.

"Daddy's Girl," The Scorpions (2006)
About a girl whose father sexually abuses her while her mother is in denial.

"Date Rape," Sublime (1991)
About a date rape whose perpetrator goes to prison and is raped in turn by other inmates. Key line: "Come on, baby, don't be afraid/If it wasn't for date rape I'd never get laid."

"Dear John," Taylor Swift (2010)
From the perspective of a survivor rebuking "John" for having sexual relations with her when she was "too young."

"Every Breath You Take," The Police (1983)
From the perspective of a man who is obsessed with a woman and is stalking her. Key line: "Every move you make/I'll be watching you."

"Face to Face," Garth Brooks (2000)
About dealing with bullies in a variety of contexts including a date-rape situation.

"Fight Back," Holly Near (2000)
From the perspective of a woman urging others to stand up and fight back against domestic and sexual violence. Key line: "Fight back, I can't make it alone/Fight back, in large numbers/Together we can make a safe home."

"Goodbye Earl," Dixie Chicks (1999)
About an abusive husband who evades legal consequences but not vigilantism.

"He Hit Me (It Felt Like a Kiss)," Crystals (1992)
About a victim of domestic violence who sympathizes with her abuser. Key line: "He hit me/And it felt like a kiss."

"He's Hurting Me," Maria Mena (2006)
About a woman pleading for help from her abusive partner. She blames herself for his violence.

"Hey Joe," Jimi Hendrix (1962)
About a man who shot and killed his wife for cheating on him and is planning to flee to Mexico. Key line: "I'm going down to shoot my old lady. . . . I caught her messing around with another man."

"Hold Her Down," Toad the Wet Sprocket (1991)
From the perspective of a man expressing shame about a rape.

"I'm OK," Christina Aguilera (2002)
About a grown daughter confronting her father about his physical abuse of her mother. Key line: "Hurt me to see the pain across my mother's face/ Every time my father's fist would put her in her place."

"(The) Incest Song," Buffy Sainte-Marie (1964)
About a girl who has a child as a result of an incestuous relationship with her brother.

"Janie's Got a Gun," Aerosmith (1989)
About a woman who gets revenge on her father for sexually abusing her by shooting him.

"La Nina," Aventura (2005)
About a 9-year-old girl being sexually abused in her bed (in Spanish).

"Lily of the Valley," Judy Collins (1995)
About a woman who kills her abusive husband and is hanged as a result.

"Luka," Suzanne Vega (1987)
About domestic violence from the perspective of a little girl. Key line: "They only hit until you cry/After that you don't ask why."

"Me and a Gun," Tori Amos (1992)
About a woman being raped by a man and the accompanying victim-blaming. This song inspired the Rape, Abuse & Incest National Network (RAINN), which the singer sponsored.

"Mercy Street," Peter Gabriel (1986)
About the psychological and emotional effects of childhood incest.

"Never Again," Nickelback (2001)
About a woman being physically abused by her male partner and ultimately shooting him. Key line: "I hear her scream from down the hall/Amazing she can even talk at all."

"977," The Pretenders (2004)
About a physically violent relationship whose victim believes the batterer loves her and sympathizes with him. Key line: "He hit me with his belt/His tears were all I felt."

"99 Biker Friends," Bowling for Soup (2006)
About domestic violence from the perspective of a male friend of the victim. He mocks and threatens the batterer with retaliation.

"Oh Father," Madonna (1989)
From the perspective of a woman reflecting on her abuse as a child at the hands of her father and empathizing with him. Key line: "Oh Father you never wanted to live that way/You never wanted to hurt me."

"Only Women Bleed," Alice Cooper (1975)
About the cycle of domestic violence with a woman as the victim and a man as the perpetrator.

"Polly," Nirvana (1991)
About the real-life abduction, rape, and torture of a 14-year-old girl who escaped from her attacker.

"Rape Me," Nirvana (2002)
About a rape victim goading the attacker. Key line: "Rape me/Rape me my friend."

"Run for your Life," The Beatles (1965)
From the perspective of a jealous male lover warning his female partner. Key line: "Well I'd rather see you dead, little girl/Than to be with another man."

"Runaway Love," Ludicris & Mary J. Blige (2006)
About a 9-year-old girl who is being sexually abused by the men her mother brings over to the house and beaten by her stepfather.

"Smooth Criminal," Michael Jackson (1987)
About a woman named Annie who was attacked in her apartment by a "smooth criminal."

"That Guy," Tori Amos (2009)
About a man who takes the stress of his life out on his family. Key line: "Just brings his war home she cries/Why can't Daddy leave his war outside?"

"Valentine's Day Is Over," Billy Bragg (1988)
From the perspective of a woman decrying the rough state of her marriage. Key line: "Thank you for the card/Thank you for the things you taught me when you hit me hard."

"Wash Away Those Years," Creed (1999)
About a sexual assault survivor reflecting on the past and finding ways to move forward.

"Where the Wild Roses Grow," Nick Cave and Kylie Minogue (2002)
From the perspective of women being assaulted by men in a romanticized way.

POPULAR BOOKS (FICTION; 2000–PRESENT)

Axel, Harper Sloan (2013)
About a woman attempting to deal with an angry, violent ex-husband.

Backseat Saints, Joshilyn Jackson (2010)
About a woman with a taste for violent men who is caught up in her wayward mother's legacy.

Bastard out of Carolina, Dorothy Allison (2005)
Ruth Anne "Bone" Boatwright, born a bastard, is abused and watched the abuse of her mother by her stepfather.

Behind Closed Doors, Susan Sloan (2005)
Valerie and her children endure abuse from her husband Jack, but when he begins attacking his grandson it is the last straw.

Bitter End, Jennifer Brown (2011)
About a young woman dealing with a jealous boyfriend.

Consequences, Aleatha Romig (2011)
About a woman who is kidnapped by a wealthy tycoon.

Don't Make Me Beautiful, Elle Casey (2013)
About an abused woman's journey toward freedom from her abuser.

Dreamland, Sarah Dessen (2000)
Shows the dynamics of abusive teen relationships and the difficulties victims have in leaving abusers.

An Early Frost, Jenna Brooks (2014)
About a family law attorney who represents battered mothers and kids suffering from abuse.

Fifty Shades of Grey, E. L. James (2011)
About a young woman who falls in love with a rich entrepreneur who is obsessed with the need to control.

Gone Girl, Gillian Flynn (2014)
Nick and Amy seem to have everything until she disappears. As the story unfolds, Amy alleges abuse and sexual assault. But there's far more to the story.

Heart on a Chain, Cindy C. Bennett (2010)
About a woman victimized by poverty, bullying, and her drug-addicted mother.

Into the Darkest Corner, Elizabeth Haynes (2011)
About a woman who struggles to deal with a violent and controlling male partner.

Just Listen, Sarah Dessen (2006)
Annabel hides from everyone, including her best friends, that she was raped by the popular boyfriend of her former best friend.

October Snow, Jenna Brooks (2012)
Josie finally escapes from her abuser and begins working with battered women and has a good friend who is abused, prompting her rage and revenge efforts against her friend's abuser.

Picture Perfect, Jody Picoult (2002)
Cassie and Alex seem to have the perfect marriage, but all is not what it seems.
Reason to Breathe, Rebecca Donovan (2011)
About a woman who suffers from abuse and tries to hide it while seeking true love.

The Rules of Survival, Nancy Werlin (2006)
About a family suffering at the hands of a physically abusive mother and searching for someone to rescue them.

Safe Haven, Nicholas Sparks (2010)
Newcomer Katie slowly starts a relationship with a man in town and makes a new friend. Over time, she reveals the abuse that prompted her to relocate.

Shelter Mountain, Robyn Carr (2007)
About a marine who meets a battered woman and her young child and tries to help them.

Split, Swati Avasthi (2010)
About a teenage boy who runs away from an abusive father.

A Thousand Splendid Suns, Khaled Hosseini (2006)
About Afghan women who suffer cruelty and violence at the hands of their husbands.

Appendix B: Recommended Resources on Rape, Domestic Abuse, and Popular Culture

Adichie, C. (2014). *We should all be feminists*. New York: Vintage.

Aldarondo, E., & Mederos, F. (Eds.). (2002). *Programs for men who batter*. New Jersey: Civic Research Institute.

Anderson, I., & Doherty, K. (2007). *Accounting for rape: Psychology, feminism and discourse analysis in the study of sexual violence*. Oxford: Routledge.

Badley, L. (1995). *Film, horror, and the body fantastic*. Westport, CT: Greenwood.

Bancroft, L. (2003). *Why does he do that? Inside the minds of angry and controlling men*. New York: Berkley.

Barnett, O., Miller-Perrin, C., & Perrin, R. (2011). *Family violence across the lifespan: An introduction*, 3rd ed. Thousand Oaks, CA: Sage.

Baumgardner, J., & Richards, A. (2005). *Grassroots: A field guide for feminist activism*. New York: Farrar, Straus, & Giroux.

Benedict, H. (1992). *Virgin or vamp: How the press covers sex crimes*. Oxford: Oxford University Press.

Benedict, J. (1997). *Public heroes, private felons*. Boston, MA: Northeastern University Press.

Benedict, J. (1998). *Athletes and acquaintance rape*. Thousand Oaks, CA: Sage.

Benedict, J. (1998). *Pros and cons: The criminals who play in the NFL*. New York: Grand Central Press.

Benedict, J. (2004). *Out of bounds: Inside the NBA's culture of rape, violence & crime*. New York: HarperCollins.

Bourke, J. (2008). *Rape: A history from 1860 to the present*. London: Virago.

Boyle, K. (2005). *Media violence: Gendering the debates*. London: Sage Publications.

Brownmiller, S. (1993). *Against our will: Men, women and rape*. New York: Ballantine.

Buchwald, E., Fletcher, P., & Roth, M. (2003). *Transforming a rape culture*. Minneapolis, MN: Milkweed Editions.

Buzawa, E., & Buzawa, C. (2002). *Domestic violence: The criminal justice response.* Thousand Oaks, CA: Sage.

Ching-In, C., Dulani, J., & Piepzna-Samarasinha, L. (Eds.). (2011). *The revolution starts at home: Confronting intimate violence within activist communities.* Boston: South End.

Clover, C.(1992). *Men, women and chainsaws: Gender in the modern horror film.* Princeton, NJ: Princeton University Press.

Collins, G. (2003). *American women.* New York: Harper Perennial.

Cook, P. (2009). *Abused men: The hidden side of domestic violence.* Westport, CT: Praeger.

Cose, E. (1995). *A man's world: How real is male privilege—and how high is its price?* New York: HarperCollins.

Cuklanz, L. (1996). *Rape on trial: How the mass media construct legal reform and social change.* Philadelphia: University of Pennsylvania Press.

Cuklanz, L. (2000). *Rape on prime time: Television, masculinity and sexual violence.* Philadelphia: University of Pennsylvania Press.

Daniel, O., & Erica, M. (Eds.). (2009). *Psychological and physical aggression in couples: Causes and interventions.* Washington, D.C.: American Psychological Association Press.

Davies, J., Lyon, E., & Monti-Cantania, D. (1998). *Safety planning with battered women: Complex lives, different choices.* Thousand Oaks, CA: Sage.

Dines, G. (2010). *Pornland: How porn has hijacked our sexuality.* Boston: Beacon Press.

Durham, M. (2008). *The Lolita effect.* Woodstock, NY: Overlook Press.

Dutton, D. (2007). *Rethinking domestic violence.* Toronto: UBC Press.

Ehrlich, S. (2003). *Representing rape: Language and sexual consent.* Oxford: Routledge.

Estrich, S. (1987). *Real rape: How the legal system victimizes women who say no.* Cambridge, MA: Harvard University Press.

Faludi, S. (1991). *Backlash: The undeclared war against American women.* New York: Doubleday.

Finley, L. (Ed.). (2013). *Encyclopedia of domestic violence and abuse.* Santa Barbara, CA: ABC-CLIO.

Finley, L., & Stringer, E. (Eds.). (2010). *Beyond burning bras: Feminist activism for everyone.* Santa Barbara, CA: Praeger.

Fleisher, S., & Krienart, J. (2009). *The myth of prison rape: Sexual culture in American prisons.* Lanham, MD: Rowman & Littlefield.

Freedman, E. (2002). *No turning back: The history of feminism and the future of women.* New York: Ballantine.

Freedman, E. (2013). *Redefining rape: Sexual violence in an era of suffrage and segregation.* Cambridge, MA: Harvard University Press.

Friedman, J. (2011). *What you really, really want: The smart girl's shame-free guide to sex and safety.* New York: Seal.

Friedman, J., & Valenti, J. (2008). *Yes means yes! Visions of female power and a world without rape.* New York: Seal.

Gay, R. (2014). Bad feminist: Essays. New York: Harper Perennial.

Girschik, L. (2002). *Woman-to-woman sexual violence: Does she call it rape?* Boston, MA: Northeastern University Press.

Gordon, L. (2002). *Heroes of their own lives: The politics and history of family violence.* Champaign, IL: University of Illinois Press.

Gould, J. (2007). *The innocence commission: Preventing wrongful convictions and restoring the criminal justice system. New York:* New York University Press.

Green, P. (1998). *Cracks in the pedestal: Ideology and gender in Hollywood.* Amherst, MA: University of Massachusetts Press.

Grossman, D., & DeGaetano, G. (2014). *Stop teaching our kids to kill: A call to action against TV, movie, & video game violence.* New York: Harmony.

Groves, B. (2002). *Children who see too much: Lessons from the child witness to violence project.* Boston, MA: Beacon.

Haaken, J. (2010). *What does storytelling tell us about domestic violence? Hard knocks: Domestic violence and the psychology of storytelling.* London: Routledge.

Hamel, J. (2005). *Gender-inclusive treatment of intimate partner abuse: A comprehensive approach.* New York; Springer.

Hansen, M., & Harway, M. (Eds.). (2002). *Battering and family therapy: A feminist perspective.* Thousand Oaks, CA: Sage.

Haskell, M. (1987). *From reverence to rape: The treatment of women in the movies.* Chicago, IL: University of Chicago Press.

Healey, K., Smith, C., & O'Sullivan, C. (2009). *Batterer intervention: Program approaches and criminal justice strategies.* Washington, D.C.: U.S. Department of Justice.

Hines, D., & Malley-Morrison, K. (2005). *Family violence in the United States: Defining, understanding, and combating abuse.* Thousand Oaks, CA: Sage.

Holland, J. (2006). *Misogyny: The world's oldest prejudice.* New York: Carroll & Graf.

hooks, b. (1981). *Ain't I a woman: Black women and feminism.* Boston, MA: South End.

hooks, b. (2004). *The will to change: Men, masculinity, and love.* New York: Atria.

Horeck, T. (2004). *Public rape: Representing violation in fiction and film.* London: Routledge.

Incite! Women of Color against Violence. (2007). *The revolution will not be funded: Beyond the non-profit industrial complex.* Boston: South End.

Jones, A. (2000). *Next time, she'll be dead: Battering and how to stop it.* Boston: Beacon.

Katz, J. (2006). *The macho paradox.* Naperville, IL: Sourcebooks, Inc.

Kimmel, M. (2006). *Manhood in America* (2nd ed.). New York: Oxford University Press.

Kimmel, M. (2008). *Guyland: The perilous world where boys become men.* New York: Harper.

Kimmel, M. (2010). *Misframing men: The politics of contemporary masculinities.* New Brunswick, NJ: Rutgers University Press.

Kimmel, M. (2013). Angry white men: Masculinity at the end of an era. New York: Nation Books.

Kimmel, M., & Messner, M. (Eds.). (2001). *Men's Lives*. Boston, MA: Allyn & Bacon.

Kirk, G., & Okazawa-Rey, M. (2007). *Women's lives, multicultural perspectives*, 4th ed. Boston: McGraw-Hill.

Krakauer, K. (2015). *Missoula: Rape and the justice system in a college town*. New York: Doubleday.

Kristof, N., & WuDunn, S. (2009). *Half the sky: Turning oppression into opportunity for women worldwide*. New York: Alfred A. Knopf.

La Violette, A., & Barnett, O. (2000). *It could happen to anyone: Why battered women stay*, 2nd ed. Thousand Oaks, CA: Sage.

Lamb, S., & Brown, L. (2006). *Packaging girlhood: Rescuing our daughters from marketers' schemes*. New York: St. Martin's.

Laughlin, K., & Castledine, J. (2010) *Breaking the wave: Women, their organizations, and feminism 1945–1985*. New York: Routledge.

Leonard, E. (2002). *Convicted survivors: The imprisonment of battered women who kill*. New York: SUNY Press.

Levy, B. (1998). *Dating violence: young women in danger*, 2nd ed. Seattle, CA: Seal.

Levy, B. (Ed.). (1998). *In love and danger: A teen's guide to breaking free of abusive relationships*, 2nd ed. Seattle, WA: Seal.

Lobel, K. (Ed.). (1986). *Naming the violence: Speaking out about lesbian battering*. Seattle, WA: Seal Press.

Logan, T. K., Cole, J., Shannon, L., & Walker, R. (2006). *Partner stalking: How women respond, cope, and survive (Springer Series on Family Violence)*. New York: Springer Publishing Company.

Loseke, D., Gelles, R., & Cavanaguh, M, (Eds.). (2004). *Current controversies on family violence*, 2nd ed. Newbury Park, CA: Sage.

Madriz, E. (1997). *Nothing bad happens to good girls: Fear of crime in women's lives*. Berkeley, CA: University of California Press.

Magestro, M. (2015). *Assault on the small screen: Representations of sexual violence on primetime television dramas*. London: Rowman & Littlefield.

McGuire, D. (2010). *At the dark end of the street: Black women, rape, and resistance—A new history of the civil rights movement from Rosa Parks to the rise of Black Power*. New York: Vintage.

McNulty, F. (1989). *The burning bed*. New York: Avon.

Miedzian, M. (2002). *Boys will be boys: Breaking the link between masculinity and violence*. New York: Lantern Books.

Muhammad, M. (2009). *Scared silent: The Mildred Muhammad story*. New York: Strebor Books.

Mulla, S. (2014). *The violence of care: Rape victims, forensic nurses and sexual assault intervention*. New York: New York University Press.

Moorti, S. (2002). *Color of rape: Gender and race in television's public spheres*. Albany, NY: State University of New York Press.

Moss, A., & Jones, D. (2014). *Relationship red flags: Domestic violence, dating abuse, pathological bonds, toxic partners, & more decoded.* Dubois, WY: Saxony Hill Press.

Murray, A. (2008). *From outrage to courage: Women taking action for health and justice.* Monroe, ME: Common Courage.

Parrott, A., & Cummings, N. (2006). *Forsaken females: The global brutalization of women.* Lanham, MD: Rowman & Littlefield.

Pearson, P. (1997). *When she was bad: Violent women and the myth of innocence.* New York: Viking.

Pinals, D. (2007). *Stalking: Psychiatric perspectives and practical approaches.* New York: Oxford University Press.

Pleck, E. (1989). *Domestic tyranny: The making of American social policy against family violence from colonial times to the present.* New York: Oxford.

Quart, A. (2004). *Branded: The buying and selling of teenagers.* New York: Basic Books.

Raine, A. (2013). *The anatomy of violence: The biological roots of crime.* New York: Vintage.

Raphael, J. (2013). *Rape is rape: How denial, distortion, and victim blaming are fueling a hidden acquaintance rape crisis.* Chicago: Lawrence Hill Books.

Reed, J. (2000). *The new avengers: Feminism, femininity and the rape-revenge cycle.* Manchester: Manchester University Press.

Renzetti, C. (1992). *Violent betrayal: partner abuse in lesbian relationships.* Thousand Oaks, CA: Sage.

Richards, T., & Marcum. C. (Eds.). (2015). *Sexual victimization: Then and now.* Thousand Oaks, CA: Sage.

Robson, P., & Silbey, J. (Eds.). *Law and justice on the small screen.* Hart Publishing.

Rowland, D. (2004). *The boundaries of her body: The troubling history of women's rights in America.* Naperville, IL: Sphinx.

Russell, B. (2010). *Battered Woman Syndrome as a legal defense: History, effectiveness and implications.* North Carolina: McFarland.

Russell-Brown, K. (2008). *The color of crime: Racial hoaxes, white fear, black protectionism, police harassment and other microaggressions,* 2nd ed. New York: New York University Press.

Sanday, P. (2007). *Fraternity gang rape: Sex, brotherhood and privilege on campus.* New York: New York University Press.

Sanday, P. (2011). *A woman scorned: Acquaintance rape on trial.* New York: Anchor.

Scarce, M. (2001). *Male on male rape: The hidden toll of stigma and shame.* New York: Basic.

Schechter, S. (1982). *Women and male violence: The visions and struggles of the battered women's movement.* Cambridge, MA: South End Press.

Shaw, S., & Lee, J. (2007). *Women's voices, feminist visions,* 3rd ed. Boston: McGraw Hill.

Sielke, S. (2002). *Reading rape: The rhetoric of sexual violence in American literature and culture, 1790–1990*. Princeton, NJ: Princeton University Press.

Singular, S., & Singular, J. (2015*). The spiral notebook: The Aurora theater shooter and the epidemic of mass violence committed by American youth*. Berkeley, CA: Counterpoint.

Smith, A. (2005). *Conquest: Sexual violence and American Indian genocide*. Boston: South End Press.

Sokoloff, N., Smith, B., West, C., & Dupont, I. (2005). *Domestic violence at the margins: Readings on race, class, gender and culture*. New Jersey: Rutgers University Press.

Solnit, R. (2014). *Men explain things to me*. Chicago, IL: Haymarket Books.

Stark, E. (2009). *Coercive control: How men entrap women in personal life*. New York: Oxford University Press.

Stith, S., McCollum, E., & Rosen, K. (2011). *Couples therapy for domestic violence: Finding safe solutions*. Washington, D.C.: American Psychological Association.

Straus, M., Gelles, R., & Steinmetz, S. (2009). *Behind closed doors: Violence in the American family*. New Brunswick, NJ: Transaction Publishers.

Tazlitz, A. (1999). *Rape and the culture of the classroom*. New York: New York University Press.

Tifft, L. (1993). *Battering of women: The failure of intervention and the case for prevention*. Boulder, CO: Westview.

Valenti, J. (2009). *The purity myth: How America's obsession with virginity is hurting young women*. New York: Seal.

Vlachova, M., & Biason, L. (Eds.). (2005). *Women in an insecure world: Violence against women facts, figures and analysis*. Geneva: Centre for the Democratic Control of Armed Forces.

Walker, L. (1980). *The battered woman*. New York: Harper.

Walker, L. (2000). *The battered woman syndrome*, 2nd ed. *New York: Springer*.

Warshaw, R. (1994*). I never called it rape: The MS report on recognizing, fighting, and surviving date and acquaintance rape*. New York: Harper Perennial.

Weatherholt, A. (2008). *Breaking the silence: The church responds to domestic violence*. Atlanta, GA: Morehouse.

Welchman, L., & Houssain, S. (Eds.). (2005). *Honour: Crimes, paradigms, and violence against women*. London: Zed Press.

Wooten, C., & Mitchell, R. (Eds.). *The crisis of campus sexual violence: Critical perspectives on prevention and response*. London: Routledge.

Journals

Contemporary Justice Review
Feminist Criminology
Gender & Society
Journal of Interpersonal Violence

Men and Masculinities
Trauma Violence Abuse
Violence against Women: An International and Interdisciplinary Journal
Violence and Victims
The Voice: A Journal of the Battered Women's Movement

SELECTED JOURNAL ARTICLES, 2000–2015

Anderson, D., & Saunders, D. (2003). Leaving an abusive partner: An empirical review of predictors, the process of leaving, and psychological well-being. *Trauma Violence Abuse, 4*(2), 163–191.

Angelone, D., Mitchell, D., & Grossi, L. (2015). Men's perceptions of an acquaintance rape: The role of relationship length, victim resistance, and gender role attitudes. *Journal of Interpersonal Violence, 30*(13), 2278–2303.

Ascione, F., Weber, C., Thompson, T., Heath, J., Maruyama, M., & Hayashi, K. (2007). Battered pets and domestic violence: Animal abuse reported by women experiencing intimate violence and by non-abused women. *Violence against Women, 13*(4), 354–373.

Babcock, J., Green, C., & Robie, C. (2004). Does batterers' treatment work? A meta-analytic review of domestic violence treatment. *Clinical Psychological Review, 23*, 1023–1053.

Banyard, V., Moynihan, M., & Crossman, M. (2009). Reducing sexual violence on campus: The role of student leaders as empowered bystanders. *Journal of College Student Development, 50*(4), 446–457.

Bennett, L., & Williams, O. (2003). Substance abuse and men who batter: Issues in therapy and practice. *Violence against Women, 9*, 558–575.

Betancourt, G., Breitbart, V., & Colarossi, L. (2010). Barriers to screening for intimate partner violence: A mixed-methods study of providers in family planning clinics. *Perspectives on Sexual and Reproductive Health, 42*(4), 236.

Bhuyan, R., & Senturia, K. (2005). Understanding domestic violence resource utilization and survivor solutions among immigrant and refugee women. *Journal of Interpersonal Violence, 20*(8), 895–901.

Bhuyan, R., Mell, M., Senturia, K., Sullivan, M, & Shiu-Thornton, S. (2005). "Women must endure according to their karma": Cambodian immigrant women talk about domestic violence. *Journal of Interpersonal Violence, 20*(8), 902–921.

Black, B., & Weistz, A. (2003). Dating violence: help-seeking behaviors of African American middle schoolers. *Violence against Women, 9*(2), 187–206.

Bui, H. N. (2003). Help-Seeking behavior among abused immigrant women. *Violence against Women, 9*(2), 207–239.

Burke, J., Thieman, L., Gielen, A., O'Campo, P., & McDonnell, K. (2005). Intimate partner violence, substance abuse, and HIV among low-income women: taking a closer look. *Violence against Women, 11*(9), 1140–61

Burn, S. (2009). A situational model of sexual assault prevention through bystander intervention. *Sex Roles, 60*(11), 779–792.

Carlson, B., & Worden, A. (2005). Attitudes and beliefs about domestic violence: Results of a public opinion survey: I. Definitions of domestic violence, criminal domestic violence, and prevalence. *Journal of Interpersonal Violence, 20*(10), 1197–1218.

Carlson, M. (2008). I'd rather go along and be considered a man: Masculinity and bystander intervention. *Journal of Men's Studies, 16*(1), 3–17.

Carlyle, K. E., Slater, M. D., & Chakroff, J. L. (2008). Newspaper coverage of intimate partner violence: Skewing representation of risk. *Journal of Communication, 58*(1), 168–186.

Chiu, E. (2010). That guy's a batterer! A scarlet letter approach to domestic violence in the information age. *Family Law Quarterly, 44*(2), 255.

Cismaru, M., & Lavack, A. M. (2011). Campaigns targeting perpetrators of intimate partner violence. *Trauma, Violence, & Abuse, 12*(4), 183–197.

Coker, D. (2006). Restorative justice, Navajo peacemaking and domestic violence. *Theoretical Criminology, 10*(1), 67–85.

Danis, F. (2003). Domestic violence and crime victim compensation: A research agenda. *Violence against Women, 9*(3), 374–390.

Dick, A., & McMahon, S. (2011). "Being in a room with like-minded men": An exploratory study of men's participation in a bystander intervention program to prevent intimate partner violence. *Journal of Men's Studies, 19*(1), 3.

Edleson, J., Mbilinyi, L., Beeman, S., & Hagemesiter, A. (2003). How children are involved in adult domestic violence: Results from a four-city telephone survey. *Journal of Interpersonal Violence, 18*(1), 18–32.

Fabiano, P., Perkins, H. W., Berkowitz, A., Linkenbach, J., & Stark, C. (2004). Engaging men as social justice allies in ending violence against women: Evidence for a social norms approach. *Journal of American College Health, 52*(3), 105–112.

Faver, C., & Strand, E. (2003). Domestic violence and animal cruelty: Untangling the web of abuse. *Journal of Social Work Education, 39*(2), 237–253.

Feder, L. & Wilson, D. B. (2005). A meta-analytic review of court-mandated batterer intervention programs: Can courts affect abusers' behavior? *Journal of Experimental Criminology, 1*(2), 239–262.

Finley, L. (2010). Where's the peace in this movement?: A domestic violence advocates reflections on the movement. *Contemporary Justice Review, 13*(1), 57–69.

Finley, L. (2011). Examining domestic violence and South Asian immigrants in the U.S. Satyam: The Chicago-Kent College of Law's Journal on South Asia and the Law. Available at: http://sites.google.com/site/chicagokentsatyam/issue-1-articles.

Finley, L., & Esposito, L. (2012). Neoliberalism and the non-profit industrial complex: The limits of a market approach to service delivery. *Peace Studies Journal, 5*(3), 4–26.

Fischer, P., Greitemeyer, T., Pollozek, F., & Frey, D. (2006). The unresponsive bystander: Are bystanders more responsive in dangerous emergencies? *European Journal of Social Psychology, 36*(2), 267–278.

Foubert, J., & Perry, B. (2007). Creating lasting attitude and behavior changes in fraternity members and male student athletes. *Violence against Women, 13*(1), 70–86.

Fox, J., & Tierney, S. (2011). Trapped in a toxic relationship: comparing the views of women living with anorexia nervosa to those experiencing domestic violence. *Journal of Gender Studies, 20*(1), 31–41.

Frohmann, L. (2005). The framing safety project: Photographs and narratives by battered women. *Violence against Women, 11*(11), 1396–1419.

Gondolf, E., & Beeman, A. (2003). Women's accounts of domestic violence versus tactics-based outcome categories. *Violence against Women, 9*(3), 278–301.

Goodkind, J., Gillum, T., Bybee, D., & Sullivan, C. (2003). The impact of family and friends' reactions on the well-being of women with abusive partners. *Violence against Women, 9*(3), 347–373.

Hampton, R., Oliver, W., & Maragan, L. (2003). Domestic violence in the African American community: An analysis of social and structural factors. *Violence against Women, 9*(5), 533–557.

Hernandez-Ruiz, E. (2005). Effect of music therapy on the anxiety levels and sleep patterns of abused women in shelters. *Journal of Music Therapy, XLII* (2), 140–158.

Johnson, R. (2014). Rape and gender conflict in a patriarchal state. *Crime and Delinquency, 60*(7), 1110–1128.

Kantor, G., & Little, L. (2003). Defining the boundaries of child neglect: When does domestic violence equate with parental failure to protect? *Journal of Interpersonal Violence, 18*(4), 338–354.

Kennedy, A. (2005). Resilience among urban adolescent mothers living with violence: Listening to their stories. *Violence against Women, 11*(12), 1490–1514.

Kocot, T., & Goodman, L. (2003). The roles of coping and social support in battered women's mental health. *Violence against Women, 9*(3), 323–346.

Lehrner, A., & Allen, N. E. (2009). Still a movement after all these years?: Current tensions in the domestic violence movement. *Violence against Women, 15*, 656–677.

Lippy, C., Perilla, J., Vasquez-Serrata, J., & Wienberg, J. (2012). Integrating women's voices and theory: a comprehensive domestic violence intervention for Latinas. *Women and Therapy, 35*(1–2), 93.

Loya, R. (2014). Rape as an economic crime: The impact of sexual violence on survivor's employment and economic well-being. *Journal of Interpersonal Violence, 30*(16), 2793–2813.

McMahon, M., & Pence, E., (2003). Making social change reflections on individual and institutional advocacy with women arrested for domestic violence. *Violence against Women, 9*(10), 47–74.

McMahon, S., Postmus, J. L., & Koenick, R. A. (2011). Conceptualizing the engaging bystander approach to sexual violence prevention on college campuses. *Journal of College Student Development, 52*(1), 115–130.

Mears, D. (2003). Research and interventions to reduce domestic violence revictimization. *Trauma Violence Abuse, 4*(2), 127–147.

Menjívar, C., & Salcido, O. (2002). Immigrant women and domestic violence: Common experiences in different countries. *Gender & Society, 16*(6), 898–920.

Moynihan, N., Banyard, V., Arnold, J., Eckstein, R., & Stapleton, J. (2010), Engaging intercollegiate athletes in preventing and intervening in sexual and intimate partner violence. *Journal of American College Health, 59*(3), 197–204.

Murphy, J. C., & Rubinson, R. (2005). Domestic violence and mediation: Responding to the challenges of crafting effective screens. *Family Law Quarterly, 39*(1), 53–85.

Nash, S. (2005). Through black eyes: African American women's constructions of their experiences with intimate male partner violence. *Violence against Women, 11*(11), 1420–1440.

Neighbors, C., Walker, D. D., Mbilinyi, L. F., O'Rourke, A., Edeison, J., Zegree, J., et al. (2010). Normative misperceptions of abuse among perpetrators of intimate partner violence. *Violence against Women, 16*(4), 370–386.

Page, A. (2010). True colors: Police officers and rape myth acceptance. *Feminist Criminology, 5*(4), 315–344.

Patterson, N., & Sears, C. (2011). Letting men off the hook? Domestic violence and postfeminist celebrity culture. *Genders, 53*, 1–17. Retrieved January 10, 2016, from http://www.academia.edu/4049475/Letting_Men_Off_the_Hook_Domestic_Violence_and_Postfeminist_Celebrity_Culture.

Patton, T., & Snyder-Yuly, J. (2007). Any four black men will do: Rape, race, and the ultimate scapegoat. *Journal of Black Studies, 37*(6), 859–895.

Raj, A., & Silverman, J. (2007). Domestic violence help-seeking behaviors of South Asian battered women residing in the United States. *International Review of Victimology, 14*(1), 143–170.

Rich, K., & Seffrin, P. (2014). Birds of a feather or fish out of water? Policewomen taking rape reports. *Feminist Criminology, 9*(2), 137–159.

Rogers, B., McGee, G., Vann, A., Thompson, N., & Williams, O. (2003). Substance abuse and domestic violence: stories of practitioners that address the co-occurrence among battered women. *Violence against Women, 9*(5), 590–598.

Rosen, L. (2007). Rape rates and military personnel in the United States: An exploratory study. *Violence against Women, 13*(9), 945–960.

Russell, B., & Melillo, L. (2006). Attitudes toward battered women who kill: Defendant typicality and judgments of culpability. *Criminal Justice and Behavior, 33*(2), 219–241.

Shetty, S., & Edleson, J. (2005). Adult domestic violence in cases of international parental child abduction. *Violence against Women, 11*(1), 115–138.

Slote, K., Cuthbert, C., Mesh, C., Driggers, M., Bancroft, L., & Silverman, J. (2005). Battered mothers speak out: Participatory human rights documentation as a model for research and activism in the United States. *Violence against Women, 11*(11), 1367–1395.

Stayton, C., & Duncan, M. (2005). Mutable influences on intimate partner abuse screening in health care settings: A synthesis of the literature. *Trauma Violence Abuse, 6*(4), 271–285.

Stotzer, R., & MacCartney, D. (2015). The role of institutional factors on on-campus reported rape prevalence. *Journal of Interpersonal Violence,* published online, April 2015.

Stuart, G. I., Temple, J. R., & Moore, T. M. (2007). Improving batterer intervention programs through theory-based research. *Journal of the American Medical Association, 2*(5) 560–562.

Swanberg, J., Logan, T., & Macke, C. (2005). Intimate partner violence, employment, and the workplace: Consequences and future directions. *Trauma Violence Abuse, 6*(4), 286–312.

Taylor, J. (2005). No resting place: African American women at the crossroads of violence. *Violence against Women, 11*(12), 1473–1489.

Tower, L. E. (2006). Barriers in screening women for domestic violence: A survey of social workers, family practitioners, and obstetrician-gynecologists. *Journal of Family Violence, 21*(4), 245–257.

Tyler, K. A., Brownridge, D. A., & Melander, L. A. (2011). The effect of poor parenting on the male and female dating violence perpetration and victimization. *Violence and Victims 26*(2), 218–230.

Ventura, L., & Davis, G. (2005). Domestic violence: Court case conviction and recidivism. *Violence against Women, 11*(2), 255–277.

Weiss, K. (2010). Male sexual victimization: Examining men's experiences of rape and sexual assault. *Men and Masculinities, 12*(3), 275–298.

Wilson, L., & Miller, K. (2015). Meta-analysis of the prevalence of unacknowledged rape. *Trauma, Violence and Abuse.*

WEBSITES

Alianza: National Latino Alliance for the Elimination of Domestic Violence: http://www.dvalianza.org/
Addresses the needs of Latino/a victims of abuse.

American Bar Association Commission on Domestic Violence: www.abanet.org/domviol
Legal resources and information related to abuse.

American Civil Liberties Union (ACLU): www.aclu.org
Advocating for civil rights broadly.

American Domestic Violence Crisis Line: www.866uswomen.org
Crisis line and resources for civilian and enlisted Americans living overseas.

American Humane Association: www.americanhumane.org
Information about pet abuse and domestic violence.

American Institute on Domestic Violence: www.aidv-usa.com
Focuses on workplace violence.

American Medical Association: http://www.ama-assn.org/ama/pub/
physician-resources/public-health/promoting-healthy-lifestyles/violence
-prevention.page
Provides information and resources regarding healthcare and domestic
violence.

Amnesty International USA: www.amnestyusa.org
Human rights group includes work on violence against women.

Asian and Pacific Islander Institute on Domestic Violence: www.apiahf.org/
apidvinstitute
"Works to eliminate domestic violence in Asian and Pacific Islander
communities."

Asian Task Force against Domestic Violence: www.atask.org
Helping end abuse in Asian communities.

The Audre Lorde Project: www.alp.org
Promotes community wellness and economic and social justice.

Ayuda: www.ayudainc.org
Resources and information about the rights of battered immigrant women.

Bureau of Justice Statistics Clearinghouse: www.ojp.usdoj.gov/bjs
Provides statistics and research on a variety of topics.

Center for Media Literacy: www.medialit.org
Provides education and professional development related to media literacy.

Child Welfare League of America: www.cwla.org
Focuses on the welfare of children.

Childhelp USA: www.childhelpusa.org
Addressing the prevention and treatment of child abuse.

Children's Defense Fund: www.childrensdefense.org
A voice for the health and safety of children.

Code Pink for Peace: www.codepink4peace.org
Female-led initiative to stop war and promote peace.

College Brides Walk: www.collegebrideswalk.org
Coordinates annual walk to raise awareness and end abuse.

Communities against Violence Network (CAVNET): www.cavnet.blogspot.org
Wealth of resources on all topics related to abuse.

Corporate Alliance to End Partner Violence: http://www.caepv.org/
Information and resource primarily about domestic violence in the workplace.

Do Something: www.dosomething.org
Teen-focused website providing information and support to empower young people to be agents of change.

Faith Trust Institute: www.cpsdv.org
Largely focused on abuse in faith communities.

The Feminist Majority and the Feminist Majority Foundation: www.feminist.org
Promotes gender equality.

Futures without Violence: www.futureswithoutviolence.org
Wealth of information and resources related to abuse.

Human Rights Watch: www.hrw.org
Global human rights watchdog.

INCITE! Women of Color against Violence: www.incite-national.org
Grassroots organization addressing violence against women of color.

Indigenous Women's Network: www.indigenouswomen.org
Provides information and support for indigenous women.

Institute on Domestic Violence in the African American Community: www.dvinstitute.org
Promoting research and resources related to abuse in the African American community.

Jewish Women International: www.jewishwomen.org
Addresses abuse involving the Jewish community.

The Joyful Heart Foundation: www.joyfulheart.org
Founded in 2002 by actress Mariska Hargitay with the aim of helping survivors heal.

LAMBDA GLBT Community Services: www.lambda.org
Legal resources for LGBT persons.

Legal Momentum: www.nowldef.org
Focuses on legal resources for victims.

Love Is Not Abuse: http://loveisnotabuse.com
Provides resources and information related to teen dating violence.

Love Is Respect: http://www.loveisrespect.org
Focuses on promoting healthy teen relationships.

Media Education Foundation: www.mediaed.org
Provides educational documentaries available for purchase by schools, universities, and libraries on social issues.

Mediawatch: www.mediawatch.com
Devoted to decreasing racism, sexism and violence in media.

Men Can Stop Rape: www.mencanstoprape.org
Advocates for men to address societal sexism and stop sexual harassment and assault.

Men Stopping Violence: www.menstoppingviolence.org
"Works to dismantle belief systems, social structures, and institutional practices that oppress women and children and dehumanize men."

Mending the Sacred Hoop: www.mshoop.org
"Working to end violence against Native American Women"

Motion Picture Association of America: www.mpaa.org
Provides information about movie ratings and information about television guidelines for parents.

MS. Foundation for Women: www.ms.foundation.org
Grants and support for domestic violence shelters.

The National Center for Children Exposed to Violence: www.nccev.org
Promotes public and professional awareness of the many forms of violence endured by children and provides information and resources on its effects, healing, and prevention.

National Center for Elder Abuse: www.elderabusecenter.org
Clearinghouse of information related to elder abuse.

National Center for Victims of Crime: www.ncvc.org
Information and advocacy for domestic violence victims and other crime victims.

National Center on Domestic and Sexual Violence: www.ncdsv.org
Provides information on all forms of abuse.

National Center on Elder Abuse: www.ncea.aoa.gov
Clearinghouse of information and resources related to elder abuse.

National Clearinghouse for the Defense of Battered Women: http://www.ncdbw.org/
"Working for justice for battered women charged with crimes."

National Clearinghouse on Abuse in Later Life: www.ncall.us
Focuses on elder abuse.

National Coalition for the Homeless: www.nationalhomeless.org
Advocacy for the homeless.

National Coalition of Anti-Violence Programs: www.ncavp.org
Brings together numerous antiviolence efforts.

National Domestic Violence Hotline: www.ndvh.org
Information and hotline for victims.

National Gay and Lesbian Task Force: www.ngltf.org
Advocacy and empowerment for LGBT persons.

National Immigration Forum: www.immigrationforum.org
Promoting immigrants' rights.

National Latino Alliance for the Elimination of Domestic Violence (ALIANZA): www.dvalianza.org
Focuses on domestic violence in Latino/a communities.

National Network for Immigrant and Refugee Rights: www.nnirr.org
"Works to defend and expand the rights of all immigrants and refugees, regardless of immigration status."

National Network to End Domestic Violence: www.nnedv.org
Coordinates annual 24-hour census on domestic violence, among other things.

National Organization for Men against Sexism: www.nomas.org
Male-led feminist organization devoted to ending sexism and violence against women.

National Organization for Victim Assistance: www.try-nova.org
Promotes dignity and compassion for victims of crime.

National Resource Center on Domestic Violence: www.nrcdv.org
Information and research on all forms of abuse.

National Runaway Switchboard: www.nrscrisisline.org
Resources for preventing and responding to runaways.

National Sexual Violence Resource Center: www.nsvrc.org
Provides information and resources related to sexual violence.

National Women's Political Caucus: www.nwpc.org
Promoting women's issues and women's involvement in the political system.

No More Tears: www.nmtproject.org
Grassroots nonprofit assisting victims.

Office for Victims of Crime: www.ovc.gov
U.S. governmental office for crime victims resources and support.

Planned Parenthood Federation of America: www.plannedparenthood.org
"The nation's leading sexual and reproductive health care provider and advocate."

Rape, Abuse & Incest National Network (RAINN): www.rainn.org
Statistics, research, and resources related to sexual violence and abuse.

Rural Assistance Center: www.raconline.org
"Health and human service information for rural America."

The Sister Fund: www.sisterfund.org
"Private foundation that supports and gives voice to women working for justice from a religious framework."

Soroptimist International of the Americas: www.soroptimist.org
"International organization for business and professional women who work to improve the lives of women and girls."

Stop Abuse for Everyone: http://www.safe4all.org
"A human rights organization that provides services, publications, and training to serve those who typically fall between the cracks of domestic violence services: straight men, GLBT victims, teens, and the elderly."

Students Active for Ending Rape: www.safer.org
"Empowers students to hold their universities accountable for having strong campus sexual assault policies and programming."

Third Wave Foundation: www.thirdwavefoundation.org
Supports third-wave feminists in their efforts to promote gender equality.

Violence against Women Office, U.S. Department of Justice: www.ojp.usdoj .gov/vaw
Information and grant funding for domestic violence services.

Women's e-news: www.womensenews.org
Compilation of news articles related to women's issues or of interest to women.

Women's Independence Scholarship Program, The Sunshine Lady Foundation: www.sunshineladyfdn.org
Scholarship for domestic violence victims.

WomensLaw.org: www.womenslaw.org
"Providing legal information and support to victims of domestic violence and sexual assault."

Index

The Accused, 8–9, 10, 116
Actors, in comedy, 43–44, 45, 75; in dramas, 47–49, 78, 95, 129, 133, 136; in made-for-TV movies, 58, 62, 94, 108, 135, 136
Adverse Childhood Experiences (ACEs), 19–20
Aerosmith, 139
Aguilera, Christina, 21
Alexander, Marissa, 127–28
All the Rage, 120–21
American History X, 29
American Psycho, 46, 94
American Psychological Association (APA), xxvi
Amnesty International, 25
Amos, Tori, 74
Anatomy of a Murder, 132
Anderson, Laurie Halse, 121–22
Angel Dance, 71–72
Anger control, 95–96
The Associate, 58
Authors, of dramatic fiction, xxvi–xxxiv, 3, 11, 15, 20, 22–23, 28, 40–41, 55, 70, 71–72, 75–76, 94–95, 128–29; of young adult fiction, 49, 77, 82–83, 109, 120–23, 124, 145–46

Bancroft, Lundy, 40–41, 96
Bandura, Albert, 97–98
Bastard Out of Carolina, 9–10, 71–72
Battered Woman's Syndrome, 94–95, 128–29
Beccaria, Cesare, 96
"Behind the Wall," 111
Bentham, Jeremy, 96
"Better Man," 83
Big Little Lies, 11, 21–22
Birth of a Nation, 51–52, 54
"Black and Blue," 22–23
"Black Eyes Blue Tears," 125
"Blame It," 74
The Bluest Eye, 15, 71–72
"Blurred Lines," 73
Bond films, xxxvi
Bone, 54
Book of Mormon, 20
Boys Don't Cry, 25–26
The Boys of St. Vincent, 60
Breathing Underwater, 49, 109
"Brutal black bucks," 52–56
The Burning Bed, 95, 129
Busta Rhymes, 20

Canary, 57
Censorship, 144

Centers for Disease Control and Prevention (CDC), xx, xxii, 2, 12, 147
Chapman, Tracy, 111
Child custody, 19
Children, and custody, 19; and domestic violence, 17–24; and media consumption, xxiv; and media effects 97–98; and music about, 13, 22, 47, 111, 119, 121, 138–39; and sexual assault, 23–24, 143–44
"Cleaning out My Closet," 20
The Color Purple, 10, 16
Comedians and rape, 43–44, 75
The Commish, 136
The Confessions of Nat Turner, 54
Cosby, Bill, 45, 75
Crank, 73
Cries Unheard: The Donna Yalkich Story, 108
Crime films, 87–89
Crime Scene Investigation (CSI), 15
Criminal justice responses, 105–118; restraining orders, 106–9
Criminological theory, xiv, 87–104; biological theories, 90–94; choice, 96–97; drug and alcohol use, 93–94; feminist, 100–101; hormones, 93–94; lead, 91; learning, 97–98; neurocriminology, 91; psychology, 94–96; sociological, 98–100; strain, 98–99; traumatic brain injury, 91–93; techniques of neutralization, 99–100
A Cry for Help: The Tracey Thurman Story, 108
Courts, and Battered Woman Syndrome, 94–95, 128–29; and child custody, 19; and restraining orders, restraining orders, 106–9
Cycle of violence, 128–29

"Daddy," 121
"Daddy's Girl," 121

Dark figure of crime, xxiii
Dating violence, and alcohol, xxii; breakup violence, xxi; and bullying, xxii; college students, xxi; male victims, xx, xxi; normalizing, 80–82; pregnancy, xx–xxi; reporting, xxi–xxii; restraining orders, xxi–xxii; statistics, xx
"Dear John," 95
Death Wish, 134–35
Death Wish 2, 54
DeGaetano, Gloria, xxvi–xxvii, xxvii, xxxiv
Del Ray, Lana, xl
Deliver Us from Evil, 60
Deliverance, 13–14
Demented, 136
Descent, 138
Differential Association theory, 97–98
Differential Identification theory, 98
Dixie Chicks, 6, 139
Domestic violence, and athletes, 57; child victims, 17–24; and elder victims, 30–31; and immigrants, 26–28; and language, 77–78; and LGBT victims, 24–26; and male victims, 11–14; and middle and upper class victims, 10–11; and military, 58–60; and poor and homeless victims, 9–10; and race, 14–17, 51–57; statistics, xx; and suicide, 83
Donoghue, Emma, 20
Doom, xxxii
Dr. Dre, 47–48
Dreamland, 122–23
Dugdale, Richard, 90
Duke Nukem, xxxii
Duluth Model, 101

Education, 148–50
Eminem, 6, 20, 80–81
Empowerment, 148–50, 151
Enough, 120, 123, 130
"Every Breath You Take," 7

Every Last Promise, 120
Extremities, 133
Eye for an Eye, 136

Fallout 3, xxxii
False allegations, 60–61, 68–69,
    75–76
Family Guy, 43
"Family Portrait," 22
The Far End of Happy, 83
Fatal Attraction, 94
Fault Line, 77
Fawcett, Farrah, 95, 129, 133
Fear, 135–36
Felicity, 76
Female abusers, 50
Female rapists, 50
Feminism, 100–101, 133–34, 150–51
50 Shades of Grey, 5–6
Fight Club, xxix–xxx
Films, xxix–xxxviii, 2, 5–6, 8–9, 10,
    16; action, xxix–xxx, 134–36;
    comedy, 21, 29, 30, 44–45, 81, 91;
    dramatic, 2, 8–9, 10, 13–14, 16,
    23–24, 25–26, 27–28, 29, 46,
    51–52, 54, 57, 60, 71, 94, 95, 129,
    130–32, 135–36, 138; documentary,
    62; horror/slasher, xxxviii–xl; 94–95
Fish, 29
For the Love of a Daughter, 94
Forced sterilization, 90
Forms of abuse, 3–8; emotional, 5–6;
    physical, 3, 6–7; power and control,
    4–5; psychological, 4; revenge
    porn, 4, 78–79; sexual, 3–4, 6–7;
    stalking, 3–4, 7–8; technology, 4
*From reverence to rape: The treatment
    of women in the movies*, xxxvi, 3

Game of Thrones, 8
General Strain theory, 98–99
The General's Daughter, 60
Gerbner, George, xxvii, xxx
Get Hard, 30
Girl on the Train, 61

The Girl with the Dragon Tattoo, 10,
    46, 127, 137–38
Glaser, Daniel, 98
Gone Girl, 61
Gone with the Wind, 71
Gonzales, Jessica, 108–109
"Goodbye Earl," 6, 139
Grand Theft Auto, xxxii–xxxiii
"Gray rape," 70–71
Green, Cee Lo, 74–75
Green Day, 13
Grossman, Dave, xxv–xxvii, xxvii, xxxiv
Groupthink, 119–20

Hand of God, 60
Happy violence, xxx
Harris, Eric, xxxiii
Haskell, Molly, xxxvii–xxxviii, 3
"He Hit Me and It Felt Like
    a Kiss," 82
"He Never Got Enough Love," 98
Helping offenders, 61
Hill, Lauryn, 125
Holmes, James, xxvii
hooks, bell, 55
Horrible Bosses, 29
Horrible Bosses 2, 50–51
Hosseini, Khalid, 28
Hounddog, 23–24
House of Cards, 125
Hughes, Francine, 95, 129
Human Rights Watch, 116
Hunt, Sam, 23

"I Get Out," 124
Ice Cube, 47–49
Ice T, 47–49
"I'm Ok," 21
Immigrants, 56
"Independence Day," 138–39
Inexcusable, 57
Instrumental violence, xxix
Into the Darkest Corner, 46–47
The Invisible War, 60
Is This Rape? Sex on Trial, 146–47

"Janie's Got a Gun," 139
Johnny Belinda, 72
Just Listen, 125

Klebold, Dylan, xxxiii
Knoll, Jessica, 122
Korn, 121

Lady Gaga, 136
Law & Order, 55, 89–90
*Law & Order: Special Victims Unit
    (SVU),* xliii–xliv, 7, 13, 15, 29, 61,
    111, 112–13, 114–15
Lawrence, Jennifer, 78
Lifetime network, 58, 62, 94, 108,
    135, 136
Lipstick, 132
Lolita effect, xxxvi
Lombroso, Cesare, 90
*The Lost Marble Notebook of Forgotten
    Girl & Random Boy,* 83
Love is Respect, xxiii
"Love the Way You Lie," 80–81
The Lovely Bones, 123–24
Luckiest Girl Alive, 122
Lucky, 115
Ludacris, 75
"Luka," 119
Lynchings, 52–54
Lyrics, xl–xlii, country, 6, 23, 125, 139;
    popular, 7, 20, 21, 22–23, 53, 73, 74,
    75, 80–81, 82, 83, 94, 95, 98, 111,
    124, 125, 136, 138–39; rap, 47–49;

Mad Men, 74
Magazines, 146
Male gaze, 8–9
"Man Down," 138
Mandatory arrest laws, 96–97,
    109–110
Manhunt 2, xxxiii
Manson, Marilyn, xl
McBride, Martina, 138–39
"Me and a Gun," 74
Mean world syndrome, xxvii

Media consumption, xxiv; and
    children, xxiv; and aggression,
    xxvii–xxviii; and desensitization,
    xxviii, xxxix–xxx; and third-person
    effect, xxviii; and violence, xxiv–xxx,
Media literacy, 144–47
Meyer, Stephenie, 49, 81–82
Military, 58–60
Misery, 94
Misogyny, xxxv–xxxvi
Mitchell, Joni, 124
Morrison, Toni, 15, 71–72
Mortal Kombat, xxxiii
A Mother's Revenge, 135
Ms. 45, 132
Music videos, country, 6, 23,125,
    138–39; popular, xl, 73, 80–81,
    136, 138; rap, 20, 47–49, 75, 80–81
Musicians, country, 6, 23, 95, 98,
    125, 138, 139; popular, xl, 13, 21,
    22, 23, 47–49, 74, 75, 94, 80–81,
    121, 125, 139; rap, 20, 75; rock, 7,
    13, 47–49, 83, 121, 139
Myths about abusers, 40–41

National Domestic Violence Hotline,
    xxiii
National Family Violence Survey, 12
National Football League, 41
National Task Force on Children
    Exposed to Violence, 19
Native Americans, 16–17,
    56–57
Native Son, 54
"Never Again," 23, 94, 139
Nickelback, 23, 94, 139
Nirvana, 47
No One Could Protect Her, 136
Non-profit organizations, xxiii, 25,
    116, 147–48
"Not to Blame," 124
Not to People Like Us, 11
Not Without My Daughter, 27–28
Novels, popular, 10, 16, 15, 17, 20,
    46–47, 61, 71–72, 75–76, 94, 122,

123–24, 136–38; young adult, 49, 81–82, 83, 121–22, 124, 125
N.W.A., 47–49
NYPD Blue, 55, 89–90

Oates, Joyce Carol, 75–76
Observe and Report, 73–74
Offenders, 40–66; and drugs and alcohol, 87–104; and evil, 46–49; and hormones, 93–94; and lead exposure, 91; and mental illness, 46–49, 94–96; and traumatic brain injury, 91–93
"Oh Mother," 21
Orange Is the New Black, 125
Outlander, 13
"Outside of That," 5, 81

"Paparazzi," 136
Past Forgiving, 82–83
Patriarchy, 2–3, 100–101
Pearl Jam, 83
The Perks of Being a Wallflower, 81
Pink, 13, 22
Pitch Perfect 2, 45
Playboy, 13, 70
Polanski, Roman, 45
The Police, 7
Police, and LGBT victims, 25–26, 112; as perpetrators, 108–9, 114
"Polly," 47
Pornland: How pornography has hijacked our sexuality, xxxvi–xxxvii
Pornography, xxxvi–xxxvi, 6
Post-Traumatic Stress Disorder, 18, 19
The Practice, 89–90
Precious, 24
Prevention programs, 147–48
Production Code, xxxviii
Professional athletes, 57, 113
Professional wrestling, xliv
Prosecutions, 114–16
Psychiatrists, 95, 122–23, 128–29
Psycho, xxxviii, 94

Quindlen, Anna, 22–23

Raine, Adrian, 91
Rap music, 47–49
Rape, and athletes, 57; and children, 23–24; and elder victims, 30–31; and fraternities, 57–58, 112; and immigrants, 26–28; and LGBT persons, 24–26; and male victims, 12–13; and military, 58–60; in prisons, 28–30; and race, 14–17, 51–57; and religious institutions; and slavery, 14–15, 51–52; and strangers, 97
Rape, Abuse and Incest National Network (RAINN), xxii
Rape: A Love Story, 75–76
Rape culture, xiii, 43–46, 67–77; and clothing, 43–44
Rape Girl, 124
Rape jokes, 43–44
Rape kits, 114–15
Rape myths, xiv, 12–13, 60–61, 67–77, 105–6, 113–14, 147
Rational choice theory, 96
Redneck Rampage, xxxii
Reporting, 110
Restraining orders, 106–9
Rice, Ray, 41
Rihanna, 80–81, 138
Risk factors for abuse, 1–2, 41–42
Rob Roy, 136
Roethlisberger, Ben, 113
Roiphe, Katie, 70
Room, 20
Rosewood, 55
The Round House, 17
Routine Activity theory, 96

Safe in Hell, 132
The Scorpions, 121
Scream, xxxviii
Sebold, Alice, 115, 123–24
Seductions of crime theory, 96
Sexual assault, and alcohol, xxiii; and acquaintances, xxiii; athletes, 112;

children, 143–44; college students, xxii–xxiii, 112; reporting, xxiii; sororities, xxiii; statistics, xxii–xxiii;
The Shanghai Express, 132
She Cried No, 58
The Shield, 111
The Simpsons, 43
Singular, Stephen and Joyce, xxvii–xxvii, xxx
Sinister 2, 21
Sisters, 78
Sixteen Candles, 44–45
Slasher films, xxxviii–xl; 94–95
Sleepers, 28
Sleeping with the Enemy, 47, 123, 130
Slumdog Millionaire, 28
Smith, Bessie, 81
The Sopranos, 136–37
South Park, 14, 43
"Southern Hospitality," 75
Speak, 121–22
The Spiral Notebook, xxvii
Spring Breakers, 72
Stalking, xxi
Stand Your Ground Laws, 127–28, 129–30
"Stone Cold Dead in the Market (He Had it Coming)," 138
Straight Outta Compton, 45–46
Strain theory, 98–99
"Strange Fruit," 53
Straw Dogs, 72
The Street, 15, 71–72
Streetcar Named Desire, 4–5
Sudden Impact, 136
Sutherland, Edwin, 97–98
Swift, Taylor, 95

"Take Your Time," 23
Television, British, 146–47; comedy, xliii–xliv, 7, 13, 15, 29, 50, 55, 61, 89–90, 111, 112–13, 114–15, 136–37; comedy, 14, 43, 124; drama, 76, 78; HBO, 8, 13, 74, 111, 125

Temptations: Confessions of a Marriage Counselor, 74
Thelma and Louise, 133–34
A Time to Kill, 16
Tommy Boy, 91
Too $hort, 47–49
True Blood, 50
Trust, 143–44
Twain, Shania, 125
21 Jump Street, 54–55
Twilight series, 49, 81–82
Twist of Faith, 60
2 Broke Girls, 45
Tyson, Mike, 45

Uniform Code of Military Justice (UCMJ), 59–60

Vega, Suzanne, 119
Veronica Mars, 124
Victim-blaming, 4–5, 8–9, 10, 12–13, 69–77, 89–90, 97, 99–100, 126–27
Victim responses, 119–42; psychiatrists, 122; self-defense, 131; revenge, 131–41; shelters, 122–23
Video games, xxvii–xxviii, xxxi–xxxiv, 144–47

Walker, Lenore, 94–95, 128–29
Warning signs of abuse, 1–2, 39–40
Water for Elephants, 136
Weitzman, Susan, 11
What's Love Got to Do with It, 55, 81, 101, 130–31
Williams, Lucinda, 98
Wilson, Rainn, 45
The Wire, 111
Without a Trace, 15
The Woodsman, 61
Wrestling with Manhood, xliv

Young adult literature, 49, 77, 82–83, 109, 120–23, 124, 145–46

About the Author

LAURA L. FINLEY, Ph.D., is Associate Professor of Sociology and Criminology at Barry University, Miami Shores, Florida. She is the author, co-author, editor, or co-editor of 15 books as well as numerous book chapters and journal articles. Dr. Finley has been involved in training and education about dating and domestic violence for more than 10 years and currently serves as Board Chair of No More Tears, a South Florida nonprofit that provides services to victims. She is also co-organizer of the College Brides Walk, an educational initiative held each February in South Florida. Dr. Finley has twice been the recipient of the Broward County Domestic Violence Volunteer of the Year award. In 2013 she received the Public Peace Intellectual Award from PeaceVoice and the Social Justice Collaboration Award from ACPA. She has also received several awards from her university for engaged scholarship and mentorship of students.